Cosmology and Eschatology
in Jewish and Christian Apocalypticism

Cosmology and Eschatology in Jewish and Christian Apocalypticism

Adela Yarbro Collins

BRILL

LEIDEN • BOSTON • KOLN

This journal is printed on acid-free paper.

Design: TopicA (Antoinette Hanekuyk), Leiden

On the cover: Rogier van der Weyden.
The Last Judgment (ca. 1445).
Detail of Central Altarpiece.
Hotel Dieu, Beaune, France.

Library of Congress Cataloging-in-Publication Data

The Library of Congress Cataloging-in-Publication Data
are also available.

ISBN 90 04 11927 2

PRINTED IN THE NETHERLANDS

CONTENTS

ABBREVIATIONS

AAAbo.H	Acta Academiae Aboensis, Series A, Humaniora
AB	Anchor Bible
AGJU	Arbeiten zur Geschichte des antiken Judentums und des Urchristentums
AJS	Association of Jewish Studies Review
AOT	H.F.D. Sparks, ed., *The Apocryphal Old Testament*
APOT	R.H. Charles, ed., *Apocrypha and Pseudepigrapha of the Old Testament*
ASGW.PH	Abhandlungen der Königlichen Sächsischen Gesellschaft der Wissenschaften, Philologisch-historische Klasse
As. Mos.	*Assumption of Moses* or *Testament of Moses*
ASNU	Acta Seminarii Neotestamentici Upsaliensis
ASTI	*Annual of the Swedish Theological Institute*
AThANT	Abhandlungen zur Theologie des Alten und Neuen Testaments
ATR	*Anglican Theological Review*
b.	born
b.	*Babylonian Talmud*
BAGD	W. Bauer, W.F. Arndt, F.W. Gingrich, and F.W. Danker, *Greek-English Lexicon of the NT*
BCE	Before the Common Era, Before Christ
BDB	F. Brown, S.R. Driver, and C.A. Briggs, *Hebrew and English Lexicon of the Old Testament*
BDF	F. Blass, A. Debrunner, and R.W. Funk, *A Greek Grammar of the NT*
Bib	*Biblica*. Roma
BibLeb	Bibel und Leben
BJRL	*Bulletin of the John Rylands University Library of Manchester*
BR	*Biblical Research*
BT	Bibliothèque de théologie. Paris
BWANT	Beiträge zur Wissenschaft vom Alten und Neuen Testament
BZAW	Beihefte der Zeitschrift für die Alttestamentliche Wissenschaft

BZNW	Beihefte der Zeitschrift für die Neutestamentliche Wissenschaft
c.	circa, approximately
CBA	Catholic Biblical Association
CBQ	*Catholic Biblical Quarterly*
CBQMS	Catholic Biblical Quarterly Monograph Series
CE	Common Era, year of our Lord
col.	collegit, collected
CP	*Classical Philology*
CSS	Collected Studies Series
DJD	Discoveries in the Judaean Desert
EBSK	Erlanger Beiträge zur Sprach- und Kunstwissenschaft
ET	English Translation
EtB	Études Bibliques
ETL	*Ephemerides Theologicae Lovanienses*
FBBS	Facet Books, Biblical Series
fl.	floruit, flourished
FRLANT	Forschungen zur Religion und Literatur des Alten und Neuen Testaments
GCS	Griechische Christliche Schriftsteller
GNS	Good News Studies
HAT	Handbuch zum Alten Testament
HDR	Harvard Dissertations in Religion
HNT	Handbuch zum Neuen Testament
HNTC	Harper's New Testament Commentaries
HSM	Harvard Semitic Monographs
HTR	*Harvard Theological Review*
HTS	Harvard Theological Studies
HUCA	*Hebrew Union College Annual*
ICC	International Critical Commentary
IDB	G.A. Buttrick (ed.), *Interpreter's Dictionary of the Bible*
IDBSup	Supplementary volume to *IDB*
Irenaeus	
Adv. Haer.	*Adversus Haereses, Against Heresies*
JBL	*Journal of Biblical Literature*
JJS	*Journal of Jewish Studies*
Josephus	
Ant.	*Antiquities of the Jews*
Bell.	*Bellum Judaicum, The Jewish War*
Vita	the *Life of Josephus*

JQR	*Jewish Quarterly Review*
JSJ	*Journal for the Study of Judaism in the Persian, Hellenistic and Roman Period*
JSNT	*Journal for the Study of the New Testament*
JTC	*Journal for Theology and the Church*
JTS	*Journal of Theological Studies*
KEK	Kritisch-Exegetischer Kommentar über das Neue Testament, begr. von H.A.W. Meyer
LCL	Loeb Classical Library
LD	Lectio Divina
lit.	literally
ln.	line
LSJ	Liddell-Scott-Jones, *Greek-English Lexicon*
m.	*Mishnah*
MHUC	Monographs of the Hebrew Union College
MS(S)	Manuscript(s)
n(n).	note(s)
NHS	Nag Hammadi Studies
NovT	*Novum Testamentum*
NovTSup	Novum Testamentum, Supplements
n.s.	new series
NT	the New Testament
NTApoc	Schneemelcher, *New Testament Apocrypha*
NTS	*New Testament Studies*
OCD	*Oxford Classical Dictionary*
OTP	J.H. Charlesworth (ed.), *The Old Testament Pseudepigrapha*
OTS	*Oudtestamentische Studiën*
Pap.	Papyrus
par(s).	parallel(s)
Ps. Sol.	*Psalms of Solomon*
PTA	Papyrologische Texte und Abhandlungen
PVTG	Pseudepigrapha Veteris Testamenti Graece
PW	Pauly-Wissowa, *Realencyclopädie der classischen Altertumswissenschaft*
RB	*Revue Biblique*
RevQ	*Revue de Qumran*
RSR	*Recherches de Science Religieuse*
RSV	Revised Standard Version
SANT	Studien zum Alten und Neuen Testament
SB	Sources Bibliques

SBLDS	Society of Biblical Literature, Dissertation Series
SBLMS	Society of Biblical Literature, Monograph Series
SBLSCS	Society of Biblical Literature, Septuagint and Cognate Studies
SBLTT	Society of Biblical Literature, Texts and Translations
SJLA	Studies in Judaism in Late Antiquity
SJT	*Scottish Journal of Theology*
SNTSMS	Society for New Testament Studies Monograph Series
SPB	Studia Post-Biblica
StHu	Studies in the Humanities
t.	*Tosephta*
TB, NT	Theologische Bücherei, Neues Testament
TDNT	G. Kittel and G. Friedrich (eds.), *Theological Dictionary of the New Testament*
ThBü	Theologische Bücherei
TSAJ	Texte und Studien zum Antiken Judentum
TU	Texte und Untersuchungen
UCOP	University of Cambridge Oriental Publications
USQR	*Union Seminary Quarterly Review*
VC	*Vigiliae Christianae*
vs	verse
VTSup	Vetus Testamentum, Supplements
WMANT	Wissenschaftliche Monographien zum Alten und Neuen Testament
WUNT	Wissenschaftliche Untersuchungen zum Neuen Testament
ZAW	*Zeitschrift für die Alttestamentliche Wissenschaft*
ZNW	*Zeitschrift für die Neutestamentliche Wissenschaft*
ZThK	*Zeitschrift für Theologie und Kirche*

CHAPTER ONE

MEANING AND SIGNIFICANCE IN APOCALYPTIC TEXTS

The hermeneutical problem may be posed by asking whether textual infidelity is a vice, a virtue, or a necessity. This way of posing the question both suggests that there is an ethics of interpretation and alludes to the difficult philosophical questions involved. The ethics of interpretation, it seems to me, includes not only the value "textual fidelity," but also fidelity to the author, as E.D. Hirsch has argued.[1] There is something inhumane at least, even immoral, about using a text without regard for the author's intention in creating it. Even advocates of interpretive freedom and play object when reviewers misunderstand their books. Liberation and feminist theologians have pointed out a further responsibility. Some texts, like the Bible, are used to maintain social structures which prevent people of color, the poor, and women from achieving their full human potential. Indeed, sometimes texts are used to legitimate injustice and physical violence. These facts suggest that interpreters are responsible for the social effects of their readings.[2]

The philosophical questions are well known. One could discuss whether a text is a valuable, even sacred, entity in its own right or a mere reminiscence of what we know or should be taught orally, as Socrates argued in the Phaedrus. The link between the phrase "textual infidelity" and "necessity" raises the question whether fidelity to a text is even possible. One could, with Stanley Fish, dispute even the existence of a text as an objective entity apart from any act of interpretation.[3]

I propose to explore some of these questions in relation to ancient apocalyptic texts. As a Biblical scholar educated at Harvard and

---

[1] E.D. Hirsch, Jr., *The Aims of Interpretation* (Chicago: University of Chicago Press, 1976) especially 74–92.

[2] See, for example, the presidential address of Elisabeth Schüssler Fiorenza to the Society of Biblical Literature, "The Ethics of Interpretation: De-Centering Biblical Scholarship," *JBL* 107 (1988) 3–17.

[3] Stanley Fish, "How to Recognize a Poem When You See One," Chapter 14 in *Is There A Text in This Class?: The Authority of Interpretive Communities* (Cambridge, MA: Harvard University Press, 1980) especially p. 331.

belonging to the post-Vatican II Catholic Church, I am inclined to
say that the interpretation of all religious texts involves two stages or
moments. At least religious texts from a time or culture different
from those of the interpreter require interpretation in two stages. My
education in Biblical studies was centered on the historical-critical
method. The Second Vatican Council affirmed the importance of
studying the Biblical texts in light of the literary conventions and
historical circumstances in which they were written.[4] The document
"The Interpretation of the Bible in the Church," presented by the
Pontifical Biblical Commission to the Pope in April, 1993, was published by the Vatican in November of that year.[5] This document
confirms the necessity of the historical-critical method in the study of
Scripture and the importance of the circumstances in which a text
was composed for the illumination of its meaning, while also insist-
ing that the task of interpretation is complete only with a serious
treatment of how the text may be appropriated in the present.

We may think of interpretation as a process involving the author,
the text, and the interpreter.[6] The first stage or moment of the interpretation of religious texts should focus on the author and the text.
A great deal may be known about the actual author; more often
virtually nothing is known about who produced the text. The goal of
this stage, then, is not only, or even primarily, to determine the
author's intention, but to understand and explain the text within its
original context. It is in this process that the meaning of the text is
discerned. Fish is persuasive in his argument that a text "has" no
meaning in itself. Meaning is perceived only in a particular social
context. Fish makes his point with an anecdote from a contemporary
American classroom that illustrates two interpretations of the question "Is there a text in this class?"[7] An anecdote that more clearly
illustrates the problems in interpreting ancient religious texts comes
from one of Art Linkletter's books about children's amusing sayings.

---

[4] "The Divine Inspiration and the Interpretation of Sacred Scripture," Chapter
III of "Dogmatic Constitution on Divine Revelation," in Walter M. Abbott, S.J.,
ed., *The Documents of Vatican II* (New York: America Press, 1966) 119–120.

[5] Pontifical Biblical Commission, "The Interpretation of the Bible in the Church,"
Origins: CNS Documentary Service vol. 23: no. 29 (January 6, 1994) 497, 499–524.

[6] For an exploration of this model in relation to hermeneutical systematic the-
ologies, see David Tracy, *The Analogical Imagination: Christian Theology and the Culture of
Pluralism* (New York: Crossroad, 1981) 99–153.

[7] Fish, "Is There a Text in This Class?", Chapter 13 in *Is There a Text in This
Class?*, 303–321.

When asked to draw a picture of his favorite Biblical story, one child drew a long sports car with three people in it. The teacher asked, "What story does that show?" The child responded, "That's God driving Adam and Eve out of Paradise."

So I would agree with Hirsch that the term "meaning" should be reserved for the intelligibility of the text in its original context. Whatever doubts one may have about the independence and objectivity of a text, it is clear that texts are produced by human beings for particular reasons. They are artifacts in that sense. It is also clear that the meanings of the words and the larger semantic meanings are culturally determined. If one does not understand a text in terms of its original cultural context, then one must understand it through some other cultural context. It seems reasonable and ethical to acknowledge the origins of a text as determinative of its meaning, including, as far as possible, the author's intention. This of course does not imply that a text has only one "correct" meaning, but suggests that a particular range of interpretations has a better claim to represent meaning in the original context than others.

The second stage or moment of interpretation focuses on the text and the interpreter. The goal in this case is to experience and articulate the significance of the text for the interpreter, including the social context in which the act of interpretation is carried out. It is primarily at this stage that the questions of the truth and utility of religious texts arises. These questions arise whether a text is canonical or not, although they are more urgent for interpreters of their tradition's normative texts. When a text is being used to support injustice or violence, there may be tension between the values of the author and the values of the interpreter, between the values of the two cultures to which they belong, and between the authority of the tradition and emerging moral sensitivity on particular issues.

This two-stage model presupposes that, however revelatory a text may be of the world of the Spirit, it is a human product and that human productions are deeply conditioned by their historical contexts. It also takes as a premise that the origins of a text are constitutive of its meaning and must be taken into account if genuine understanding is to take place. In these convictions I have been influenced by Krister Stendahl, an historical critic and leader in the Church, who argued in an article on Biblical theology that interpreters of the Bible must distinguish between what the text meant in its original historical context and what it means for the believer and

the Church in the present day.[8] Later, I found the terminology of
E.D. Hirsch to be useful in making the same point in a more precise
way, namely, his distinction between meaning and significance.[9]

Although I continue to maintain the normative character of the
original meaning of the text, I am aware that other points of view
are held, both in the discipline of the study of religion and in the
Christian tradition. Wilfred Cantwell Smith, formerly Director of the
Harvard Center for World Religions, has argued that what distinguishes the interpreter of Scripture from those who interpret other
texts is that the believing exegete of Scripture assumes that the normative meaning of the text is the best or highest meaning that the
interpreter can devise.[10] This principle is a way of reconciling the
interpreter's convictions about truth and reality with his or her commitment to the Scripture as the Truth or the Word of God. The
further away the interpreter is from the origin of the Scripture in
time, space, and cultural context, the greater the gap is likely to be
between those convictions and the "literal" or original meaning of
the Scriptural text.

Smith's principle of the interpretation of Scripture is exemplified
in Augustine's *Confessions*. In his discussion of Genesis 1 in Book 12
of the *Confessions*, Augustine mentions several different interpretations
of the first verse of Genesis: "In the beginning God created the heaven
and the earth." He then comments that every reader of Genesis,
presumably every Catholic Christian reader, attempts to understand
what the author wished to convey. Since these interpreters believe
the author to speak truly, they dare not suppose that he has spoken
anything which they know or suppose to be false. But Augustine
goes further. He allows for the possibility that "the light of all true-
speaking minds" may show the interpreter some truth which the author
did not understand. Augustine assumes that the author understood a
truth, but not necessarily the same truth revealed to the interpreter.[11]
A little further on, he remarks that readers may disagree in two ways
about interpretation "when by signs anything is related, even by true

---

[8] Krister Stendahl, "Biblical Theology, Contemporary," *IDB* (1962) 1. 418–32.
[9] Hirsch, *The Aims of Interpretation*, especially 79–81.
[10] This conclusion follows from his discussion of Scripture in various publications, for example, Wilfrid Cantwell Smith, *Towards a World Theology: Faith and the
Comparative History of Religion* (Philadelphia: Westminster, 1981) 163–64.
[11] Augustine, *Confessions*, Book 12, Chaper 18 (= § 27).

reporters."[12] Interpreters may differ concerning the truth of the things or concerning the meaning of him who reports them. With regard to the first, Augustine declares, "let all those depart from me who imagine themselves to know as true what is false. And as for the other also, let all depart from me who imagine Moses to have spoken things that are false."[13] It is clear that for Augustine, the primary criterion for interpretation is truth. Yet charity plays a role also. He urges readers so to honor the author as to believe that, when he wrote the text, he intended "that which in [it] chiefly excels both for light of truth and fruitfulness of profit."[14] Near the end of this discussion, he prays that he may attain the meaning which the author of the text intended. If not, he asks that any other true meaning be made known to him through the occasion of the same words.[15] When the modern reader peruses Augustine's allegorical interpretation of Genesis 1,[16] it is only too clear how his philosophical and religious presuppositions have shaped his reading of the text. From the point of view of the historical critic and in terms of the two stage model of interpretation, he has articulated the significance of Genesis 1 for those Catholic Christians of the fourth century who conceived of reality in Neo-Platonic terms. Augustine's notions of truth and charity are suggestive and valid for the appropriation of a text, but not for discerning the meaning of a text. For the latter, historical reconstruction and historical imagination are the requisite tools.

Before discussing apocalyptic texts as such, I would like to return briefly to an issue mentioned earlier, whether a text is valuable or even sacred in itself. Susan Handelman has argued recently that Jewish interpreters, especially the rabbis of the Talmud, take the Jewish Scripture, especially the Torah, as sacred, even divine.[17] The Torah is the closest entity to God that humans can relate to directly in this world. It provides more direct knowledge of God than nature, for example, because the Torah itself was the blueprint for the creation

---

[12] Ibid., Chapter 23 (= § 32). The translation cited is by J.G. Pilkington (1876) reprinted in *A Select Library of the Nicene and Post-Nicene Fathers of the Christian Church* (ed. Philip Schaff [1886]; Grand Rapids: Eerdmans, 1983) 185.

[13] Ibid.

[14] Ibid., Chapter 30 (= § 41); (page 188 in *Nicene and Post-Nicene Fathers*).

[15] Ibid., Chapter 32 (= § 43); (page 189).

[16] Summarized in ibid., Book 13, Chapter 34 (= § 49); (pages 206–207).

[17] Susan A. Handelman, *The Slayers of Moses: The Emergence of Rabbinic Interpretation in Modern Literary Theory* (Albany: State University of New York Press, 1982) 27–50, especially 37–42.

of the material world. It is more authoritative even than a voice
from heaven, a vision, or an ascent to the divine throne or chariot.
Interpretation is therefore an end in itself. In contrast, for the Greeks,
the text is not an end in itself, but represents an experience. The
Christians took over this notion from the Greeks in such a way that
the Jewish Scripture was seen as a figure or type of Jesus Christ.
What came to be called the New Testament, likewise, is a representation of the reality of the living Christ. Experience of God through
this living Christ became the ultimate goal of Christian interpretation.[18] Typically Christian interpretation, therefore, is not an end in
itself, but represents an experience and is intended to evoke an experience in the audience. The following discussion of the apocalypses
will suggest that these texts, both the Jewish and the Christian ones,
are closer to Handelman's "Christian" model of interpretation than
to the "rabbinic."

INTERPRETING THE APOCALYPSES: MEANING

The ancient apocalyptic genre was not confined to a single culture
or religious tradition. It appears in Jewish, Christian, Gnostic, Greek,
Latin, and Persian literature.[19] The genre continued to be employed
in Byzantine and Islamic cultures, as well as in medieval Europe.[20]
The term "apocalypse" comes from the Greek word ἀποκάλυψις,
which means "revelation." Its use to name a genre derives from the
opening words of the last book of the New Testament, the Book of
Revelation: "A revelation of Jesus Christ. . . ." In defining and discussing the genre, some scholars emphasize the interest in history and
the future, that is, the eschatological dimension.[21] Others emphasize
the interest in the heavenly world, that is, the mystical dimension.[22]
My position is that the classic apocalypses combine the two concerns,
so that contact with and knowledge of the heavenly world provides

---

[18] Ibid., 83–120.

[19] See John J. Collins, ed., *Apocalypse: The Morphology of a Genre, Semeia* 14 (1979).

[20] See Paul J. Alexander, *The Byzantine Apocalyptic Tradition* (ed. with an introduction, Dorothy deF. Abrahamse; Berkeley/Los Angeles/London: University of California Press, 1985); Bernard McGinn, *Apocalypticism in the Western Tradition* (CSS;
Aldershot, Hampshire, UK/Brookfield, Vermont, USA: Variorum, 1994).

[21] For example, Paul Hanson, *The Dawn of Apocalyptic* (Philadelphia: Fortress, 1975).

[22] For example, Christopher Rowland, *The Open Heaven* (New York: Crossroad,
1982).

an understanding of history and supports a particular way of life. The definition of the genre presupposed here is as follows:

"Apocalypse" is a genre of revelatory literature with a narrative framework, in which a revelation is mediated by an otherworldly being to a human recipient, disclosing a transcendent reality which is both temporal, insofar as it envisages eschatological salvation, and spatial, insofar as it involves another, supernatural world; such a work is intended to interpret present, earthly circumstances in light of the supernatural world and of the future, and to influence both the understanding and the behavior of the audience by means of divine authority.[23]

A definition is important first of all because it determines which works are to be included as belonging to the genre. It is important also because it indicates which related works are the most similar. These similar, related works provide evidence for inferring what the meaning and function of the apocalypses were. They constitute a kind of context for interpretation or a framework within which the apocalypses are to be understood.

One important key for interpretation lies in the definition of an apocalypse as a narrative account of a revelatory experience. It has been debated whether these accounts represent actual ecstatic experiences.[24] Whether they do or not, it is clear that the narratives represent a revelatory experience to the audience in such a way that the audience has a virtual revelatory experience.[25] Even if such an account is a literary convention, the result is that the text points beyond itself to a mystical experience and is legitimated by the claim that the author had such an experience.

---

[23] This definition is taken from *Semeia* 14 (1979) 9 and supplemented by the suggested addition to the definition in Adela Yarbro Collins, ed., *Early Christian Apocalypticism: Genre and Social Setting, Semeia* 36 (1986) 7.

[24] For an intermediate position on this issue, see R.H. Charles, *A Critical and Exegetical Commentary on the Revelation of St. John* (ICC; New York: Scribner's Sons, 1920) 1. civ–cix. More detailed discussions may be found in Johannes Lindblom, *Gesichte und Offenbarungen: Vorstellungen von göttlichen Weisungen und übernatürlichen Erscheinungen im ältesten Christentum* (Skrifter utgivna av Kungl. Humanistiska Vetenskapssamfundet i Lund 65; Lund: Gleerup, 1968); Lars Hartman, *Prophecy Interpreted: The Formation of Some Jewish Apocalyptic Texts and of the Eschatological Discourse Mark 13 Par.* (CB.NT 1; Lund: Gleerup, 1966); and Martha Himmelfarb, "The Practice of Ascent in the Ancient Mediterranean World," in John J. Collins and Michael Fishbane, eds., *Death, Ecstasy, and Other Worldly Journeys* (Albany, NY: State University of New York Press, 1995) 123–37.

[25] See David Aune, "The Apocalypse of John and the Problem of Genre," in *Semeia* 36 (1986) 65–96.

The definition presupposed here suggests that there are three important bodies of literature which, as closely related works, provide the context for interpretation. The concern of the genre with temporal matters, the interpretation of history and salvation in the future, indicates a link with the prophetic literature of Israel and Judah. The emphasis on mystical experience leads in two directions. The apocalypses generally describe the mystical experience, a vision, audition, or extraordinary journey, as spontaneous. There are hints, however, that such experiences require preparation and that there may be techniques for inducing them. These hints lead the historian to the Greek magical papyri and the Demotic spells which focus on techniques for getting in touch with supernatural beings.[26] The actual descriptions of heavenly beings and places in the apocalypses are similar to those in a few contemporary and many later Jewish mystical texts. In general terms then, the apocalypses present a view of reality and attempt to lure the reader to accept it and to live in accordance with it. Each apocalypse contains a "program for life." I would suggest that this "program for life" has two major dimensions: how to live in the material world and how to transcend that world. Living in the material world is first and foremost a matter of survival and thereafter a matter of power.

Recently a number of students of early Christianity, second temple Judaism, and the Hellenistic Near East have suggested that the insights and methods of sociologists and anthropologists studying millenarian movements in a cross-cultural manner might be applied fruitfully to Jewish and early Christian apocalypticism. Sheldon Isenberg noted that most previous study had been devoted to the literary products of Jewish apocalyptic communities rather than to the communities themselves. In a brief article, he attempted to interpret the community at Qumran as a Jewish millenarian movement and to study it in terms of social anthropology's language of power, access to power, redemption and redemptive media.[27] Isenberg's conceptual framework

---

[26] The Greek magical papyri are available in K. Preisendanz et al., eds., *Papyri Graecae Magicae: Die Griechischen Zauberpapyri* (2 vols.; 2nd ed.; Stuttgart: Teubner, 1973–74); English translations of the Greek magical papyri and the Demotic spells are available in Hans Dieter Betz, ed., *The Greek Magical Papyri in Translation: Including the Demotic Spells*, vol. 1: *The Texts* (Chicago: The University of Chicago Press, 1986; 2nd ed. 1992).

[27] Sheldon Isenberg, "Millenarism in Greco-Roman Palestine," *Religion* 4 (1974) 26–46.

was based on Kenelm Burridge's *New Heaven, New Earth*.[28] Shortly
thereafter, a slim monograph by John Gager appeared, *Kingdom and
Community: The Social World of Early Christianity*.[29] Gager's book makes
a case for viewing earliest Christianity as a millenarian movement in
the anthropological sense. Jonathan Z. Smith has suggested that the
studies of "new" religions in tribal societies, such as the cargo cults,
can be helpful in assessing the social forces which led to the rise of
Christianity.[30] These studies are illuminating, especially when one
recognizes that religious and political institutions were much less
differentiated in the ancient world than in modern times.

These broad, comparative studies have been complemented by
continuing historical and literary studies of apocalypses and related
works themselves.[31] Some of that work has focused on the social
settings of individual apocalypses.[32] Like the prophets of Israel and
Judah, the visionaries of the earliest apocalypses bring a religious
message to bear on the political and social situation of their times.
The two oldest Jewish apocalypses are contained in a work preserved
only in Ethiopic in its entirety, but fragments in Aramaic have also
been found among the Dead Sea Scrolls.[33] This larger, composite
work is called Ethiopic Enoch or *1 Enoch*.[34] The two shorter, incorporated works have been entitled by modern scholars "The Book of
the Watchers" and "The Astronomical Book" or "The Book of the
Heavenly Luminaries." The Book of the Heavenly Luminaries seems
to be a sectarian work concerned with the calendar. The Book of

---

[28] Kenelm O.L. Burridge, *New Heaven, New Earth* (New York: Schocken, 1969).
[29] John Gager, *Kingdom and Community: The Social World of Early Christianity* (Engle-
wood Cliffs, NJ: Prentice-Hall, 1975).
[30] Jonathan Z. Smith, "The Social Description of Early Christianity," *Religious
Studies Review* 1 (1975) 19–25, especially 20; idem, *Map Is Not Territory* (Leiden: Brill,
1978) 67–87 and 289–309; idem, *Imagining Religion: From Babylon to Jonestown* (Chicago: University of Chicago Press, 1982) 90–101.
[31] See, for example, John J. Collins, *The Apocalyptic Imagination* (New York: Crossroad, 1984), Christopher Rowland, *The Open Heaven* (New York: Crossroad, 1982),
and Martha Himmelfarb, *Tours of Hell* (Philadelphia: University of Pennsylvania
Press, 1983) and *Ascent to Heaven in Jewish and Christian Apocalypses* (New York/Oxford:
Oxford University Press, 1993).
[32] Such as, Adela Yarbro Collins, *Crisis and Catharsis: The Power of the Apocalypse*
(Philadelphia: Westminster Press, 1984); Leonard L. Thompson, *The Book of Revelation: Apocalypse and Empire* (New York/Oxford: Oxford University Press, 1990).
[33] See the discussion in Collins, *Apocalyptic Imagination*, 33.
[34] An English translation by M.A. Knibb is available in H.F.D. Sparks, ed., *The
Apocryphal Old Testament* (Oxford, Clarendon Press, 1984) 184–319. See also the translation by E. Isaac in James H. Charlesworth, ed., *The Old Testament Pseudepigrapha*
(Garden City: Doubleday, 1983) 1. 13–89.

the Watchers is an adaptation of the flood story; in it a story about
the Beginning becomes a story about the End. The "sons of God"
who, according to the book of Genesis, descended from heaven to
marry human women before the flood, are identified as fallen angels
or Watchers in the later Enoch literature. These Watchers corrupt
the earth by begetting violent and predatory giants and by teaching
humanity forbidden secrets, like the arts of war and cosmetology.
Cosmetology is condemned as conducive to fornication.[35]

It is evident that both of these texts arose in situations of cultural
conflict, including conflict over what we would call religious and
political values and power. Different Jewish groups had different
notions of what the correct calendar was. The calendar represented
not only a view of the fundamental nature of reality, but also a
practical guide for the observance of the temple cult and the festivals
of the religious year. The Watchers seem to be types or allegories of
oppressive foreign rulers, who claimed to be the offspring of the gods,
and of aristocratic priests, who, in the eyes of some of the common
people and their scribes, were marrying the wrong women and had
therefore become impure.[36] These two apocalypses were written in
the third century BCE, while Judah and Galilee were under the control
of the Greco-Egyptian kings and thus open to Hellenistic influence.
Such influence led to conflict between traditional Jewish and Hellenistic values.

As is well known, the book of Daniel is the oldest canonical apocalypse. It is not more than a century later than the two apocalypses
already mentioned. In the meantime, control over Judah and Galilee
had passed from the successors of Alexander in Egypt to those in
Syria. Daniel was written during a time of crisis, 164–168 BCE. This
crisis resulted from the interaction of a struggle for power among
Jewish aristocrats and the policies of the Greco-Syrian king, Antiochus
IV Epiphanes.[37] The purpose of Daniel is to interpret that crisis and

---

[35] See Max Küchler, *Schweigen, Schmuck und Schleier: Drei neutestamentliche Vorschriften
zur Verdrängung der Frauen auf dem Hintergrund einer frauenfeindlichen Exegese des Alten Testaments im antiken Judentum* (NTOA 1; Freiburg, Schweiz: Universitätsverlag Freiburg;
Göttingen: Vandenhoeck & Ruprecht, 1986) 258–75.

[36] See George W.E. Nickelsburg, "Apocalyptic and Myth in 1 Enoch 6–11," *JBL*
96 (1977) 383–405 and David W. Suter, "Fallen Angel, Fallen Priest. The Problem
of Family Purity in 1 Enoch 6–16," *HUCA* 50 (1979) 115–35; see also Paul D.
Hanson, "Rebellion in Heaven, Azazel and Euhemeristic Heroes in 1 Enoch 6–11,"
JBL 96 (1977) 195–233.

[37] For a recent analysis of the historical situation, see Klaus Bringmann, *Hellenistische*

to move its audience to live in accordance with the interpretation offered. The king is symbolized as a little horn on a monster that rises from the sea. This beast in turn symbolizes chaos, the force opposing the creator God who maintains proper order. Abandonment of Jewish tradition and Hellenization is tantamount to collaboration in a rebellion against heaven. Even if death results from resistance, potential martyrs are assured, through an adaptation of older prophecy (Isa 26:19), that they will rise from the dust and shine like the stars (Dan 12:2–3).

Similarly, the New Testament Book of Revelation expresses conflict between Christian and Roman social structures, cultural values, and ideology. This fundamental conflict is portrayed in Revelation in terms of the competing claims of Christian messianism and the Roman imperial cult. The book denies Roman claims to embody the golden age of Apollo by co-opting the story of Apollo's birth in a narrative about the birth of the messiah (chapter 12).[38] Revelation adapts prophetic oracles about the defeat of the nations and the popular Eastern expectation of the fall of Rome to maintain the imminent demise of the empire. The primary concern of the text is that its audience reject Roman propaganda and opt out, as far as possible, of Roman social structures and relations. The Christian people are to live within the Roman empire as if they had come out of it (see, for example, Rev 18:4).

It was noted earlier that the apocalyptic genre was not confined to one culture in the ancient world. The extension of the genre suggests that the virtual experience provided by the apocalypses had cross-cultural plausibility. This plausibility may be explored with regard to visions and visionary journeys. The visions of the apocalypses are of two types. Both types have their roots in prophecy. One is the symbolic vision, whose images are not intended to be literally true, but whose interpretation refers to heavenly and earthly beings and events. The vision of the statue composed of four metals in Daniel 2 and the four beasts arising out of the sea in Daniel 7 are examples of this type.

Reform und Religionsverfolgung in Judäa: Eine Untersuchung zur jüdisch-hellenistischen Geschichte (175–163 v. Chr.) (AAWG.PH 3. 132; Göttingen: Vandenhoeck & Ruprecht, 1983); see also John J. Collins, *Daniel: A Commentary on the Book of Daniel* (Hermeneia; Minneapolis, MN: Fortress, 1993) 61–71.

[38] Adela Yarbro Collins, *The Combat Myth in the Book of Revelation* (HDR 9; Missoula, MT: Scholars Press, 1976) 101–155.

The other type involves visions of heavenly beings, places and events, usually revealed in the course of a journey. In these cases, the referential character of the visions is crucial, because the view of reality expressed by the apocalypses depends on them. Further, the way of life implicitly advocated by the apocalypses is sanctioned by them, especially by the descriptions of the places of reward and punishment.

The apocalyptic visionaries have their counterparts in what historians of religion and anthropologists call the holy man, the divine man, or the shaman.[39] Such figures hold an important place in Greek tradition and are specially linked to the god Apollo.[40] The pre-Socratic philosopher, Parmenides, wrote a didactic poem which opens with a description of his journey on the chariot of the sun from the House of Night to the House of Day. Parmenides and other legendary or famous Greeks were remembered as healers; as seers; as purifiers, for example, of a city after bloodshed; and as thaumaturges. Such men were capable of making long journeys, sometimes "in spirit" and sometimes "in the body."

Abaris, the legendary servant of Apollo, was said to have traveled to the land of the Hyperboreans, a legendary people of the far North. He was said to have made the journey riding astride a golden arrow, a symbol of the god. Aristeas, another legendary servant of Apollo, was capable of ἔκστασις, that is, the literal separation of the soul from the body. He was said to have produced the semblance of his death in northern Asia Minor and then appeared in southern Italy to spread the worship of Apollo. Like Abaris, he is also said to have traveled to the land of the Hyperboreans. Epimenides was a thaumaturge from Crete. It was said that, while his body appeared lifeless, his soul visited the gods. Empedocles, a pre-Socratic philosopher like Parmenides, was believed to have been called to heaven by a divine voice. Instead of dying, he was taken up to the gods.

These phenomena seem to be cross-cultural. Mircea Eliade has noted that shamans from various cultures are visionaries who are taken to heavenly realms in their visions.[41] In other words, they experience the ascent type of vision. They report sensations of flying

---

[39] Susan Niditch, "The Visionary," in J.J. Collins and G.W.E. Nickelsburg, eds., *Ideal Figures in Ancient Judaism: Profiles and Paradigms* (SBL Septuagint and Cognate Studies 12; Chico, CA: Scholars Press, 1980) 153–79.

[40] Ioan P. Couliano, *Expériences de L'Extase* (BH; Paris: Payot, 1984) 25–43.

[41] Mircea Eliade, *Shamanism: Archaic Techniques of Ecstasy* (Bollingen Series 76; Princeton, NJ: Princeton University Press, 1964; French ed., 1951) 181–214.

through the sky, or of being carried into the sky. Some seers speak of the ascent in terms of their spirits or souls taking leave of their bodies. In another Jewish apocalypse attributed to Enoch, the Similitudes of Enoch, Enoch is presented as saying:

> And it came to pass after this that my spirit was carried off, and it went up into the heavens (*1 Enoch* 71:1).

This passsage is evidence for the notion and probably the experience of ἔκστασις among Jewish apocalyptists.

Although Paul wrote letters, not apocalypses, it is generally agreed that his letters presuppose an apocalyptic world view. For example, in 2 Corinthians 12 Paul speaks about "visions and revelations of the Lord," remarking:

> I know a man in Christ who fourteen years ago was caught up to the third heaven—whether in the body or out of the body I do not know, God knows. And I know that this man was caught up into Paradise—whether in the body or out of the body I do not know, God knows—and he heard things that cannot be told, which man may not utter. On behalf of this man I will boast, but on my own behalf I will not boast, except of my weaknesses (2 Cor 12:2–5).

Most commentators are agreed that Paul here is speaking about his own experience, because in vs 7 he says "And to keep me from being too elated by the abundance of revelations, a thorn was given me in the flesh, . . . to keep me from being too elated."

Paul's comments that he did not know whether his journey to the third heaven and to Paradise took place in the body or out of the body, show at least that he was aware of visionary lore which distinguished between two types of ascent.

As has been noted, the apocalyptic visions of the ascent-type are related to Jewish mystical texts. According to these texts, meditation on the Merkabah, the divine chariot or throne, is an important means of contact with the divine. The root of this activity, which is usually called Merkabah mysticism, is meditation on Isaiah 6 and especially Ezekiel 1. Evidence of this practice can be found in Jewish apocalyptic and other intertestamental literature, especially in a text from Qumran, the *Songs of the Sabbath Sacrifice*, edited and published by Carol Newsom.[42] This is a liturgical text consisting of thirteen separate

---

[42] Carol Newsom, *The Songs of the Sabbath Sacrifice: A Critical Edition* (HSS; Atlanta: Scholars Press, 1985).

compositions, one for each of the first thirteen Sabbaths of the year.[43] These thirteen compositions call forth angelic praise, describe the angelic priesthood and the heavenly temple, and give an account of the worship carried out in the heavenly sanctuary on that particular Sabbath. The fragmentary condition of the text makes interpretation tentative, but the song seems to progress from the praise sung by the outer parts of the temple to the innermost room, the Holy of Holies. There appears to be a brief description of the divine throne.

The seventh Sabbath song, as the center of the thirteen compositions, is in an emphatic position. The first two Sabbath songs are didactic and informational; in them the role of the worshipping human community is fairly prominent. The language of the sixth through the eighth, in contrast, is formulaic and repetitive. Newsom suggests that the repetition had a hypnotic effect on the community reciting the songs.[44] The middle three songs contain several lists and sequences of seven. A list of numbered elements involves an almost involuntary participation of the audience, who anticipate the execution of the sequences. Since the community believed that the number seven was holy and had cosmic significance, the combination of the "external" fact of its being the seventh Sabbath and the "internal" or literary repetition of the number would have had a strong emotional effect. In other words, the song has an ecstatic quality and may have evoked mystical or even visionary experiences for the members of the community.

The book of Revelation is an interesting parallel. The book is an account of a visionary experience of the early Christian prophet John. It was intended to be read aloud to the seven congregations mentioned in chapters 1–3. The reading of the book was a representation of the ecstatic experience of the seer for the members of those congregations. The number seven is used in Revelation as a structuring principle and as an explicit literary device of sequencing. The repetition of the number and its sacred character may have had an emotional impact on the audience of this book as well.[45]

---

[43] Since the calendar of the book of *Jubilees* and of Qumran divided the year into four periods of thirteen weeks, it may be that the recitation of the songs began anew for each period; see Israel Knohl, "Between Voice and Silence: The Relationship between Prayer and Temple Cult," *JBL* 115 (1996) 17–30, especially 26, n. 26.

[44] Newsom, *Songs of the Sabbath Sacrifice*, 13–15.

[45] On the sacred character of the number seven, see Chapter Three below, "Numerical Symbolism in Jewish and Early Christian Apocalyptic Literature."

The two emphases of the ancient apocalypses, historical and heavenly, suggest that their original meaning conveys a revealed interpretation of history: past, present, and future. That meaning is rendered plausible by the visionary's claim to mystical experience. The virtual mystical experience of the audience lured them to accept the interpretation of their historical situation offered and to shape their lives in accordance with it.

INTERPRETING THE APOCALYPSES: SIGNIFICANCE

Among those who have recognized the social and political concerns of the apocalypses, some have taken their visions as literal prophecies of political and military events to be fulfilled in the twentieth century. The most famous of these is Hal Lindsey.[46] Even though he has had to adjust the date of the End at least once, this way of reading apocalyptic texts is still widespread. This mode of reading the apocalypses is inadequate because of its aesthetic, religious, and moral poverty. It is aesthetically and religiously poor because it takes apocalyptic symbols as steno-symbols[47] or flat allegories, missing their multivalent symbolic meaning and their rich traditional connotations. It is morally poor because it associates the dragon, the beast and other symbols of chaos and evil only with the "other," the current enemy, leaving the audience to imagine themselves and their institutions as pure and innocent.

When the apocalyptic meaning of the message of Jesus was rediscovered near the end of the nineteenth century by the German scholar Johannes Weiss, he suggested that modern Christians reinterpret the end of the world in terms of the end each one of us must face, namely, death.[48] Many in the twentieth century, for whom the apocalyptic vision had been a broken myth, have rediscovered its power in contemplating the possibility of a nuclear winter, major nuclear

---

[46] Hal Lindsey, *The Late Great Planet Earth* (59th printing; Grand Rapids: Zondervan, 1977); for a critique of this mode of interpretation, see Robert Jewett, "Coming to Terms with the Doom Boom," *QR* 4 (1984) 9–22.

[47] The term "steno-symbol" derives from Philip Wheelwright; see idem, *Metaphor and Reality* (Bloomington: Indiana University Press, 1962) and *The Burning Fountain* (rev. ed.; Bloomington: Indiana University Press, 1968).

[48] Johannes Weiss, *Jesus' Proclamation of the Kingdom of God* (Lives of Jesus Series; ed. R.H. Hiers and D.L. Holland; Germ ed., 1892; Philadelphia: Fortress, 1971) 135–36.

accidents, and ecological disasters.[49] The vision of a new Jerusalem has sustained the likes of Martin Luther King in this country and Allan Boesak in South Africa, as they struggled against racism.[50]

Many Biblical scholars prefer the prophetic literature to the apocalypses, admiring the realism of the prophets and deploring the fantasies and bizarre visions of the apocalyptic seers.[51] Others have pointed out that apocalyptic language is born of extreme social dislocation and anomie.[52] It is not a frivolous or arbitary choice of a fantasy-world, but a profound expression of crisis among those who are cut off from the sources of social and religious power.

It is relatively easy to make a case for the significance of the apocalypses with regard to social relations, conflict, and issues of power. Rather than seeing apocalyptic symbols as flat allegories or stenosymbols of historical events or as products of deluded fantasy and wish-fulfillment, one can argue that they comprise an alternative symbolic system to the conventional wisdom of their time. In other words, human beings are symbol-makers, social structures are based on symbolic systems, and social change is correlated with the creation of new symbolic systems. Those who see themselves as oppressed by the dominant social system need an alternative symbolic system to the dominant one in order to imagine what kind of social change is needed.

It is much more difficult to retrieve the mystical dimension of the meaning of the apocalypses. The modern mentality rejected language about the supernatural world as ontologically meaningless; it was seen, at best, as an expression of emotion. In the post-modern mentality, pluralism is accepted and each community of "faith," including reli-

---

[49] Michael Barkun, "Divided Apocalypse: Thinking About the End in Contemporary America," *Soundings* 66 (1983) 257–80, especially 263–66.

[50] Allan A. Boesak, *Comfort and Protest: Reflections on the Apocalypse of John of Patmos* (Philadelphia: Westminster, 1987).

[51] Such a value judgment is implied, for example, in Paul Hanson's remark that "the visionaries have largely ceased to translate [the cosmic vision of God's sovereignty] into the terms of plain history, real politics, and human instrumentality due to a pessimistic view of reality growing out of the bleak post-exilic conditions within which those associated with the visionaries found themselves" (*Dawn of Apocalyptic* [Philadelphia: Fortress, 1975] 11–12).

[52] For example, Amos Wilder, "The Rhetoric of Ancient and Modern Apocalyptic," *Interpretation* 25 (1971) 436–53; reprinted as "Apocalyptic Rhetorics," in idem, *Jesus' Parables and the War of Myths* (ed. James Breech; Philadelphia: Fortress, 1982) 153–68. Paul Hanson also expresses this point of view in "Apocalyptic Consciousness," *QR* 4 (1984) 23–39.

gious and secular groups centered on some tradition or ideology, is expected to live in accordance with their inherited or chosen, unprovable perspective. Even in post-modern circles, at least in academia, there is still a pervasive practical atheism and materialism. What is real is what can be perceived with the senses, measured and tested, or at least verbalized.

In this cultural context, the satisfactions derived from a naive reading of the apocalypses constitute a faint cry to their cultured despisers that the world of spirit be rediscovered or at least taken more seriously. Rudolf Otto's reflections on the *mysterium tremendum*[53] and Mircea Eliade's on the sacred[54] may seem unduly subjective nowadays when theologians and social scientists alike emphasize the cultural and linguistic more than the cognitive and experiential.[55] The forms and contents of the apocalyptic visions are certainly conditioned by the cultural and linguistic contexts in which they arose. But cross-cultural similarities suggest a common root in the psychology of religion and perhaps even in experience.

The trembling, violent quaking, fainting and similar descriptions of the seer's physical and emotional state in the apocalypses recall trance states described by I.M. Lewis in his book *Ecstatic Religion*.[56] Prayer, solitude, fasting and penance are the activites most commonly narrated prior to the apocalyptists' visionary experiences. Mourning may have been one of the most important techniques in inducing an alternate psychic state.[57] The last and longest vision of Daniel was preceded in the narrative by three weeks of mourning. The vision of Daniel 9 came in response to Daniel's seeking the Lord "by prayer and supplications with fasting and sackcloth and ashes" (vs 3).

The deutero-canonical Apocalypse of Ezra (2 Esdras 3–14; also referred to as *4 Ezra*) and the Syriac Apocalypse of Baruch (*2 Baruch*)

---

[53] Rudolf Otto, *The Idea of the Holy* (New York: Oxford University Press, 1958; Germ. ed. 1917).

[54] Mircea Eliade, *Patterns in Comparative Religion* (New York: World, 1963).

[55] See the reference to George Lindbeck by Wayne Meeks in Meeks, *The First Urban Christians: The Social World of the Apostle Paul* (New Haven: Yale University Press, 1983) 7.

[56] I.M. Lewis, *Ecstatic Religion* (Baltimore: Penguin Books, 1971).

[57] This is the thesis of Daniel Merkur which he presented in a paper, "The Visionary Practices of Jewish Apocalyptists," at the Annual Meeting of the Society of Biblical Literature in Boston, December 5, 1987. For a different type of psychological interpretation of texts involving ascent, see David J. Halperin, *The Faces of the Chariot: Early Jewish Responses to Ezekiel's Vision* (Tübingen: Mohr [Siebeck], 1988). For a historical interpretation, see Himmelfarb, *Ascent to Heaven*, 69–71.

were both composed near the end of the first century CE in response to the Jewish War with Rome that resulted in the second
destruction of Jerusalem and the temple.[58] They present themselves
as written in response to the first destruction in the sixth century
BCE and thus draw an analogy between the two catastrophes. In
both these works mourning plays a major role, both as a response to
the political crisis and perhaps as a visionary technique. At the end
of Ezra's first vision, which consisted of a dialogue between the seer
and the angel Uriel, the angel tells him "if you pray again, and
weep as you do now, and fast for seven days, you shall hear yet
greater things than these" (*4 Ezra* 5:13). Ezra follows the instructions
and has a second visionary dialogue. The same procedure is followed for a third visionary experience. Since the visions occurred at
night (6:30, 36; 7:1), it may be that sight and sleep deprivation were
additional inductive techniques. In *2 Baruch*, the actual destruction of
the temple is described. Then the seer says:

> And I, Baruch, came, together with Jeremiah,. . . . And we rent our
> clothes and wept, and we mourned and fasted seven days. And after
> seven days the word of God came to me and said to me (there follows
> a message for Jeremiah) (*2 Baruch* 9:1–10:1).

Baruch's other revelatory experiences are preceded by grief, laments
and fasts of seven days. Ruth Underhill and Ake Hultkrantz have
shown that the visionaries among North American Indians induced
their visions by similar techniques, including prayers, weeping while
calling for the help and pity of the spirits, solitude, fasting, thirst,
sexual abstinence, sleep deprivation and sometimes self-mutilation
and torture.[59] The similarities do not imply historical connections between North American Indians and the ancient apocalypses, but
suggest a common basis in the psychology of religion.

The mourning which leads to visions is often spontaneous. Great
grief can lead quite naturally, if not inevitably, to an inadequate diet,
loss of sleep, solitude, complaint and fatigue. Whether spontaneous

---

[58] An English translation of *4 Ezra* is available, for example, in *The New Oxford
Annotated Bible with the Apocrypha* (ed. H.G. May and B.M. Metzger; New York:
Oxford University Press, 1977). *2 Baruch* may be found in an English translation by
A.F.J. Klijn in Charlesworth, *OTP*, 1. 621–52.

[59] Ruth M. Underhill, *Red Man's Religion: Beliefs and Practices of the Indians North of
Mexico* (Chicago: University of Chicago Press, 1965) 96–98, 99–100, 102–103; Ake
Hultkrantz, *The Religions of the American Indians* (Berkeley: University of California
Press, 1979; Swedish ed., 1967) 70–71, 73, 94–96, 108, 121–22.

or deliberate, these conditions produce depression which triggers an unconscious process leading to a waking dream state. The visions themselves were not always or only terrifying, but also exhilarating. This aspect is not explicit in all the apocalypses, but may be implied. On one occasion Ezra says:

> O sovereign Lord, . . . show me, thy servant, the interpretation and meaning of this terrifying vision, that thou mayest fully comfort my soul. For thou hast judged me worthy to be shown the end of the times and the last events of the times (*4 Ezra* 12:7–9).

The exhilaration is explicit in a later Jewish apocalypse that was probably composed in Egypt. In the Slavonic Apocalypse of Enoch, usually referred to as *2 Enoch*, Enoch is taken on a journey through the seven heavens.[60] In the fourth heaven he sees an armed host, worshipping God with cymbals, organs, and unceasing voices. When he hears this host, he says, "And I was delighted as I listened to them" (*2 Enoch* 17:1). Psychologists speak of this shift from depression to elation as an unconscious defense against depression, which Freud and others have called "a bi-polar mechanism of the psyche."[61] Psychological language, however, is as much a subjective interpretation of the phenomena as the accounts of the visionaries themselves, who attribute the experiences to the world of the Spirit.

In the ancient world, mystical experiences often constituted the basis for legitimation of a leader or played a role in the formation of the legend of some hero of the past. In the United States of the twentieth century such experiences are suspect, at least in the public discourse of the elite. Recent developments, like the growth of New Age religion and the consultation of an astrologer in the White House, suggest that the needs of the human spirit are not being dealt with adequately in that discourse.

CONCLUSION

This discussion of the ancient apocalypses is based on the premise that the intention of these texts is to point beyond themselves to

---

[60] See the English translation by F.I. Andersen in Charlesworth, *OTP*, 1. 102–213.

[61] The term was used by Merkur; see note 56.

social situations and to mystical experiences. They are not independent sacred objects, but are context-bound. The most appropriate
constructions of "the world in front of the text" are those which are
analogous to the way in which the text functioned in "the world
behind the text."[62] The two main emphases of the apocalypses, social-
religious critique and mystical experience, were mutually supportive
in their original context. Any retrieval of these texts should take into
account, not only their aesthetic and traditionally religious qualities,
but also their latent transformative power.

---

[62] Paul Ricoeur has called for interpretations which pay attention to "the world
in front of the text," rather than to "the world behind the text," on which the
historical-critics usually concentrate. See the discussion by Lewis S. Mudge, "Paul
Ricoeur on Biblical Interpretation," in Paul Ricoeur, *Essays on Biblical Interpretation*
(ed. with an Introduction by Lewis S. Mudge; Philadelphia: Fortress, 1980) 25–27
and Ricoeur's own comments, ibid., 98–104.

CHAPTER TWO

THE SEVEN HEAVENS IN JEWISH AND CHRISTIAN APOCALYPSES

The *religionsgeschichtliche Schule* of the late nineteenth and early twentieth centuries attempted to explain the origin and development of
the Israelite, Jewish and early Christian religions in terms of their
interaction with other cultural traditions. The traditions of Sumer,
Babylon, and Persia and the phenomena of "Hellenistic Oriental
syncretism" were brought to bear on Israelite, Jewish and Christian
texts because the explanation of origins was thought to go a long
way toward illuminating meaning and function. The complex of ideas
related to the motif of the ascent to heaven was a major topic
addressed by members of the history of religions school. Although
some scholars argued for the origin of the tradition in Babylon and
others in Persia, they shared the assumption that the number of
heavens involved was an indication of the cultural origin of the notion
of ascent.

The first influential study of ascents to heaven in antiquity was
Anz's *Ursprung des Gnostizismus*, published in 1897.[1] Study of the Mithras mysteries and Gnostic systems suggests that the later teaching
is connected with belief in seven planetary star-gods.[2] Anz argued
that the teaching of seven heavens was connected with the seven
planetary gods and that the whole complex originated in Babylonian
tradition.

Even more influential than Anz's study, was that of Wilhelm
Bousset, "Die Himmelsreise der Seele," published in 1901.[3] Bousset
argued that Persian religion is the home of the notion of the ascent
of the soul. This notion involved both the ecstatic ascent during a
human being's lifetime and a final ascent after death. He agreed
with Anz that the teaching of seven heavens originated in late

---

[1] Wilhelm Anz, *Zur Frage nach dem Ursprung des Gnostizismus: Ein religionsgeschicht-
licher Versuch* (TU 15.4; Leipzig: Hinrichs, 1897).
[2] Wilhelm Bousset, "Die Himmelsreise der Seele," *ARW* 4 (1901) 236–37, with
reference to Anz.
[3] Wilhelm Bousset, "Die Himmelsreise der Seele," *ARW* 4 (1901) 136–69, and
229–73.

Babylonian religion, but argued that many texts contain evidence
for an older view, namely, that there were three heavens and over
these, Paradise. This older view, according to Bousset, was Persian
in origin. Therefore, one can speak only of a secondary influence of
Babylonian religion.

The views of these two scholars have been challenged by Ioan
Culianu. He has argued that the motif of the seven planetary heavens could not be derived from Babylonian religion because, for the
Babylonians, the seven planets moved on the same plane, that is, at
the same distance from the earth. It was the Greek astronomers during the time of Plato who first conceived the idea that the planets
moved at different distances from the earth. This idea arose as an
explanation for the differing lengths of time it took each planet,
supposedly, to circle the earth.[4] He argued further that the Babylonian
cosmology made use of a variable number of heavens, from one to
ten, with the exception of six. The notion of three heavens was no
less conventional than seven. But since the Babylonians never arrived
at the idea that the planets circled at different distances from the
earth, there was never a link between the vaults of heaven and the
planets. Thus, he rejected the argument of the history of religions
school that a cosmological scheme involving seven planetary spheres
was borrowed from the Babylonians.[5]

In discussing the Jewish and Jewish-Christian apocalypses, Culianu
has remarked that an important feature of all these works is the
absence of any relation between the seven heavens and the seven
planets.[6] His own proposal for a classification of ascents involves two
types: (1) the "Greek" type, in which beliefs concerning ascent are
conformed to scientific hypotheses; and (2) the "Jewish" type, involving a journey through three or seven heavens which are never identified with planetary heavens. He indicated that the myth of Er in
book ten of Plato's *Republic* and the eschatological myths of Plutarch
either belong to the "Jewish" type or to a third, "mixed" type. With
regard to the second, "Jewish" type, he suggested that it may have
developed under Babylonian influence, but he did not pursue this
point at all.[7]

---

[4] Ioan P. Culianu, *Psychanodia I* (EPRO; Leiden: Brill, 1983) 27–28.
[5] Ioan P. Coulianu, *Expériences de l'extase: Extase, ascension et récit visionnaire de l'Hellén-
isme au moyen âge* (Paris: Payot, 1984) 10.
[6] Culianu, *Psychanodia*, 56.
[7] Culianu, *Expériences de l'extase*, 20.

Culianu's criticism of the theories of Anz and Bousset has reopened the question of the origin of the motifs of the three and the seven heavens in the Jewish and early Christian apocalypses. His brief suggestion that these motifs may have been borrowed from Babylon without any link to the seven planets requires exploration. If the seven heavens were not linked to the seven planets, what did they signify? This is the question to be addressed in this chapter.

I shall begin with a brief discussion of the usage of the Hebrew Bible and its Greek translation, raising the question whether they presuppose multiple heavens. After a brief look at The Book of the Watchers, I shall examine the oldest Jewish and Christian texts that speak of a plurality of heavens and give them a definite number. These texts date to the period from the end of the second century BCE to the second century CE. Some are apocalypses and the others manifest an apocalyptic perspective. Among the texts that I will discuss, three are Jewish works, that is, *The Life of Adam and Eve*, the *Apocalypse of Abraham*, and *2 Enoch*. Two are Christian in their present form, but were probably Jewish compositions originally, namely, the *Testament of Levi* and *3 Baruch*. The *Martyrdom and Ascension of Isaiah* as a whole is a Christian work in two parts. The first part, the story of Isaiah's martyrdom, may have been based on a Jewish work. The account of Isaiah's ascent, however, which is the part relevant to this study, is a Christian composition. Paul's account of his ascent in 2 Corinthians 12 is of course a Christian text, but it may provide evidence also for the practice of ascent in the type of Judaism to which Paul had belonged. I shall also mention The Similitudes of Enoch, another Jewish work, since it seems to reflect the motif of three heavens.

THE HEBREW BIBLE AND ITS OLD GREEK TRANSLATION

The word for heaven in the Hebrew Bible is הַשָּׁמַיִם. According to von Rad, this abnormal plural can only be regarded as a secondary shortening. Its etymology is obscure.[8] He concludes that Israel was not acquainted with the idea of many intersecting heavenly spheres, although there may be an echo of this Babylonian view in the phrase שְׁמֵי הַשָּׁמַיִם. This phrase could be translated "heaven of heavens," as

---

[8] Gerhard von Rad, "οὐρανός, B. Old Testament," *TDNT* 5 (1967) 502.

von Rad does, or "heaven of heaven," as Bietenhard takes it.[9] If the translation "heaven of heavens" is correct, the phrase implies the existence of at least three heavens. If "heaven of heaven" is the meaning, the phrase distinguishes two heavens: the heaven above the earth that human beings see and a heaven that is above the visible heaven.[10] The phrase occurs in the climax of the historical review of Deuteronomy (10:14), in the prayer of Solomon at the dedication of the temple (1 Kings 8:27), in Ezra's confession in Nehemiah 9:6, and in other contexts involving prayer.[11] Though the phrase may reflect Babylonian ideas, it may have been used simply as rhetorical hyperbole.[12]

In the Old Greek translation of the Hebrew Bible, the singular of the Greek word for heaven, οὐρανός, is the almost exclusive translation of the Hebrew שָׁמַיִם and its Aramaic equivalent.[13] In the Old Greek, οὐρανός occurs 51 times in the plural. This usage is rare in classical Greek and probably came into Greek usage through the Septuagint, the Greek translation of the Hebrew Bible. In the earlier writings of the Septuagint, the plural οὐρανοί should probably be taken as a "translation-plural," reflecting the hyperbole or fullness of expression typical of hymnic and liturgical style.[14] In later writings, the plural is more common and should be taken, in many cases, as a true plural.[15] In the phrase "who created the heavens and the earth," which occurs in Judith, the Psalms, and Proverbs, οὐρανοί is probably a true plural, reflecting the idea of a plurality of heavens. This idea most likely became more common among Jews from the time of the Babylonian exile and indicates the influence of Babylonian cosmology on Jewish writers.

THE BOOK OF THE WATCHERS

The oldest part of the composite work known as *Ethiopic Enoch* or *1 Enoch* consists of the first thirty-six chapters, usually called The

[9] Ibid., 503; Hans Bietenhard, *Die himmlische Welt im Urchristentum und Spätjudentum* (WUNT 2; Tübingen: Mohr [Siebeck], 1951) 11.
[10] Bietenhard, *Die himmlische Welt*, 11.
[11] Ps 148:4, 2 Chr 2:5, 6:18.
[12] von Rad, "Old Testament," 503.
[13] Helmut Traub, "οὐρανός, C. Septuagint and Judaism," *TDNT* 5 (1967) 509.
[14] Ibid., 510.
[15] 2 Chr 28:9; 2 Macc 15:23; 3 Macc 2:2; Wis 9:10, 16; 18:15; Tob 8:5; see Traub, "Septuagint and Judaism," 511.

Book of the Watchers. It is characterized by the story of the fallen angels or Watchers, found in chapters 6–11, and by Enoch's journeys to heaven and to the ends of the earth. In chapter 1:4, Enoch utters a "parable," regarding an eschatological epiphany of God. In the Greek version, it is said that God will appear in the power of his strength from the heaven of the heavens.[16] It is likely that this phrase is hyperbolic, since, when Enoch travels to the heavenly throne of God in chapter 14, there is no indication of a plurality of heavens.[17]

THE TESTAMENT OF LEVI

The work entitled the *Testaments of the Twelve Patriarchs* has been preserved in Greek, Armenian and Slavonic versions. All three versions are Christian in their present form. A number of scholars have argued that this work was originally a Jewish composition and that it has been revised by one or more Christian editors. If the probably Christian passages are left aside, internal evidence suggests a date toward the end of the second century BCE.[18] Since 1955 several fragments of one or more Aramaic Levi-documents have been discovered at Qumran.[19] One of these fragments shows clearly that at least one such document contained an account of a vision of Levi that involved more than one heaven.[20] Some of the Aramaic fragments overlap with the Greek version. Thus, the conclusion is warranted that the Christian Greek version was based on a Jewish work written in Aramaic.

[16] ἀπὸ τοῦ οὐρανοῦ τῶν οὐρανῶν; see Matthew Black, *Apocalypsis Henochi Graece* (Leiden: Brill, 1970) 19.

[17] But the motif of the seven stars in the Book of the Watchers probably reflects an understanding of the seven planets which was already outdated at the time the work was composed; see Chapter Three below, "Numerical Symbolism in Jewish and Christian Apocalyptic Literature," the section on "Order in the Macrocosmos."

[18] Robert Henry Charles, *The Greek Versions of the Testaments of the Twelve Patriarchs* (Oxford: Clarendon, 1908; reprint, Hildesheim: Olms Verlagsbuchhandlung, 1960) ix.

[19] 4Q213 TestLevi^a; originally published by J.T. Milik in *RB* 62 (1955) 398–406; see the discussion in H.W. Hollander and M. de Jonge, *The Testaments of the Twelve Patriarchs: A Commentary* (SVTP; Leiden: Brill, 1985) 17–18. Another fragment is 4Q Test Levi^a 8 III, published and discussed by J.T. Milik, *The Books of Enoch: Aramaic Fragments of Qumran Cave 4* (Oxford: Clarendon, 1976). Milik has announced the discovery of fragments of a second document, 4Q Test Levi^b (*RB* 73 [1966] 95, n. 2 and *The Books of Enoch*, 214). Fragments of an Aramaic Levi-document were also found in the first cave at Qumran (Hollander and de Jonge, *The Testaments of the Twelve Patriarchs*, 18).

[20] 4Q TestLevi^a col. II, lines 11–18.

The *Testament of Levi* contains an account of Levi's ascent into heaven
(chapters 2–3). There are two recensions of the Greek version. The
earlier of these involves three heavens; the later speaks of seven.[21]
Both recensions may have existed in Aramaic. Another possibility is
that the Aramaic Levi-documents involved only three heavens and
the motif of seven heavens was first added at some stage in the Greek
transmission of the work. Thus the possibility must also be kept in
mind that it was a Christian redactor who added the motif of the
seven heavens.

The first Greek recension describes Levi's ascent as follows:

> And behold, the heavens were opened, and an angel of the Lord said
> to me, "Levi, Levi, come in." And I entered the first heaven and I saw
> there much water hanging. And I saw yet a second heaven that was
> much brighter and more radiant. For there was unlimited height[22] in
> it. And I said to the angel, "Why are these things so?" And the angel
> said to me, "Do not marvel concerning this (heaven), for you will see
> another heaven more radiant and beyond comparison (with it). And
> when you go up there, you will stand near the Lord, and you will be
> a minister to him, and you will announce his mysteries to human beings,
> and you will make a proclamation concerning the coming redemption
> of Israel.[23] (*T. Levi* 2:6–10).

In the following chapter (*T. Levi* 3), the angel instructs Levi about
the heavens. The lower heaven is sad or gloomy because it sees all
the unrighteous deeds of humanity. It contains fire, snow, and ice,
prepared for the day of judgment. In it also are the winds or the
spirits associated with the punishment of humanity. In the second
heaven are the heavenly powers that are to punish the spirits of error
and of Beliar. And in the highest dwelling of all is the Great Glory
above all holiness.

It is possible that the notion of the three heavens in this work
results from an inner Jewish development, based perhaps on a reading of שְׁמֵי הַשָּׁמַיִם in the Hebrew Bible as "heaven of heavens," that
is, as implying three heavens. It is more likely that its use implies a
picture of the world based on Babylonian cosmology.

---

[21] Charles argued that the two Greek recensions were translations of two Hebrew
recensions; since the Aramaic fragments have been discovered, the hypothesis of a
Hebrew original has been discarded (*The Greek Versions of the Testaments of the Twelve
Patriarchs*, xxxviii).

[22] Charles emends to "light" (ibid., 30, n. 38).

[23] Charles considered the words "the coming redemption of" to be a Christian
modification of the text (ibid., 31, n. 55).

According to W.G. Lambert, the basic picture of the universe current in Mesopotamia in the first millennium BCE involved "superimposed levels, the earth being roughly in the middle, the stars and heaven above, and cosmic water and the underworld below."[24] He also notes that the Babylonians had a doctrine of several superimposed heavens.[25] He implies that the most conventional number of heavens, at least in the second and early first millennia BCE, was three.[26] He notes that the fullest exposition of the levels of the Babylonian universe occurs in a non-literary text that has been preserved in a short and a long form. Both forms speak of three heavenly levels: the upper heavens, the middle heavens, and the lower heavens.[27] In the shorter, older form, the upper heavens are the abode of Anu, the nominal ruler of the universe. Each level is made of a different precious stone. The lower heavens are made of jasper, from which the sky derives its blue color. The stars are visible to those on earth from this level.[28]

An indication that the cosmology of the *Testament of Levi* may be based on Babylonian tradition is that what is called "the first heaven" in *T. Levi* 2:7 is called "the lower (heaven)" in 3:1.[29] In chapter 3, the third heaven is called "the upper dwelling" (3:4).[30] The terms "lower" and "upper" with respect to heavenly levels are reminiscent of typical Babylonian expressions.

The "much water hanging" that Levi sees in the first heaven reflects the idea that there are waters above the firmament expressed in Gen 1:7.[31] This motif probably derives from Babylon also, since it appears in the *Enuma elish* IV 139–140. The notion that the first heaven contains fire, snow, ice, and winds prepared for the day of judgment, is probably based on older Jewish tradition.[32]

---

[24] W.G. Lambert, "The Cosmology of Sumer and Babylon," in Carmen Blacker and Michael Loewe, eds., *Ancient Cosmologies* (London: Allen & Unwin, 1975) 44–45.

[25] Ibid., 58.

[26] See also Alasdair Livingstone, *Mystical and Mythological Explanatory Works of Assyrian and Babylonian Scholars* (Clarendon: Oxford, 1986) 82–86.

[27] Livingstone's translation of the same or a similar text speaks of "the upper heaven," "the middle heaven," and "the lower heaven" (ibid., 82–83).

[28] Lambert, "The Cosmology of Sumer and Babylon," 58–59.

[29] ὁ κατώτερος; see Charles, *The Greek Versions*, 32.

[30] τῷ ἀνωτέρῳ . . . καταλύματι; ibid., 33.

[31] For further references in the Bible, the apocrypha, and the pseudepigrapha, see Hollander and de Jonge, *The Testaments of the Twelve Patriarchs*, 134.

[32] Compare Job 38:22–24, Sir 39:28–29; for further references see Hollander and de Jonge, *The Testaments*, 137.

Unfortunately, there does not seem to be sufficient evidence to
determine when the recension of the *Testament of Levi* that refers to
seven heavens originated. All that we can say is that it was created
sometime after the end of the second century BCE.[33] It is striking
that this recension does not add any new information about the
contents of the heavens. It simply divides the information given in
the first recension among a greater number of heavens. This state of
affairs supports Charles' conclusion that the notion of seven heavens
is secondary.

It is not likely that the motif of seven heavens is the result of an
inner-Jewish development. Like the notion of three heavens, it was
probably inspired by Babylonian tradition. According to Francesca
Rochberg-Halton, the two most common numbers of the heavens in
Babylonian and Assyrian tradition are three and seven.[34] In an article on Mesopotamian cosmology, she argued that the plurality of
heavens and earths is not an innovation of first millennium Babylonia.
Sumerian incantations of the late second millennium already refer to
seven heavens and seven earths.[35] As an example, she cites a short
incantation which has the frequently used incipit "heavens are seven,
earths are seven," expressing a common mythological theme.[36] Since
their nature and extent are not discussed in this early literature, she
suggests that the seven heavens may be another derivation from the
magical properties of the number seven, like the seven demons or
the seven thrones, rather than evidence of an early stage in the
development of a consistent cosmography.[37]

According to R. Campbell Thompson, the Babylonians cultivated
one of the most elaborate and intricate systems of ancient magic that
we know.[38] Much of Babylonian magic is concerned with "the Seven,"

---

[33] See the discussion of date in Charles, *The Greek Versions*, xlii–xliv.

[34] Personal communication.

[35] Francesca Rochberg-Halton, "Mesopotamian Cosmology," in Norriss S.
Hetherington, ed., *Encyclopedia of Cosmology: Historical, Philosophical, and Scientific Foundations of Modern Cosmology* (New York/London: Garland Publishing, 1993) 398–407,
especially 401.

[36] J. van Dyjk, A. Goetze, and M.I. Hussey, eds., *Early Mesopotamian Incantations
and Rituals* (Yale Oriental Series, Babylonian Texts 11. 67b; New Haven: Yale
University Press, 1985) 44; cf. 13 and Plate LXVI.

[37] Rochberg-Halton, "Mesopotamian Cosmology," 402; cf. Livingstone, *Mystical and
Mythological Explanatory Works*, 159. On the seven thrones, see a Sumerian blessing of
the royal throne in van Dyjk, Goetze, and Hussey, eds., *Early Mesopotamian Incantations
and Rituals*, 39; cf. 12 and Plate LIX. On the seven demons or evil spirits, see below.

[38] R. Campbell Thompson, *Semitic Magic: Its Origins and Development* (New York:
Ktav, 1971; originally published in 1908) 1.

seven malefic spirits who were thought to cause much evil and destruction.[39] The number seven appears frequently in magical ritual. One of the Assyrian incantation texts in the series *Maqlû* involves two sets of seven figures representing two sets of seven female magicians.[40] In an incantation for healing, "the seven wise ones of Eridu" are called upon for help.[41]

According to a certain spell, a person suffering from chills and fever was to be anointed seven times with water from a bowl to which various preparations had been added.[42] An Assyrian tablet dealing with the laying of ghosts calls for seven small loaves.[43] A prayer to use when a dead man appears to a living man for evil, to turn him back, involves a ceremony in which seven knots are tied in a thread.[44] An incantation to break a spell is to be recited seven times.[45] A text on the seventh tablet of the *Šurpu* series specifies that seven loaves of pure dough should be prepared to cure a person who has fallen sick.[46] Another incantation in the same collection seeks absolution for one in danger of death. Among others, the seven winds are adjured to release his oath.[47]

The hypothesis that the seven heavens in Sumerian and Babylonian tradition derives from magical thought and practice fits the usage of the motif in the second recension of the *Testament of Levi*. In that recension there is no mention of seven planets. A simple distinction seems to have been introduced into the second recension between the lower three heavens which are concerned with the punishment of evil and the upper four heavens which are holy.[48] But for the most

---

[39] R. Campbell Thompson, *The Devils and Evil Spirits of Babylonia* (London: Luzac, 1903) 1. 50–53, 62–65, 68–69, 72–79, 154–55, 190–199. Cf. Erica Reiner, *Šurpu: A Collection of Sumerian and Akkadian Incantations* (AfO 11; Graz: Ernst Weidner, 1958) 24, l. 172. See also the enumeration of seven prayers, the seventh of which involves "the Seven" (Reiner, 27, ll. 60–66).

[40] Gerhard Meier (ed.), *Die assyrische Beschwörungssammlung Maqlû* (AfO 2; Berlin: Ernst F. Weidner, 1937) 33; cf. 43, l. 79. The majority of the tablets of this series comes from the libraries of Assurbanipal and Assur.

[41] Ibid., 48, l. 49; cf. 17, l. 24.

[42] Thompson, *Semitic Magic*, lii–liii.

[43] Ibid., 32.

[44] Ibid., 33; cf. 166–167, 170; cf. Meier, *Maqlû*, 60, l. 73.

[45] Ibid., 188.

[46] Ibid., 206–207; cf. 208. See the edition and translation of this text by Reiner, *Šurpu*, 37, ll. 54–59. The majority of the tablets of the series *Šurpu* also come from the libraries of Assurbanipal and Assur.

[47] Reiner, *Šurpu*, 17, ll. 166–67. Cf. the reference to seven generations (ibid., 19, l. 6).

[48] Compare the last sentence of *T. Levi* 3:3 in the two versions (Charles, *The Greek Versions*, 33).

part, there is little interest in the contents and layout of each of the heavens. What seems to be of primary importance is the number of the heavens itself.

If the motif of seven heavens was added by a Christian redactor at some time in the first or second century CE, other influences may have been at work. Such influences will be discussed below.

THE SIMILITUDES OF ENOCH

Another part of the composite work known as Ethiopic Enoch or *1 Enoch* consists of chapters 37 to 71, and is usually called The Similitudes of Enoch. The latest historical allusion in it is to the activity of Herod the Great. Thus it probably dates to around the turn of the era. The similitudes or parables involved contain divine revelation focusing on a heavenly savior, based on Daniel 7, who is called that Son of Man, Messiah, and the Elect One. Another important motif in this work is the translation of the living Enoch to a heavenly existence (chapters 70–71). None of the Similitudes has been preserved in Aramaic or Greek; only the Ethiopic version attests them, so we are rather far removed from the wording of the original. Nevertheless, it should be noted that a plurality of heavens seems to be presupposed in two passages of chapter 71. Verse 1 reads, "And it came to pass . . . that my spirit . . . went up into the heavens."[49] Verse 5 speaks about Enoch being carried off into "the highest heaven"[50] or "the heaven of heavens."[51] Bietenhard interprets verse 5 as a reference to three heavens.[52] This chapter of the Similitudes may reflect the Babylonian notion of three heavens, but, if so, the motif is undeveloped.

---

[49] Translation by M.A. Knibb in H.F.D. Sparks, ed., *The Apocryphal Old Testament* (Oxford: Clarendon, 1984) 255; E. Isaac also translates with the plural "heavens" in James H. Charlesworth, ed., *The Old Testament Pseudepigrapha* (Garden City: Doubleday, 1983) 1. 49.

[50] Knibb, 255.

[51] Isaac, 49.

[52] Bietenhard, *Die himmlische Welt*, 11.

PAUL THE APOSTLE

2 Corinthians 10–13 come from a "painful letter" or "letter of tears" (cf. 2:3–9) that Paul wrote to defend his apostleship against some "super-apostles" who were threatening Paul's leadership role among the Christians at Corinth. One of the legitimating characteristics of these "super-apostles" was apparently their extensive experiences involving "visions and revelations of the Lord" (2 Cor 12:1). Although he acknowledges that it is foolish to boast of such things, Paul proceeds to recount his own experience in that regard (12:2–10). He begins in the third person, either out of modesty or as a gesture toward the preservation of the esoteric character of the experience, but soon lapses into the first person (cf. vs 2 with vss 6–7).

Thus this passage provides a first person account of an ascent to heaven, dating from the 50s of the first century of the Common Era:

> I know a person in Christ who fourteen years ago was caught up to the third heaven—whether in the body or out of the body I do not know; God knows. And I know that such a person—whether in the body or out of the body I do not know; God knows—was caught up into Paradise and heard things that are not to be told, that no mortal is permitted to repeat (2 Cor 12:2–4).

Bousset argued that "the third heaven" (vs 2) and "Paradise" (vs 4) represent two different stations on the heavenly journey. Otherwise, the repetition would be senseless.[53] The repetition, however, could be for rhetorical effect, so it is not so clear that Paul envisioned Paradise as a place above the third heaven, that is, as a fourth heavenly region. If Paul envisioned three heavens, this passage may be taken as evidence that the originally Babylonian tradition of three heavens had become conventional, probably already in the Judaism to which Paul belonged before becoming an apostle of Christ.

The Greek word παράδεισος and its Hebrew equivalent come from an Old Persian word meaning "park" or "garden" without any particularly religious significance. The Hebrew form of the word does not occur in the story of Adam and Eve in Genesis 2–3. The Greek form, however, was used in the Septuagint version of these chapters. When the idea of an abode of the righteous after death had developed, this dwelling was identified with the Garden of Eden, that is,

---

[53] Bousset, "Die Himmelsreise der Seele," 143.

Paradise. This identification may be presupposed already in *1 Enoch* 20:7 (third century BCE) and probably in *Ps Sol* 14:3 (first century BCE).[54] The location of Paradise is not specified in these early texts. For Paul, it is apparently in the third heaven.

There does not seem to have been a consistent world-picture among Christians in the first two centuries CE. As we have just seen, Paul speaks of three heavens. The letter to the Colossians, probably written in the 60s, speaks of a plurality of heavens without indicating their number (Col 1:5). The situation is the same with the letter to the Ephesians, written somewhat later (4:10, 6:9). The book of Revelation, probably written around 95 CE, seems to know only one heaven. The letter to the Hebrews, written sometime between 60 and 115,[55] clearly envisages more than one heaven, but this motif is not developed (4:14, 7:26).

THE LIFE OF ADAM AND EVE

Rabbinic literature contains many legends regarding Adam and Eve and their children. But no pre-Christian collection of such legends in Hebrew or Aramaic has survived. Many Christian Adam books have been preserved in various languages. The following discussion relates to the Latin "Life of Adam and Eve" and to a closely related Greek work published by Tischendorf in 1866 under the title "The Apocalypse of Moses."[56] M.D. Johnson has dated the original composition upon which both the Greek and the Latin depend to the period from 100 BCE to 200 CE, more probably to the end of the first century CE.[57]

In the Latin version, chapters 25–29 contain Adam's account of his ascent to heaven, accompanied by the archangel Michael. He begins as follows:

> Listen, Seth my son, and I will tell you what I heard and saw after your mother and I had been driven out of Paradise. When we were at prayer, Michael the archangel, a messenger of God, came to me. And

---

[54] H.K. McArthur, "Paradise," *IDB* (1962) 3. 655.
[55] Harold Attridge, *The Epistle to the Hebrews* (Hermeneia; Philadelphia: Fortress, 1989) 6–8.
[56] See the discussion by M. Whittaker in Sparks, ed., *The Apocryphal Old Testament*, 141–42.
[57] M.D. Johnson in Charlesworth, ed., *OTP*, 2. 252.

> I saw a chariot like the wind, and its wheels were fiery; and I was caught up into the Paradise of righteousness. And I saw the Lord sitting; and his face was a flaming fire that no man could endure. And many thousands of angels were on the right and on the left of that chariot (25:1–3).[58]

God reveals to Ádam that he must die because of his sin. Adam asks for mercy and God promises that at least some of his descendants will always serve God. After Adam worships God, the text continues as follows:

> Michael the archangel of God immediately took hold of my hand and ejected me from the Paradise of visitation and of God's command. And Michael held in his hand a rod and touched the waters which were around Paradise and they froze. I crossed over and Michael with me, and he took me to the place from where he had seized me (29:1–3).[59]

It is apparent that in this work there is both a heavenly and an earthly Paradise. When Adam speaks about being driven out of Paradise (25:2), he refers to the earthly Garden of Eden. The Paradise of righteousness to which he ascends is clearly a heavenly place, the dwelling of God (25:3). This heavenly region is also called the Paradise of visitation (29:1).[60] This correspondence between an earthly and a heavenly entity is ultimately rooted in Babylonian thinking.[61] The notion may have already become part of Jewish tradition by this time, since it appeared in the discussion of the sanctuary built in the wilderness (Exod 25:9).

Although the Latin version gives no indication of a plurality of heavens, the Greek version speaks of seven heavens. As Adam lies dying, Eve goes out to pray. The angel of humankind, that is, Michael, comes to her, lifts her up, and says, "Rise, Eve, from your repentance, for behold, Adam your husband has gone out of his body. Rise and see his spirit borne up to meet its maker" (32:3–4).[62] As Eve watches, the divine chariot comes to fetch Adam. Eve calls Seth to come and see things that no eye has seen. When Seth arrives, Eve says:

---

[58] Translation by L.S.A. Wells, revised by M. Whittaker, in Sparks, ed., *The Apocryphal Old Testament*, 153.

[59] Translation by Johnson, in Charlesworth, ed., *OTP*, 2. 268.

[60] Wells and Whittaker translate "Paradise of God's Reckoning" (in Sparks, ed., *The Apocryphal Old Testament*, 154).

[61] Bietenhard, *Die himmlische Welt*, 14.

[62] Translation by Johnson, in Charlesworth, ed., *OTP*, 2. 287.

> Look up with your eyes and see the seven heavens opened, and see
> with your eyes how the body of your father lies on its face, and all the
> holy angels are with him, praying for him . . . (35:2).

Eventually, the Lord of all takes Adam, hands him over to Michael,
and instructs him to take him up into Paradise, to the third heaven[63]
(37:4–5). The next scene is a description of the return of the divine
chariot to heaven and the taking of Adam's body into the heavenly
Paradise (chapter 38). In the following scene, Seth is mourning over
the body of Adam in the earthly Paradise (chapter 39). In the next
scene Adam and Abel are buried in the earthly Paradise with cloths
of linen and silk and fragrances brought from the heavenly Paradise
(chapter 40).

It is unlikely that the motif of the seven heavens in the Greek
version of this work derived from the tradition of seven planetary
spheres known to Plato and Eudoxos. Virtually the only astronomical interest appears in the narration that two Ethiopians accompany
the divine chariot when it comes to fetch Adam. These two dark-
skinned persons are identified as the sun and the moon who are not
able to shine in the presence of the Light of all (35–36). Support for
the conclusion that the motif of seven heavens derives from Babylonian tradition may be found in its combination with the notion of
the correspondence between the earthly and the heavenly Paradise.
There is little interest in the planets as such. It seems that the tradition known to Paul, in which Paradise is in the third, which is the
highest, heaven has been combined with the tradition of seven heavens. This hypothesis is supported by the fact that nothing is said
about the dwelling of God being in the seventh heaven. In fact, no
information is given about any of the heavens except the third.

THE APOCALYPSE OF ABRAHAM

The *Apocalypse of Abraham* is a Jewish work dating to the latter part of
the first century, shortly after the fall of Jerusalem in 70 CE.[64] It is

---

[63] Some MSS lack the reference to the third heaven (ibid., 291, n. f).

[64] G.H. Box, *The Apocalypse of Abraham* (London: SPCK, 1919) xv. R. Rubinkiewicz dates it in the first to second century CE; idem, "Apocalypse of Abraham," in
Charlesworth, ed., *OTP*, 2. 683. A. Pennington set 350 CE as a *terminus ante quem*
for at least the embryo of the work; idem, "The Apocalypse of Abraham" in Sparks,
ed., *AOT*, 367.

preserved only in Slavonic. Chapters 1–8 consist of the story about Abraham's conversion from idolatry. Chapters 9–32 describe Abraham's ascent to heaven which is connected with the sacrifice offered by the patriarch in Genesis 15.[65]

In 10:8, the angel who accompanies Abraham on his ascent says: "I am Iaoel and I was called so by him who causes those with me on the seventh expanse, on the firmament, to shake." H.G. Lunt suggested that the words "on the firmament" may be a gloss explaining "on the seventh expanse."[66] He points out that three Slavic roots, all synonyms of the ordinary word for "heaven," appear in this work. One of these (*tvĭrdĭ*) surely translates the Greek στερέωμα, translated here as "firmament." The other two (*protjaženie* [a pulling out tightly] and *prostĭrtie* [a spreading out broadly]) probably reflect forms of the Greek τείνω and are usually translated "expanse."[67]

In 15:4–5, Abraham says "And we ascended as if (carried) by many winds to the heaven that is fixed on the expanses. And I saw on the air to whose height we had ascended a strong light which cannot be described." This is apparently the highest point of the heavenly world, for it is here that Abraham sees God as fire on a throne of fire, surrounded by many-eyed ones. This "heaven," the highest point of the heavenly world, is also called "the seventh firmament" in 19:4. One of the concerns of the description of the heavens seems to be to assure Abraham, and the reader as well, that there is no other power in any of them other than the one God (19:2–4).

Abraham is allowed to see what is in the "expanses" below the firmament on which he is standing. Their contents are described, beginning with the seventh, which is identical with the firmament on which he stands. In that place he saw a spreading fire, and light, and dew, angels, a power of invisible glory from above, the living creatures and no one else. In the sixth expanse, he saw a multitude of spiritual angels, without bodies, who do the bidding of the fiery angels on the seventh firmament; there was no power on that expanse either, only the spiritual angels. In the fifth expanse, he saw the starry powers, the commands they are bidden to fulfill, and the

---

[65] For further discussion, see Martha Himmelfarb, *Ascent to Heaven in Jewish and Christian Apocalypses* (New York/Oxford: Oxford University Press, 1993) 61–66.

[66] The translation cited is by R. Rubinkiewicz and H.G. Lunt in Charlesworth, ed., *OTP*, 1. 694; the comment by Lunt is in n. c).

[67] Ibid., 698, n. 19 a.

elements of earth that obey them (19:2–9). The description breaks
off here, and the contents of the first four expanses are not discussed.

The image of something "pulled out tightly" or "spread out
broadly" fits the Babylonian world-picture better than the Greek.
Lambert has pointed out the lack of evidence for the theory that the
Babylonians imagined the shape of the sky or heaven to be vault- or
dome-like.[68] The Hebrew term of Genesis 1 traditionally translated
as "firmament" actually means "a strip of beaten metal." This term
was used to describe the expanse stretched out to separate the upper
and the lower waters.[69] As noted earlier, this idea appears also in the
Enuma elish.[70] The later Greeks, including Plato for example, considered the seven heavens to be spherical. Since the *Apocalypse of Abraham*
includes no indication of a curved shape for the seven heavens or
"expanses," it is clear that the motif was not adapted from Greek
tradition, at least not from Greek tradition informed by astronomy.

Like the Christian situation, there was not a consistent world-
picture among Jews in the first two centuries of the Common Era.
As just noted, the *Apocalypse of Abraham* speaks of seven heavens or
"expanses." Two other Jewish apocalypses also written in reaction to
the destruction of Jerusalem, *4 Ezra* and *2 Baruch*, speak of only one
heaven. Yet a fourth apocalypse, apparently responding to the same
crisis, speaks of multiple heavens, *3 Baruch*. But before discussing that
work, an earlier one should be mentioned.

2 ENOCH

Like the *Apocalypse of Abraham*, *2 Enoch* has been preserved only in
Slavonic. There are two recensions, one long and the other short.
The consensus is that the shorter recension is more original.[71] It is
clearly a Jewish composition. It was probably written in the first
century CE, prior to the destruction of the temple, since sacrifices
play a major role in the work.[72]

---

[68] Lambert, "The Cosmology of Sumer and Babylon," 61.
[69] T.H. Gaster, "Firmament," *IDB* (1962) 2. 270.
[70] Enuma elish IV 139–140.
[71] This consensus, however, has been challenged by F.I. Andersen in his contribution on *2 Enoch* in Charlesworth, ed., *OTP*, 1. 91–213. The following discussion
is based on the shorter recension.
[72] John J. Collins, "The Jewish Apocalypses," *Semeia* 14 (1979) 40.

According to this text, Enoch experienced an ascent to heaven when he was 365 years of age. He is conducted by two angels through seven heavens. In the first heaven he sees elders, who are rulers of the stellar orders. He also sees a vast sea which is greater than the earthly sea, and the treasuries of snow, clouds, and dew (chapters 3–6).[73] In the second heaven he sees the imprisoned rebellious angels who ask him to intercede for them, a motif also found in The Book of the Watchers (chapter 7). Next the angels take him to the third heaven and set him in the midst of Paradise, which is described as the eternal inheritance of the righteous (chapters 8–9). North of the third heaven, or in the northern heaven or region, is a terrible place. It is characterized as the eternal inheritance of the wicked which involves torture as punishment for their sins (chapter 10). In the fourth heaven, Enoch is shown all the movements of the sun and moon, their doors or gates, and armed troops worshipping (chapters 11–17). In the fifth heaven, Enoch sees the non-fallen Watchers who mourn for the fallen; Enoch exhorts them to worship God again and they do (chapter 18). In the sixth heaven there are seven equal angels who rule all, seven phoenixes, seven Cherubim and seven six-winged creatures who sing songs that cannot be reported. These are God's footstool (chapter 19). In the seventh heaven he sees arch-angels, angels, ophannim, and the Lord sitting on his throne; also present are heavenly armies, glorious ones, hosts of cherubim, and six-winged angels who cover the throne, singing. At this point the two angels depart from Enoch. Gabriel presents him before the Lord, and the Lord speaks to him. Then Michael takes off his earthly garments, anoints him with oil, and clothes him with glorious garments (chapters 20–22).[74]

2 Enoch seems to share certain traditions with the *Testament of Levi* 2–3. Both speak of "much water" or a "sea" in the first heaven.[75] Both teach that there is snow and ice in the first heaven.[76] Both

---

[73] The chapter numbers correspond to those of the translation by F.I. Andersen in Charlesworth, ed., *OTP*, 1. 105–213; A. Pennington uses a different scheme in the translation in Sparks, ed., *The Apocryphal Old Testament*, 329–62.

[74] Martha Himmelfarb argues that this process is a heavenly version of priestly investiture (*Ascent to Heaven*, 40–41).

[75] Cf. the older recension of *T. Levi* 2:7 (Charles, *The Greek Versions*, 30) with *2 Enoch* 4:2.

[76] Cf. the older recension of *T. Levi* 3:2 (Charles, *The Greek Versions*, 32) with *2 Enoch* 5:1 (some MSS read "cold" instead of "ice"; see Pennington, in Sparks, ed., *The Apocryphal Old Testament*, 330, n. 3).

associate the second heaven with the wicked angels.[77] A striking difference between the two is the far greater interest in *2 Enoch* in astronomical phenomena. When Enoch is in the first heaven, the
angels show him the movements and aberrations of the stars from
year to year (4:1).[78] In the fourth heaven, they show him the movements (and in some MSS the displacements) of the sun and the moon
(11:1–2). There is interest in the shortening and lengthening of the
days and the nights (13:1). The discussion of the various gates in
the east and west through which the sun rises and sets is related to
the annual movement of the point across the horizon where the sun
appears to rise and set (13:1–15:3).[79] At the end of this discussion it
is stated that "these gates the Lord created to be an annual horo-
loge" (15:3). The idea seems to be that these gates keep track of the
days of the year in the same way as a sundial keeps track of the
hours of the day.[80] In the account of the fourth heaven, there is also
a discussion of the movements and the gates of the moon (16:1–8).
The moon goes in and out by each of these gates for a period rang-
ing from 22 to 35 days.

The astronomical notions of *2 Enoch* do not conform to the most
advanced scientific ideas of its time. For example, the fixed stars are
placed in the first heaven, rather than above the seven planetary
spheres.[81] The picture of the movement of the sun and the moon is
either mythical involves literary personification. They do not seem to
move as part of an intrinsically orderly cosmic system; rather, they
are moved, or at least directed, by the angels who accompany them.[82]

Some of these astronomical traditions are either derived from or
shared with The Book of the Heavenly Luminaries, an originally
independent work dating from the third century BCE, which is preserved in *1 Enoch* 72–82. The discussion of the gates of the sun in
the East and in the West is closely related to *1 Enoch* 72.[83] The

---

[77] Cf. the older recension of *T. Levi* 3:3 (Charles, *The Greek Versions*, 33) with
2 Enoch 7.

[78] "Movements" refers to regular movements, like the rising and setting of the
sun. "Aberrations" refers to perturbations in those regular movements, such as the
annual movement of the sunrise point across the horizon. The movement of this
point causes apparent "aberrations" in the positions of the stars (Andersen, in
Charlesworth, ed., *OTP*, 1. 111, second column of n. b).

[79] Ibid.

[80] Ibid., 127, second column of n. d.

[81] Ibid., 110, n. 4a.

[82] Ibid., 121, second column of n. g.

[83] Ibid., 123, n. 13a.

discussion of the gates of the moon has some points of contact with *1 Enoch* 73 and 75.[84] The Book of the Heavenly Luminaries could not be the source of *2 Enoch*'s idea of seven heavens, since the older work knows only one heaven. The motif of seven heavens could have been borrowed directly from Babylonian tradition, or more likely, it had already become one of several Jewish traditions about the number of heavens. The relation of the astronomical ideas of *2 Enoch* to Babylonian and Egyptian thought is a matter that requires further study. They do not seem to have much connection with Greek astronomical thought.

THE MARTYRDOM AND ASCENSION OF ISAIAH

The *Martyrdom and Ascension of Isaiah* may be a composite Christian work, made up of an originally independent Martyrdom of Isaiah and a Christian ascent text. The account of Isaiah's ascent is given in chapters 6–11 of the Ethiopic version of the work. The ascent text was written toward the end of the first or in the second century CE.[85]

The world-picture implied by the *Ascension* involves a "firmament" that separates the earth from the seven heavens. When an angel takes Isaiah up to the firmament, he sees Sammael, apparently equivalent to Satan, and his hosts. There is strife among the angels of Satan because of jealousy. Isaiah comments that what happens in the firmament happens similarly on earth (7:9–12). Then Isaiah is taken above the firmament to the first heaven. In it he sees a throne,[86] with angels on the right and left. Those on the right had greater glory; all sang praises to God and the Beloved (7:13–17).

The angel then takes him to the second heaven, whose height is the same as (the distance) from the firmament to the earth. There he sees a throne, with angels on the right and left. The one seated on this throne had greater glory than the rest. Isaiah began to worship the one seated on the throne. The angel instructed him not to worship

---

[84] Ibid., 128, n. b.

[85] There are also two recensions of the Latin version, a Slavonic recension, and Coptic and Greek fragments (see Adela Yarbro Collins, "The Christian Apocalypses," *Semeia* 14 [1979] 84–85). See also Robert G. Hall, "The *Ascension of Isaiah*: Community Situation, Date, and Place in Early Christianity," *JBL* 109 (1990) 289–306; idem, "Isaiah's Ascent to See the Beloved: An Ancient Jewish Source for the *Ascension of Isaiah?*" *JBL* 113 (1994) 463–84 and the literature cited there.

[86] There is no mention of any one sitting on the throne.

any angel or throne in the (lower) six heavens, because his own throne, garments and crown are set above these heavens. Isaiah rejoiced that those who love the Most High and his Beloved will be taken up to the seventh heaven by the angel of the Holy Spirit (7:18–23).

The arrangement of the third heaven is like that of the second. Each heaven has greater glory than the one beneath it. Here Isaiah comments that his face is being transformed, presumably into angelic glory (7:24–27). When Isaiah reaches the fourth heaven, he comments that the height from the third to the fourth is greater than the (distance) from the earth to the firmament. The contents are like those of the third, only more glorious (7:28–31). The same pattern continues in the fifth heaven (7:32–37).

Next the angel took Isaiah up first into the *air* of the sixth heaven, then into the sixth heaven itself. The glory was greater there than in the five lower heavens. Here and upwards there is no one seated in the middle on a throne and no angels on the left because they are directed by the power of the seventh heaven. When Isaiah addresses the angel with the phrase "my lord," the angel tells him that he is his companion, not his lord. Isaiah and the angel praise with the angels of the sixth heaven. The angel also tells Isaiah that he must return to earth, because his time for entering the seventh heaven permanently had not arrived yet (8:1–28).

Then they enter the *air* of the seventh heaven. Isaiah's entry is challenged by the one in charge of the praises of the sixth heaven, but he is allowed passage by the Lord Christ. Then they enter the seventh heaven itself. There is marvelous light and innumerable angels. All the righteous from the time of Adam are there: Abel, Enoch, and later Seth, are mentioned. They had been stripped of their garments of the flesh and were wearing garments of the world above, like angels, standing in great glory. They had not yet received their thrones or crowns because the Beloved had not yet descended. Then a summary of the descent and ascent of the Beloved is given. Isaiah sees many garments, thrones, and crowns stored up for those who believe in the Beloved. Isaiah sees One (Beloved), another glorious One (angel of Holy Spirit), and the Great Glory. Isaiah and the angels could not look upon the Great Glory, but the righteous could. Then all worshipped the Great Glory (9:1–42).

There follows a description of the descent and transformation of the Beloved. He was not transformed in the sixth heaven; the angels there recognized and worshipped him. But he was transformed to look like the angels of fifth and lower heavens, so they do not perceive his descent. The keepers of the gate of the third heaven demand a password and the Lord gives it. The same thing happens in the second and first heavens and in the firmament where the prince of this world dwells. Then he descended to the air and made himself like the angels there. It was not necessary to give them a password, because they were too busy doing violence to one another (10:1–31).

Chapter 11 contains stories about the birth, infancy, life, and crucifixion of the Lord. Then his ascent through the seven heavens is described. He ascends first to the firmament. Since he had not transformed himself, the angels of the firmament and Satan worship him. They lament and ask how his descent was hidden from them. The same thing happens in (the first) through fifth heavens, except the angels there do not lament. Instead they worshipped and praised him. In each heaven the praise increased. All praise in the seventh, and he sits down at the right hand of the Great Glory. The angel of the Holy Spirit is seated on the left. This angel sends Isaiah back to earth. Near the end there is an exhortation in the second person (apparently to the readers) to keep watch in the Holy Spirit so that they may receive their garments, thrones and crowns of glory that are stored up in the seventh heaven (11:1–43).

There is virtually no astronomical interest in this work. The primary distinction within the heavenly world is between the air above the earth and the firmament, on the one hand, and the seven heavens above the firmament, on the other. The air above the earth and the firmament are the abode of Satan, the prince of this world, and the wicked angels. The seven heavens appear to be holy. Yet there are distinctions among them as well. The sixth and seventh heavens are considerably more holy and glorious than the lower five. Each of the lower five has a ruler or throne in its midst and angels on the left who are inferior to those on the right. When the Beloved descends, he is not transformed in the sixth heaven, because it is in full harmony with the seventh. There is a further distinction between the third and lower heavens and the fourth and higher ones. In the third and lower heavens, and at least in theory in the firmament, a password is required for passage. Such a requirement does not seem to apply to the fourth and upper heavens.[87] This distinction between

---

[87] There is no mention of passwords as Isaiah and the angel are ascending; the motif appears only in the descent of the Beloved.

the lower three and the upper four heavens recalls an analogous distinction in the later recension of the *Testament of Levi*.[88]

The transformation of the Beloved in the fifth and lower heavens during his descent and the need for the use of a password in the lower three heavens suggest some degree of opposition between these lower heavens and the upper two. The relation of this mild opposition to the theories of the Valentinians and the Ophites requires further investigation.[89]

As noted above, each heaven, according to the *Ascension of Isaiah*, is more glorious than the one below it. The sixth heaven, in particular, has much greater light than those beneath it. This motif calls to mind the pattern in the *Testament of Levi*, in which the second heaven is brighter than the first and the third is incomparably brighter than the second (*T. Levi* 2:6–10). Another similarity between these two works is the name "Great Glory" used of God.[90]

Both the *Ascension of Isaiah* and the *Apocalypse of Abraham* associate the seventh heaven with a marvelous or indescribable light.[91] They differ, however, in a striking way. The enthroned angels or powers in the lower five heavens of the *Ascension of Isaiah* contrast vividly with the remarks in the *Apocalypse of Abraham* that there is no power besides God in all the expanses. Thus the *Ascension of Isaiah* may represent or be related to the kind of tradition against which the relevant part of the *Apocalypse of Abraham* was written.[92] The *Ascension of Isaiah* lacks the motif of Paradise as such, but it emphasizes the salvation of the faithful and their exalted destiny in the seventh heaven.[93] Unlike *2 Enoch*, the *Ascension of Isaiah* has little interest in the punishment of the wicked.

The *Ascension of Isaiah* is the oldest certainly Christian composition to make use of the motif of seven heavens. This motif was most likely borrowed from Jewish tradition.

---

[88] See the discussion above.

[89] See, e.g., Irenaeus, *Against Heresies* 1.5.2; 1.24.3–7 (Latin) (cf. Bentley Layton, *The Gnostic Scriptures* [Garden City, NY: Doubleday, 1987] 420–25); *Against Heresies* 1.30.12 (cf. Culianu, *Psychanodia*, 9); *Against Heresies* 2.30.6–7; Tertullian, *Against the Valentinians* 20.

[90] Cf. *T. Levi* 3:4 with *Asc. Isa.* 9:37.

[91] Cf. *Apoc. Abr.* 15:7 with *Asc. Isa.* 9:6.

[92] Cf. *Apoc. Abr.* 19:3–7 with *Asc. Isa.* 7:14–15, 19–21, 24–27, 29–31, 32–37.

[93] The motif of Paradise, as noted above, appears in 2 Corinthians 12, the *Life of Adam and Eve*, and *2 Enoch*.

3 BARUCH

3 Baruch is probably a Jewish composition that has undergone some Christian reworking. The Jewish form of the work was produced during the second century CE.[94] It was composed in Greek and is preserved both in Greek and Slavonic. The following discussion is based on the Greek version. It begins with the lament of Baruch, the scribe of Jeremiah, over the destruction of Jerusalem and its temple. Presumably, the earlier destruction is chosen as the fictive setting because of the parallel with the destruction of 70 CE. The Lord sends an angel to comfort Baruch and to guide him through the heavens and reveal their mysteries to him. After his ascent, Baruch is returned to earth to communicate what he has seen to others.

At the beginning of the journey, the angel takes Baruch to the place where the heaven was set fast and where there is a river which no one is able to cross (2:1). The statement that "the heaven was set fast" may imply a dome-like or semi-spherical shape for heaven.[95] Then the angel leads Baruch to a large door which is the door of heaven (2:2). They enter as on wings about the distance of a thirty days' journey. The angel says later that the door is as (thick) as the distance from earth to heaven. Inside is the first heaven that contains a plain whose width is the same distance. On the plain are men with faces of cattle and horns of deer and feet of goats and loins of sheep. These are those who built the tower of the war against God, that is, the tower of Babel (2:2–7).

Then the angel takes Baruch to a second door. They enter, flying about the distance of a sixty days' journey. Inside is the second heaven that contains a plain with men on it who look like dogs; their feet are like those of deer. These are those who plotted to make the tower, forcing people to make bricks (chapter 3).

Next the angel and Baruch pass through doors, making a journey of about 185 days. Inside is the third heaven that contains a plain and a serpent whose belly is Hades. This serpent feeds on the wicked.

---

[94] See the discussion by H.E. Gaylord in *OTP*, 1. 655–56. See also Daniel C. Harlow, *The Greek Apocalypse of Baruch (3 Baruch) in Hellenistic Judaism and Early Christianity* (SVTP 12; Leiden/New York/Köln: Brill, 1996).

[95] Gaylord translates "the heaven was set fast" and refers to *1 Enoch* 18:5 and 33:2, passages that say that heaven rests on the ends of the earth (ibid., 665 and n. 2a); H.M. Hughes and A.W. Argyle translate "where the vault of heaven was set" (in Sparks, ed., *The Apocryphal Old Testament*, 904).

In the third heaven is the place where the sun goes forth. The chariot of the sun is drawn by forty angels and accompanied by the phoenix. Apparently in the third heaven also are 365 gates of heaven by means of which light separates itself from darkness (that is, dawn; cf. 6:13–14). The sun passes through the third heaven (cf. 7:2). Baruch views the setting of the sun whose crown has to be removed and renewed because it has been defiled by the earth. The moon and the stars are also apparently in the third heaven. The moon is in the form of a woman and rides in a chariot (chapters 4–9).

The angel then takes Baruch to the fourth[96] heaven and in it he sees an unbroken plain with a lake in the middle. Around it are birds unlike those on earth. The plain is the abode of the righteous; the water is the life-giving water that is rained onto earth, the dew that produces fruit. The birds are those who continuously praise the Lord (chapter 10).

Next the angel leads Baruch to the fifth heaven, at the entrance of which is a closed gate. The angel tells him that only Michael can open it. Michael appears to receive the prayers of humanity. Angels bring baskets of flowers which represent the virtues of the righteous. Michael eventually departs and the doors close. The angel and Baruch wait while Michael carries the virtues to God. He then returns and gives oil to those who had brought flowers. When the door closes a second time, the angel returns Baruch to earth (chapters 11–17).

3 Baruch shows more interest in cosmological matters than the *Ascension of Isaiah*, but this interest is limited. The firmament (heaven) is pictured as resting on the ends of the earth. A river surrounds the earth, but it is not named. The thickness of the doors of the various heavens is emphasized, probably to dramatize the vastness and greatness of the heavenly world compared with the earthly.

The placement of Hades in the third heaven (4:3) reflects a development beyond the eschatological functions of the heavens in the *Testament of Levi*. In the latter work, fire, snow, ice, and winds are held in the first heaven for the day of judgment. These materials were apparently to be used in a way similar to the plagues in the book of Revelation. In the second heaven, according to the *Testament of Levi*, heavenly powers await the time when they will punish the spirits of Beliar and of error. In *3 Baruch*, in contrast, punishment of

---

[96] The Greek version reads "third heaven" (10:1), but it is evident that this reading is a mistake; see Gaylord in Charlesworth, ed., *OTP*, 1. 673, n. 10a.

wicked humans at least is not postponed to the final day of judgment, but presumably occurs immediately after death. *2 Enoch* also
goes beyond the *Testament of Levi* in that the rebellious angels are
already imprisoned in the second heaven (*2 Enoch* 7). But Paradise,
the "eternal inheritance of the righteous," and the "terrible place"
that is the eternal reward of the wicked are not yet occupied in the
narrative time of *2 Enoch*. They are "prepared," that is, held ready
in waiting, for use after the general resurrection and the final judgment. Thus, of the three works, the eschatology of *3 Baruch* seems to
be the most fully realized.

In both *2 Enoch* and *3 Baruch*, Hades or its equivalent is placed in
the heavenly world rather than under the earth. This placement may
reflect a new cosmography. The old view is expressed, for example,
by Plato in the *Phaedrus* 249A–B: the wicked are punished under the
earth and the good are rewarded in a heavenly place. The new view
is typical of Plutarch (c. 46-after 120 CE). According to his dialogue
On the Face of the Moon, when the soul leaves the body, it must spend
some time in the sphere of the moon. The unjust are punished there;
the just also need purification on the meadow of "Hades."[97] In another
dialogue, the widespread motif of the tortures of the wicked in the
underworld is taken up, but placed in the heavenly regions. Likewise,
the islands of the blest are shifted to the heavenly world.[98] It is not
clear whether the new cosmography was due to a more scientific
view of the world, involving the shift from the picture of a more or
less flat earth to one of a spherical earth, or simply to another form
of popular religion.[99] In any case, language about "the underworld"
continued to be used alongside descriptions reflecting the new world-
picture.[100]

Besides the discussion of Hades, the account of the third heaven
also includes matters of astronomical interest: the nature and movement of the sun; the 365 gates of heaven; the nature, movement,
waxing and waning of the moon; and the stars. This material is clearly
more mythical or poetic than scientific. The fact that the sun, moon,
and stars appear in the same heaven makes clear that the notion of
the planetary spheres as distinguished from the sphere of the fixed
stars plays no role in this work.

---

[97] Plutarch, *De facie in orbe lunae* 27–29; cf. *De genio Socratis* 590B.
[98] Plutarch *De sera numinis vindicta* 563D.
[99] See the discussion by Culianu, *Psychanodia*, 41–46.
[100] *Pistis Sophia* 102, 126–27, 144; *Apocalypse of Ezra* (Greek) 1:7–8, 4:5.

Some of the more intriguing questions about *3 Baruch* are how
many heavens the work presupposes and whether it originally described more than the four with a glimpse of the fifth that appear in
the work in its present form. The angel tells Baruch several times
that he will see the glory of God (for example, 7:2, 11:2). Yet Baruch
never does see the glory of God in the present form of the work.
The reader's expectation of a description of the divine throne may
be deliberately aroused and frustrated.[101] The descriptions of Michael
going *upward* to God from the fifth gate may imply that there are
higher heavens.[102] If the work presupposes more than five heavens,
seven is the most likely number. It may never have contained descriptions of the upper (three) heavens. It appears to be roughly a
mirror image of the *Apocalypse of Abraham*, which describes only the
upper heavens, the seventh, sixth, and fifth.

PRELIMINARY CONCLUSION

Most of the Jewish and Christian works discussed so far presuppose
that there are three or seven heavens. The main options for the
origin of the notion of three heavens are: (1) it is an inner Jewish
development, based on the phrase "heaven of heavens" in the Hebrew Bible, or (2) it was borrowed from one of the typical Babylonian
pictures of the universe. Given the basically rhetorical use of the
Hebrew phrase and the extensive contact of Jews with Babylonian
culture, the second option is more likely. The use of the terms "lower"
and "upper heaven" and the presence of a heavenly sea in the *Testament of Levi* support this conclusion. The major options for the origin of the motif of seven heavens are: (1) it was borrowed from the
Greek world-picture involving seven planetary spheres, or (2) it was
borrowed from Babylonian magical tradition. Since the later recension of the *Testament of Levi* and the other relevant works discussed
do not connect the seven heavens with planetary spheres, the second
option is more likely. I would now like to turn to texts that explicitly
link the seven heavens and the seven planets.

---

[101] So Harlow, *The Greek Apocalypse of Baruch*, 34–76.
[102] When Baruch and the angel enter the gates of the lower heavens, there is no
indication that they travel upward in order to enter the relevant heaven.

THE SEVEN PLANETS: EXPLICIT LINKS

Although there is no explicit connection between the seven heavens and the seven planets in the early Jewish and Christian apocalypses, certain other texts explicitly associate the two. The oldest of these seems to be *Poimandres*, which dates to the second century CE.[103] According to chapter 9 of this work, divine intellect engendered rationally a second intellect as craftsman. The latter created seven "controllers," that is, the planets, called "governors" in astrology,[104] which encompass the visible world in orbits. Their control is called destiny. In chapters 24–26 is a discussion about the ascent of the soul. As the human soul speeds upward through the framework of the orbits, it gives up to each of the seven zones (planetary spheres) the quality that the zone produced in it as it descended earlier to enter a body. Stripped of those undesirable qualities, the soul comes to the nature of the eighth heaven. Eventually it comes to be within god; that is, it becomes god.[105]

In his recent study, David Ulansey has shown that the Mithraic mysteries were closely related to astronomy and astology.[106] From this point of view, it is not surprising that the seven planets appear frequently in Mithraic iconography. Some of the examples are undated.[107] Two of the relevant monuments have been dated to the

---

[103] For an introduction and English translation with notes, see Layton, *The Gnostic Scriptures*, 447–62. See also Walter Scott, ed., *Hermetica: The Ancient Greek and Latin Writings which Contain Religious or Philosophic Teaching ascribed to Hermes Trismegistus* (4 vols.; Boston: Shambhala, 1985); the Greek text and an English translation are given in 1. 114–33.

[104] Layton, *The Gnostic Scriptures*, 453, n. 9b.

[105] See the translation by Layton (*Gnostic Scriptures*, 457–58). Culianu argues that the order of the vices in *Poimandres* corresponds to the so-called "Chaldaen" order of the planets (*Psychanodia*, 49).

[106] David Ulansey, *The Origins of the Mithraic Mysteries* (New York: Oxford University Press, 1989).

[107] In a marble relief of a tauroctony found in Rome, the planets are represented as seven stars beside Mithras's head, four on the left, three on the right; CIMRM 368 (*Corpus Inscriptionum et Monumentorum Religionis Mithriacae* [ed. M.J. Vermaseren; the Hague: Marinus Nijhoff, 1956] 1. 368). In a white marble low-relief, kept at Bologna, the exact find-spot being unknown, Mithras is depicted slaying the bull. On the vaulted upper border the raven and the busts of the seven planets are represented (CIMRM 693). In the center of a bronze plate (CIMRM 1727) found near the back wall of a small mithraeum in Brigetio (in Pannonia, what is now Hungary; CIMRM 1723) is Mithras slaying the bull. Behind his head, there are seven stars in the field. Below this and other scenes and separated from them by two horizontal lines are the busts of the seven planets with their attributes.

second half of the second century CE. In the Mithraeum of the Seven Spheres in Ostia,[108] the floor of the central aisle is covered with a mosaic showing representations.[109] In the white-black mosaic floor near the entrance there is a dagger and behind it follow seven half circles which represent the seven spheres of the planets. The Mithraeum of the Seven Gates, also in Ostia, is dated to about 160–170 CE.[110] On the threshold of the mosaic paved floor of this mithraeum,[111] there is a large central arch formed by two pilasters; this main arch is flanked by three minor arches on either side. The seven arches are thought to represent the seven spheres of the planets. Other evidence, to be discussed below, suggests that the initiate expected to ascend through the planetary spheres after death.

The work entitled the *Chaldaean Oracles* was probably written by Julian the Theurgist in the second half of the second century CE. An extant fragment speaks figuratively about the seven planets in connection with the ascent of the soul.[112] The initiate is instructed not to look downward, because there is an abyss that threatens to tear him from the ladder with seven gates, under which is the throne of Necessity.[113]

In book I, chapter 30 of *Against Heresies*, Irenaeus describes the teaching of "others," presumably a group of Gnostics. They say that Wisdom's offspring, Ialdabaoth, emitted an offspring; this third one did the same, until there were seven. "Thus, according to them, the septet was completed, with the mother [Wisdom] occupying the eighth position" (1.30.4).[114] The names of the seven are Ialdabaōth, Iaō, Sabaōth, Adōnaios, Elōaios, Ōraios, and Astaphaios.[115] The snake who persuaded Eve was the agent of Wisdom.[116] Ialdabaōth cast the snake, along with Adam and Eve, from heaven into this lower world. "And it . . . engendered six offspring, with itself serving as the seventh in imitation of that septet which surrounds its parent [Ialdabaōth]. And—they say—these are the seven worldly demons, which always oppose and resist the race of human beings, because it was

---

[108] CIMRM 239.
[109] The mosaic floor is CIMRM 240.
[110] CIMRM 287.
[111] CIMRM 288.
[112] Culianu, *Psychanodia*, 53–54.
[113] Bousset, "Die Himmelsreise der Seele," 263–64.
[114] Translation by Layton, *Gnostic Scriptures*, 175.
[115] Irenaeus, *Against Heresies*, 1.30.5.
[116] Ibid., 7 (Layton, *Gnostic Scriptures*, 176).

on account of these that their parent [the snake] was cast down."[117] Later it is said that this lower septet introduced humanity to all kinds of evil, beginning with apostasy from the upper, holy septet, presumably the septet associated with Ialdabaoth. The holy septet is then identified with the seven heavenly bodies called planets.[118]

Later in the same account, Irenaeus says that they teach that the anointed [pre-existent] Christ descended and entered into the human Jesus. Christ descended "through the seven heavens, having assumed the likeness of their offspring, and it gradually emptied them of any power; for—they say—the whole secretion of light rushed to it."[119] The "seven heavens" here are presumably equivalent to "the holy septet," who were identified with the seven planets earlier. The allusion to their "power" may reflect astrological ideas of destiny.

According to Origen, Celsus, following Plato, asserted that souls could make their way to and from the earth through the planets. Origen then discusses Jacob's vision of the ladder, saying that it may point to the same things Plato had in view or to something greater than these.[120] Origen goes on to say that Celsus speaks about a representation (*symbolon*) used in the Mithraic mysteries. This representation concerned a ladder with seven gates (and on the top of it, an eighth gate) which represented the soul's passage through the seven planetary spheres. Celsus apparently argued that the Mithraic teaching was similar to that of the Christians, implying some derogatory conclusion about the latter.[121] Perhaps anticipating this argument, Origen claims in the prior passage that the Christian Scriptures do not teach any specific number of heavens.[122]

Symbols for the seven initiatory stages in Mithraism are found associated with symbols of the seven planets in mosaics found in the Mithraeum of Felicissimus at Ostia, dated to the second half of the third century CE.[123] The central aisle has a mosaic pavement with the symbolic representations of the different Mithraic grades; each of these grades is associated with one of the planetary deities.

---

[117] Ibid., 8 (Layton, *Gnostic Scriptures*, 177).
[118] Ibid., 9 (Layton, *Gnostic Scriptures*, 178).
[119] Ibid., 12 (Layton, *Gnostic Scriptures*, 179–80).
[120] Origen, *Contra Celsum* 6.21.
[121] Ibid., 6.22. See Ulansey, *Mithraic Mysteries*, 18–19.
[122] Ibid., 6.21.
[123] CIMRM 299; cf. Ulansey, *Mithraic Mysteries*, 19.

THE SEVEN PLANETS: PROBABLE LINKS

Certain other texts can be taken as probably presupposing an association of the seven heavens with the seven planets, because of their
similarity to texts that make the association explicitly. One of these
texts is Irenaeus' account of the Gnostic myth according to Ptolemy,
which he attributes generally to "the Valentinians."[124] According to
this account, the Demiurge created seven heavens, above which they
say that he exists. And on this account they term him the seventh,
and his mother the eighth, "preserving the count of the primal and
first octet of the fullness. They say that the seven heavens are intellectual and postulate that they are angels;. . . . Likewise, they say that
paradise is above the third heaven and is virtually the fourth archangel; and that Adam got something from it [or him] when he passed
time within it [or conversed with him].[125] These seven heavens associated with seven angels are analogous to the holy septet that Irenaeus
says "others" identified with the seven planets.[126]

Another such text is an account of the teachings of the Gnostic
sect of the Ophites in Origen's *Contra Celsum* 6.24–38.[127] An important part of their teaching was the ascent of the soul after death
(6.27). To reach its goal in the realm of the Father and the Son, the
soul had to pass through a "Barrier of Evil" (or "fence of wickedness"—φραγμὸν κακίας), which is defined as "the gates of the archons
which are shut for ever" (6.31). There are seven archons controlling
the gates; in ascending order they are: Horaeus, Aiolaeus, Astaphaeus,
(Adonaeus), Sabaoth, Iao, and Ialdabaoth. To persuade the archons
to let him pass, the soul must address them by name, recite the
correct formula, and show to each of them a "symbol" (*symbolon*).
These symbols are perhaps to be connected with the "seal" (*sphragis*)
which, according to 6.27, was bestowed by the Father on the "Youth
and Son."[128] Having passed through the realms of the seven archons,
the soul reaches the eighth (sphere)—the Ogdoad, ruled over by "the
first power" (6.31). The Ogdoad seems to be equivalent to an eighth

---

[124] Irenaeus, *Against Heresies*, 1.1.1–1.8.5; see Layton, *Gnostic Scriptures*, 276–302.
[125] *Against Heresies*, 1.5.2; translation by Layton, *Gnostic Scriptures*, 291.
[126] See above.
[127] See the discussion by P. Alexander (in the introduction to his translation of
3 Enoch) in Charlesworth, ed., *OTP*, 1. 237.
[128] Cf. the "seals" mentioned in the Naassene hymn quoted by Hippolytus (*Refu-
tation of All Heresies* 5.10.2 = 5.5 [ANFa 5.58]).

heaven. The names of the seven archons in this text are almost the same as those given by Irenaeus in his account of "others."[129] Irenaeus says that these are the "holy septet" who are identified with the seven planets. A contrast between the two texts is that in Irenaeus, the planets seem to be ambivalent, whereas in Origen they are somewhat more malefic.

Sometime before 350 CE, a Gnostic work entitled *The Reality of the Rulers* or *The Hypostasis of the Archons* was written. According to this work, there is a "veil" (καταπέτασμα) that divides the world above and the realms that are below.[130] This veil separates the seventh heaven from the eighth.[131] When Sabaōth repented and condemned his father Sakla (= Ialtabaōth or Ialdabaōth), he was caught up and appointed in charge of the seventh heaven, below the veil between above and below.[132] Wisdom had her daughter Life sit at Sabaoth's right hand to teach him about the things in the eighth (heaven).[133] This text seems to presuppose the same basic myth and cosmography as Irenaeus' account of the "others."

Around 375 CE, Epiphanius wrote a work *Against Heresies*. This work contains a discussion of the teachings of "the Phibionites," apparently a Gnostic group. He says that they speak of many rulers, but gives the names of the ones they consider to be the greater ones. There follows a list of names associated with seven heavens. Five of the seven names agree with the list given by Irenaeus in discussing "the others." It is likely, then, that this text also is evidence for a link between seven rulers and the seven planets.[134]

Finally, at the end of the fourth or beginning of the fifth century CE, a work entitled the *Life of Joseph* (the husband of Mary) was written.[135] In chapter 21, Death, Hades, the Devil and evil demons approach Joseph on his death-bed. Jesus drives these powers away and calls Michael and Gabriel to accompany Joseph and to show

---

[129] Irenaeus, *Against Heresies* 1.30.5; see above.
[130] *Reality of the Rulers* 94, 8–13; see the discussion by Alexander in Charlesworth, ed., *OTP*, 1. 236.
[131] *Reality of the Rulers* 95, 19–22.
[132] Ibid., 95, 13–21.
[133] Ibid., 95, 31–34.
[134] Epiphanius, *Against Heresies* 26.9.6–9; see Layton, *Gnostic Scriptures*, 210–11.
[135] It is preserved in Coptic, Arabic, and Latin; see Wolfgang A. Bienert, "XI. The Relatives of Jesus. 4. Joseph, the father of Jesus," in Wilhelm Schneemelcher, ed., *The New Testament Apocrypha* (2 vols.; 2nd ed.; Cambridge, UK: James Clarke; Louisville, KY: Westminster/John Knox, 1991) 1. 484–85.

him the way until he has passed through the "seven aeons of darkness."[136] The identity of these seven aeons is not clear, but, if "aeons" may be taken as a synonym for "rulers," they may be associated with the planets. If so, they are pictured in malefic terms.

EXPLICIT REFERENCES TO THE PLANETS, BUT NOT TO SEVEN

In the Gnostic work *The First Thought in Three Forms*, one of the events of the final struggle is the undoing of planetary determinism:

> And the lots of destiny and those which traverse the houses [the planets which traverse the sectors of the celestial sphere] were greatly disturbed by a sharp thunderclap. And the powers' thrones were disturbed and overturned, and their ruler became afraid. And those which follow destiny [the planets] gave up their numerous circuits along the way.

The planets then complain to the powers that the way on which they travel is no longer established.[137] The lack of interest in the number of planets and spheres is noteworthy.

Chapter 136 of *Pistis Sophia* is usually classified as part of book IV of that work, which is dated to the first half of the third century CE.[138] In that passage it is said that Jeu bound 1800 archons and placed 360 (archons) over them, and he placed five other great archons as rulers over the 360 and over all the bound archons. These five are named in the human world as follows: Kronos, Ares, Hermes, Aphrodite, Zeus. The order given here is neither the so-called "Chaldaean" nor the Egyptian.[139] It may be that seven planets are presupposed, but that for some reason the sun and moon are omitted.

---

[136] Bousset, "Die Himmelsreise der Seele," 150.

[137] This work is also called the *Trimorphic Protennoia* or the *Triple Protennoia*; the passage quoted is 43, 13–17; the translation is by Layton and the comments in brackets are from his notes (*Gnostic Scriptures*, 96).

[138] See Francis Fallon, "The Gnostic Apocalypses," *Semeia* 14 (1979) 135–36.

[139] On these see Culianu, *Psychanodia*, 28; on the order used in Babylonian astronomical literature of the Seleucid period and on a different, older, Neo-Babylonian order, see F. Rochberg-Halton, "Benefic and Maiefic Planets in Babylonian Astrology," in Erle Leichty et al., eds., *A Scientific Humanist: Studies in Memory of Abraham Sachs* (Occasional Publications of the Samuel Noah Kramer Fund 9; Philadelphia: Samuel Noah Kramer Fund, The University Museum, 1988).

NUMBER OF HEAVENS NOT CONNECTED WITH PLANETS

In Irenaeus' account of the Gnostic myth of Basilides, he remarks:

> And out of the power together with wisdom (there were engendered)
> authorities, rulers, angels. These he calls "first" ones. And by them the
> first heaven was crafted. By an act of emission on their part, other
> angels came into being, and they made another heaven closely resem-
> bling the first one. . . . [and so forth] (up to a total of) 365 heavens.
> And it is because of them that the year has that quantity of days,
> corresponding to the number of heavens (1.24.3).
>
> They locate the positions of the 365 heavens just as astrologers do;
> for they accept the astrologers' principles, adapting them to their own
> kind of system. And the ruler of them (the heavens) is named Abrasaks,
> and that is why this (ruler) has the number 365 within it $(1 + 2 + 100 + 1 + 200 + 1 + 60 = 365)$ (1.24.7).[140]

Thus Basilides, who was active in Alexandria at about 132–35 CE,
seems to have had a more complex cosmography than many other
Gnostics.

A passage from Epiphanius was cited above as evidence that the
Phibionites presupposed seven heavens. In another passage, the implication may be that they knew 365 heavens, each ruled by an
archon.[141]

The *Apocalypse of Paul* from Nag Hammadi speaks of ten heavens
(22–23). The *First Apocalypse of James*, also from Nag Hammadi, says
that there are 72 heavens that are under the authority of the twelve
rulers (26).

Thus, it is impossible to speak of a standard Gnostic cosmography.

CONCLUSION

There is no clear indication in the early Jewish and Christian apocalyptic writings that there is any connection between the seven heavens
and the seven planets. Such a connection first becomes visible in
Hermetic texts, Mithraic monuments and Celsus' discussion of Mithraic

---

[140] Translation by Layton, *Gnostic Scriptures*, 422–25; the comments are taken from
his notes. He notes in addition that the name "Abrasaks" was widely used in Greek
magic and astrology (425, n. 1.24.7. c).

[141] Epiphanius, *Against Heresies* 26.6.6–9; see Layton, *Gnostic Scriptures*, 210. See
also the discussion by Culianu (*Psychanodia*, 64, n. 47).

mysteries. The connection is clearly made under the influence of Greek astrology. The motif of seven heavens was probably borrowed from Babylonian tradition by Jewish apocalyptic writers. The reasons for adapting this motif probably included the magical properties of the number. The tradition of the sabbath and the motif of the seven archangels may also have reinforced the choice of this motif.

If the motif of the seven heavens was added to the *Testament of Levi* by a Christian redactor, that recension and the *Ascension of Isaiah* would be the earliest Christian apocalyptic writings to make use of the motif. There is virtually no indication of any astronomical or astrological interest in these two works.

The only explicit evidence in the first three centuries that Christians connected the seven heavens with the seven planets is Irenaeus' account of the teaching of "the others," presumably a Gnostic group.[142] The connection was probably made by Ptolemy, the follower of Valentinus, and the Ophites (as described by Origen).[143] Some Gnostic groups probably combined the magical idea of seven malefic spirits or seven demons with the astrological idea of the planets as controllers of destiny.[144]

Thus Culianu was right in rejecting the hypothesis of the history of religions school that the seven heavens in Jewish and Christian apocalyptic writings derived from a Babylonian tradition concerning seven *planetary* heavens or spheres. As he conceded in an aside, however, the picture of seven heavens probably does derive from Babylon. The context of this borrowing probably involved magical rather than cosmographical ideas. The main concern of the history of religions school was to interpret Jewish and Christian *origins*. One may say that, with regard to this tradition at least, they were right in looking to Babylon.

---

[142] Irenaeus, *Against Heresies* 1.30–31.

[143] On Ptolemy, see ibid., 1.1.1.–1.8.5; on the Ophites, see Origen, *Contra Celsum* 6.24–38.

[144] See the discussion of these seven spirits or demons in Babylonian tradition in the section on *The Testament of Levi* above.

CHAPTER THREE

NUMERICAL SYMBOLISM IN JEWISH AND EARLY CHRISTIAN APOCALYPTIC LITERATURE

This chapter has grown out of my ongoing fascination with the symbols of the New Testament book of Revelation, their origins and significance.[1] The commentaries' explanations of the role of particular numbers in Revelation seem rather superficial and non-explanatory.[2] Some bold and interesting suggestions have been made in individual studies, but they appear to be tendentious and have not been well supported with evidence.[3] Rather than focusing primarily or even solely on the traditions of the Old Testament and its Mesopotamian background, as most interpreters have done on this topic, one should study numerical symbolism in literature contemporary with Revelation.[4] As far as I have been able to discover, very little

---

[1] Adela Yarbro Collins, *The Combat Myth in the Book of Revelation* (HDR 9; Missoula: Scholars Press, 1976); eadem, "The History-of-Religions Approach to Apocalypticism and the 'Angel of the Waters' (Rev 16:4–7)," *CBQ* 39 (1977) 367–381.

[2] R.H. Charles remarks, "Why the particular seven Churches mentioned in i.11 were chosen by our author cannot now be determined . . .; but the fact that seven were chosen, and no more and no less, can occasion no difficulty. For seven was a sacred number not only in Jewish Apocalyptic and Judaism generally, but particularly in our Author . . ." (*A Critical and Exegetical Commentary on the Revelation of St. John* [ICC; New York: Scribner's, 1920] 1.8–9). Wilhelm Bousset comments, "Gerade an sieben Gemeinden schreibt er wegen der Heiligkeit der Siebenzahl" (*Die Offenbarung Johannis* [KEK; 5th ed., Göttingen: Vandenhoeck und Ruprecht, 1896] 213).

[3] Austin Farrer argued that the seven messages, seals, etc. "spell out that favourite apocalyptic period, the symbolic week" (*A Rebirth of Images* [Westminster: Dacre, 1949] 37); he suggests that the seventh element in each case represents the sabbath. J. Brandis and A. Jeremias explained the dominance of the number seven in Revelation in terms of the influence of the idea of the seven planets (Brandis, "Die Bedeutung der sieben Thore Thebens," *Hermes* 2 [1867] 267–268; Jeremias, *Babylonisches im Neuen Testament* [Leipzig: Hinrichs, 1905] 24–27).

[4] I.T. Beckwith concluded that the number seven was used in a few places in Revelation in an exact sense. In other cases it was used in a typical or schematic way to denote a "completeness, entirety, sufficiency." He asserted that this typical use is based on Hebrew tradition, giving no evidence (*The Apocalypse of John* [New York: Macmillan, 1922] 253). G.B. Caird interpreted Revelation's use of seven as a symbol for completeness or wholeness; he gave no reasons for this interpretation (*A Commentary on the Revelation of St. John the Divine* [HNTC; New York: Harper & Row, 1966] 14). Both writers are probably dependent ultimately on the theories of J. Hehn (*Siebenzahl und Sabbat bei den Babyloniern und im Alten Testament* [Leipzig: Hinrichs,

has been written about the significance of numerical symbolism in apocalyptic literature.[5] Numerical symbolism plays an important role in two non-apocalyptic Jewish writers, Aristobulus and Philo. Their texts can fruitfully be compared with the apocalyptic ones. Finally, the Pythagorean and astrological traditions, widespread and influential at the time of Revelation was written, must be taken into account to determine what contribution they may have made to the numerical symbolism under study.

In all the texts and traditions mentioned above, numerical symbolism is part of the activity of discovering order in environment and experience. Such activity is a basic human impulse which finds expression in most of the world's religions. Mary Douglas has argued that rituals of purity and impurity create order in human life and in social relations. On one level, they influence behavior. On a deeper level, they express convictions about reality and social relations. Their effect is to organize the environment in conformity with an idea.[6]

Numerical symbolism creates order in two basic ways. First, it is used to order the experience of time. At root here is the observation of the sun and moon and the formation of calendars. Related to the calendar are repeated festivals and other cultic acts. In the first part of this chapter, the focus will be on attempts to perceive meaningful patterns in large blocks of time. Numerical symbolism also expresses order in the experience of space. The perception of such order is expressed in the Greek idea of the cosmos. An orderly correspondence was seen between the universe (the macrocosmos) and the human body (the microcosmos). The role of numbers in astronomy, music and grammar showed the unity and orderliness of the world. The interest in ordering large blocks of time is typical of Jewish apocalyptic texts. Such an interest is, however, also found in Greek tradition.[7] Appreciation of cosmic order expressed in numerical terms

---

1907]; idem, "Zur Bedeutung der Siebenzahl," in K. Budde, ed., *Vom Alten Testament: Karl Marti zum siebzigsten Geburtstage gewidmet* [BZAW 41; Giessen: Töpelmann, 1925] 128–136).

[5] D.S. Russell has a section on "allegorical arithmetic" in his introduction to Jewish apocalypticism (*The Method and Message of Jewish Apocalyptic* [Philadelphia: Westminster, 1964] 195–202; see also the section "History Systematically Arranged," ibid., 224–229). G.W. Buchanan has argued that all Jewish and Christian eschatology has its origins in the rules about sabbatical and jubilee years (*The Consequences of the Covenant* [NovTSup 20; Leiden: Brill, 1970] 9–18.)

[6] Mary Douglas, *Purity and Danger* (London: Routledge and Kegan Paul, 1966) 2–3.

[7] For example, Hesiod, *Works and Days* 106–201. See the discussion in Martin Hengel, *Judaism and Hellenism* (Philadelphia: Fortress, 1974) 1. 181–82.

is characteristic of the Pythagorean tradition, but it occurs in apocalyptic texts as well.[8]

As noted above, interest in the ordering of time begins with the observation of the sun and moon and the simple reckoning of time. Calendars of greater or lesser complexity and accuracy are developed. Such calculations form one of the roots of historiography, in that they are helpful in fixing the chronological order of events.

Interest in the chronology of the history of Israel seems to have been rather high in post-exilic Judaism. An Alexandrian Jew by the name of Demetrius wrote a chronological book on the kings of the Jews in the third century BCE.[9] A similar, though less learned book was written by Eupolemus, probably a Palestinian Jew of the second century BCE.[10] These writers, and of course Josephus as well, wanted to demonstrate the great antiquity of their national tradition relative to their neighbors'.[11]

The apocalyptic texts manifest minimal interest in chronology as such. An occasional remark shows familiarity with chronological data. An example can be found in the vision of the heavenly Jerusalem in *4 Ezra* 9–10. The mourning woman tells the seer that she had been barren for thirty years (9:43–45). In the interpretation of the vision, the angel explains her barrenness by saying that there were three thousand years in the world before any offering was offered in Zion (10:45).[12]

---

[8] The relevant texts will be discussed in the second half of this essay.

[9] Hengel, *Judaism and Hellenism*, 1.69; for an introduction, Greek text, English translation and notes, see Carl R. Holladay, *Fragments from Hellenistic Jewish Authors*, vol. 1, *Historians* (SBLTT 20, Pseudepigrapha 10; Chico, CA: Scholars Press, 1983) 51–91; for an introduction, English translation and notes, see John Hanson, "Demetrius the Chronographer," in Charlesworth, ed., *OTP*, 2. 843–54.

[10] Hengel, *Judaism and Hellenism*, 92–95; for an introduction, Greek text, English translation and notes, see Holladay, *Fragments from Hellenistic Jewish Authors*, 1. 93–156; for an introduction, English translation and notes, see Frank Fallon, "Eupolemus," in Charlesworth, ed., *OTP*, 2. 861–72. See also Ben Zion Wacholder, *Eupolemus: A Study of Judaeo-Greek Literature* (MHUC 3; Cincinnati, OH/New York/Los Angeles/Jerusalem: Hebrew Union College/Jewish Institute of Religion, 1974).

[11] Ibid., 69; for Josephus, see *Ap.* 1.1.

[12] The *Assumption of Moses* (which is more accurately referred to as the *Testament of Moses*) opens with the remark that Moses gave his testament in the one hundred and twentieth year of his life, which was the two thousand five hundredth year from the creation of the world. This work contains apocalyptic eschatology, but it is a

Impulses to calculate the time of the end

Throughout the centuries, from the Hellenistic period until modern times, the impulse to calculate the time of the end has been a recurring feature of the apocalyptic or millenarian mentality.[13] In spite of that fact, the ancient Jewish and early Christian apocalypses themselves contain very few passages that reflect a concerted attempt to calcucate the date of the end of the world in a rather precise way. Among the texts that for good reasons can be classified as apocalypses,[14] only the book of Daniel manifests such an attempt. Other books use particular indications of time not as elements of precise calculation but more generally to indicate that the time of tribulation will be short or that the end is near.

1. *The prophecy of Jeremiah and its interpretation*

In the Jewish and Christian apocalyptic traditions, Daniel is the oldest text which includes calculations of the time of the end. It probably inspired at least some later attempts at such calculation and served as their model. The logic of the passages which predict the end is most clear in chapter 9. At the beginning of that chapter, the purported author, the seer Daniel, notes that the Lord told Jeremiah the prophet that seventy years must pass before the end of the desolations of Jerusalem (see Jer 25:11–12, 29:10). Daniel then prays a long prayer for the city. Afterward Gabriel appears to Daniel and tells him that seventy weeks of years must pass before the desolation of Jerusalem will cease and everlasting righteousness begin (9:24). It looks very much as though this is an allegorical interpretation of certain passages in Jeremiah, an interpretation which arose in the struggle to apply earlier prophecy to the situation in the fourth decade of the second century BCE.[15]

Gabriel goes on to describe the period of seventy weeks of years,

---

testament rather than an apocalypse (see the discussion in John J. Collins, "The Jewish Apocalypses," in *Apocalypse: The Morphology of a Genre, Semeia* 14 [1979] 45–46).

[13] On the calculations of the rabbis, see Buchanan, *The Consequences of the Covenant*, 14–15; on those of ancient and medieval Christians, see Bernard McGinn, *Visions of the End: Apocalyptic Tradition in the Middle Ages* (New York: Columbia University, 1979) 51, 159.

[14] See the introduction and the articles "The Jewish Apocalypses" and "The Early Christian Apocalypses," *Semeia* 14 (1979).

[15] Russell suggests that the reinterpretation resolved the tension between the conviction that God's promises to the prophets could not fail and the realization that

dividing it into three portions of seven "weeks," sixty-two "weeks," and one "week." In the last week "the prince who is to come" (Antiochus Epiphanes) will make a strong covenant with many, and for half of the week he will cause sacrifice and offering to cease (9:27). The last period of time mentioned occurs in several other places in Daniel in various forms. In 7:25 it is said that the saints of the Most High will be given into the hand of the last king "for a time, times, and a half time." The remark may be understood as three and a half times or three and a half years, which would be the equivalent of half of the last week of years of chapter 9.

In chapter 8 a clear connection is made between a period of time and the desecration of the temple (as in 9:27). An angel asks how long the sanctuary will be defiled (8:13). The answer is for two thousand three hundred evenings and mornings (8:14). This period is probably to be understood as the time during which 2,300 evening and morning sacrifices would be offered, that is 1,150 days or three years and about two months. According to modern calculations, the desecration of the temple resulting from Antiochus' policies lasted for about three years, from about December, 167 BCE (see 1 Macc 1:54) to December, 164 BCE (see 1 Macc 4:52). It is difficult to explain the discrepancy between the calculations in Daniel and those of modern scholars. Nevertheless, Dan 8:14 should probably be read as a prophecy after the fact, and its intention was very likely to give an accurate prediction of events. The time period given, like that of 7:25, is roughly equivalent to the half "week" of 9:27.

According to 9:27, the last week of years comes to a close with the end of the desolator, Antiochus Epiphanes. In the "prediction" of events which begins with 11:2, the death of Antiochus (11:45) is immediately followed by a great time of trouble and the resurrection (12:1–3). It seems then, that the author of Daniel expected not only the restoration of the temple to occur at the end of the seventy weeks of years, but also the great turning point from this age to the next. This conclusion is supported by 12:5–13. That passage manifests great interest in the time of the end. Three calculations are given: a time, times and a half a time (vs 7; see 7:25); 1,290 days (vs 11); and 1,335 days (vs 12). The multiple computations may indicate that later hands modified the text. The last figure given in vs 12 especially

---

Jeremiah's prophecy had been fulfilled only in a very partial manner (*The Method and Message of Jewish Apocalyptic*, 196).

looks like an accommodation of the text to events. In any case, the book of Daniel in its original form manifests the conviction not only that the end was near but also that its date could be calculated.[16]

The form that the calculations took in the book of Daniel is noteworthy. It is never said that the end will come on such and such a day of a particular year. Such a prediction would have been easier to disconfirm, although reinterpretations even of a very precise prediction are possible. But the book of Daniel does not contain predictions of the day or the year. Rather, it gives periods of time until the end. In its more precise form, the prediction of the end involves a period of days whose beginning point is somewhat vague. Not only is the relation of the period to absolute chronology somewhat vague, but there is also the possibility of further allegorical interpretation of the numbers given or of the period of a "day." In its less precise form, the prediction mentions a time, times and a half a time. This designation is quite indeterminate, since the period of a "time" can be variously interpreted. It may well be that ambiguous language was used purposely to allow for adaptation to circumstances and reinterpretation.

As was already noted above, the calculations in Daniel are based on the prophecy of Jeremiah that Jerusalem would be restored after seventy years. Daniel's reinterpretation of that period as seventy weeks of years seems to have influenced three other works. None of these other writings is an apocalypse, but they all have a clearly eschatological orientation.

a) *The* Damascus Document
This work refers explicitly to the destruction of Jerusalem by Nebuchadnezzar and says that 390 years later God visited his people and caused a root of planting to spring up (1:5–12, MS A). This visitation probably refers to the founding of the sect by whose members the document was read. The text goes on to say that they were like blind men groping for the way for twenty years, until God raised up the Teacher of Righteousness for them. At another point in the same work it is said that about forty years will pass between the death of the Teacher and the end of all the men of wickedness (2:13–15,

---

[16] On the passages cited, see John J. Collins, *Daniel: A Commentary on the Book of Daniel* (Hermeneia; Minneapolis, MN: Fortress, 1993).

MS B). The end of wicked men is usually taken as a reference to God's final visitation, the eschatological turning point.

These two references to periods of time seem to indicate that the sect had calculated the time from the destruction of Jerusalem to the end of the age, the same period calculated by Daniel 9. Some time must be allowed for the activity of the Teacher of Righteousness. If forty years are added to account for that period, as F.F. Bruce suggested, the total number of years is 490.[17] This number is equivalent to Daniel's seventy weeks of years (70 × 7) and may be dependent on it.

b) Melchizedek

In the fragmentary scroll designated as 11QMelch, it is said that the exile will end and the people of the diaspora will return in the last jubilee-year, which is the tenth (1.7).[18] In the context the end of days is mentioned (1.4 and 15) and the judgment of God (1.9–13). It is likely that the members of the Qumran sect counted forty-nine years as a jubilee like the book of *Jubilees*, rather than fifty years like the Pentateuch.[19] If that is the case, the *Melchizedek* scroll reflects the expectation that the end of days would arrive 490 years (49 × 10) after the exile. This period is equivalent to the seventy weeks of years in Daniel 9 and is probably another version of its reinterpretation of the prophecy of Jeremiah.

c) Testament of Levi *15–16*

In chapter 15, Levi "predicts" that the temple will be laid waste and that the people will be captives in all the nations. Immediately after commenting on the destruction of the temple and its effects, the patriarch says that the people will go astray for seventy weeks and profane the priesthood and pollute the sacrifices (16:1). The people will remain a curse and a dispersion among the Gentiles until God visits them again (16:5). The period of time in question seems once again to be the period from the exile to the last judgment. Seventy

---

[17] F.F. Bruce, *Biblical Exegesis in the Qumran Texts*, cited by Russell, *The Method and Message of Jewish Apocalyptic*, 200, n. 1.

[18] The text and an English translation can be found in M. de Jonge and A.S. van der Woude, "11QMelchizedek and the New Testament," *NTS* 12 (1966) 301–26.

[19] In the book of *Jubilees* and in the official count of sabbatical years in the Maccabean and post-Maccabean periods, the jubilee consisted of forty-nine years (J. Morgenstern, "Jubilee, Year of," *IDB* 2 [1962] 1002).

weeks of years is probably meant. Here, not only is the length of the
period the same as in Daniel, but the wording used to describe it is
similar. It is likely that the *Testament of Levi* 15–16 is dependent on
Dan 9:24.

d) *Sabbatical logic*

G.W. Buchanan has argued that the prophecy of Jeremiah and its
interpretations are based on an extension of sabbatical rules from
the individual to the nation. When an individual borrowed money
and could not repay it he was obliged to work for his creditor at half
wages until the debt had been cancelled. In each sabbatical year,
however, debtors were to be set free and any outstanding debts were
to be cancelled. In each jubilee-year land sold out of financial need
was to be returned to the original Israelite owner.[20]

According to Buchanan, when Israel sinned she was to be treated
like a debtor. If the people failed to observe the sabbath years, then
God would enforce them by removing the people to foreign captivity
for the length of time that it took for the land to make up its sabbaths.
He has made the hypothesis that Jeremiah originally predicted the
return of the exiles in the seventh year. The basis for this theory is
that Jeremiah bought a field, evidently expecting that the captivity
would end during his lifetime. The implication is that Jeremiah
viewed the exile as an enforced sabbath rest for the land of Israel to
make up for about forty-nine years of failure to observe sabbatical
years. Buchanan argued further that Jeremiah's number was changed
from seven to seventy to accord with the number of years from the
destruction of Jerusalem to the completion of the rebuilding of the
temple. The change was made to correlate with the facts, but still in
terms of Jeremiah's sabbatical logic.[21]

Buchanan's theory goes beyond the texts he cites in its rational
and systematic character. A few texts do reflect a tendency toward
systematization (such as Lev 26:27–35, 43–45; 2 Chr 36:20–21). But
the passages in Jeremiah are much less systematic. Further, Jeremiah's
purchase of the field says nothing about the length of the exile; it
simply expresses the conviction that it is not permanent. Land will
one day be bought and sold again in Israel (Jer 32:15). One cannot
get behind the seventy years of Jer 25:11–12, 29:10–11 to an earlier

---

[20] Buchanan, *The Consequences of the Covenant*, 9.
[21] Ibid., 9–10.

form of the prophecy with any certainty. Nevertheless, Buchanan may well be correct that a certain sabbatical logic was at work in defining the length of the exile as seventy (7 × 10) years. The approximate length of time involved quite possibly reflects historical facts. The fact of the restoration would have precluded numbers like seven years or seven hundred years. There is little evidence that the concrete rules about sabbatical years as such played a role in the selection of the number seventy. Yet it is a round number and a multiple of seven. It may be that this particular round number was selected because of the prominence of the number seven in the weekly sabbath observance and in the traditions about sabbatical years.

A similar logic was apparently at work in the reinterpretation of Jeremiah's prophecy in Daniel 9. The number seventy was no longer serviceable or adequate. It could have been replaced, superseded or reinterpreted in a variety of ways. The actual course of events certainly played a role. But it is probably no accident that a new prediction of a novel period of time is achieved by multiplying Jeremiah's figure by seven. The phrase weeks of years again indicates the prominence of weekly observance of the sabbath. A deeper root may be the calculation of time according to phases of the moon, but in the time of Jeremiah and that of Daniel, any reference to the seven days of the week would certainly call sabbath to mind. In the prophecy of Jeremiah and its reinterpretation by Daniel, larger blocks of time are shown to have the same order and rhythm as the smaller unit, the week.

11QMelchizedek manifests a similar logic. The number seven and the idea of the week determine the period after the exile in an indirect way, through the idea of the jubilee. The jubilee, as a unit of time made up of seven periods of seven years, is also a projection of the rhythm of the week on a larger block of time.

The Damascus Document does not use the language of Daniel (seventy weeks of years). The author or others before him seems rather to have calculated the precise length of time implied by Dan 9:24 (490 years) and to have used it in an attempt to calculate the time of the end. The author of the Testament of Levi 15–16 uses language similar to Daniel's, but shows little interest in calculating precise dates. The symbolic character of the seventy "weeks" does seem to be of importance as the discussion of jubilees which follows (chapter 17) shows. That passage will be discussed below.

2. *Imprecise, rhetorical calculations*

It was noted earlier in this chapter that the attempt to calculate the time of the end of the world is a typical feature of the apocalyptic mentality. The book of Daniel, however, is the only ancient apocalypse which contains an attempt to make a fairly accurate calculation of that sort. Two other ancient apocalypses, *4 Ezra* and the book of Revelation, refrain from giving a particular length of time from a certain event until the end. These two books do nonetheless show some interest in calculating the time of the end. They do this in a way that is less precise than Daniel's, apparently in order to achieve certain effects upon the readers.

In one of the dialogues between Ezra and the interpreting angel, Ezra asks, in effect, when the end of the age will be (*4 Ezra* 4:33). By way of answer, the angel recounts a dialogue between the souls of the righteous in their chambers and the archangel Jeremiel. They ask, "How long are we to remain here? And when will come the harvest of our reward?" (4:35, RSV). The reply is "When the number of those like yourselves is completed; for he has weighed the age in the balance, and measured the times by measure, and numbered the times by number; and he will not move or arouse them until that measure is fulfilled" (4:36–37). The text does not reveal what the measures or numbers are; only that they exist. The reader is apparently supposed to take solace in the idea that there is indeed a fixed time for the end.

In response to the angel's remarks, Ezra raises the question whether the end is being delayed for the sake of the righteous, that they might repent (4:38–39). The angel replies, "Go and ask a woman who is with child if, when her nine months have been completed, her womb can keep the child within her any longer" (4:40). When the seer responds negatively, the angel explains that it is the same way with Hades. Not only is the time of the end fixed, but that date cannot be altered.

A similar idea is presented in the vision of the fifth seal in the book of Revelation. The souls under the altar asked when God would pass judgment and avenge their blood upon the dwellers of the earth (Rev 6:10). They were given a white garment and told to rest awhile until their fellow servants and brothers who were to be killed as they had been were fulfilled (6:11). As in *4 Ezra* 4:33–43, the idea here is that there is a fixed number of righteous souls who must go to their graves before the end could arrive. In *4 Ezra* the end was predetermined and human beings could do nothing to hasten or delay it. In Rev 6:9–11, it is implied that the more people who die for the faith, the sooner the end would come.[22] The rhetorical effect of the Revelation passage is consolation in the idea that the sufferings of the righteous have a limit. Further, the reader is encouraged to meet death bravely in order to hasten the time of divine vengeance.

In each of these passages, a rather indirect but vivid means is chosen to express the idea that the age has a predetermined length. In the chapter of *4 Ezra* cited above, the seer goes on to inquire further. He wants to know whether the greater portion of the age is already past or is still to come (4:44–46). The angel responds by showing him a "parable": a flaming furnace passed by, smoke remained; a cloud poured down a heavy rain, drops remained in the cloud. So, the angel said, the quantity (of time) that has passed is far greater (4:47–50). Clearly, the burden of this passage is that the end is near. The text is, however, strikingly reticent on the subject of dates and periods of time. This reticence is underlined by the interchange which follows. Ezra wishes to know whether he will be alive at the end. The angel says he does not know, for he was not sent to reveal things to Ezra about his life (4:51–52).

The other passages in *4 Ezra* emphasize the nearness of the end without giving precise dates or periods of time. One of these is the vision of the eagle and its interpretation (11–12). The eagle was easily recognizable to the earliest readers as a symbol of the Roman empire.[23] The twelve wings represent twelve emperors, beginning with Julius Caesar. The three heads represent Vespasian, Titus and Domitian.[24] The lion, representing the messiah, appears while Domitian is still reigning (11:35–36, 12:1–2). The implication is that

---

[22] See the discussion of this passage in Chapter Six below, "The Political Perspective of the Revelation to John."

[23] The eagle is explicitly associated with the fourth kingdom of Daniel in *4 Ezra* 12:11. Josephus provides evidence that the fourth kingdom of Daniel 7 was usually interpreted as Rome in his day (see the discussion by D. Flusser, "The four empires in the Fourth Sibyl and in the Book of Daniel," *Israel Oriental Studies* 2 [1972] 158–159). Further, the eagle was the military emblem of the Roman legions (see H.M.D. Parker and George Ronald Watson, "signa militaria," in N.G.L. Hammond and H.H. Scullard, eds., *OCD* [2nd ed., 1970] 988).

[24] These interpretations of the twelve wings and the three heads are generally accepted; see J.M. Myers, *I and II Esdras* (AB 14; Garden City: Doubleday, 1974) 301; cf. Michael Edward Stone, *Fourth Ezra: A Commentary on the Book of Fourth Ezra* (Hermeneia; Minneapolis, MN: Fortress, 1990) 365.

the messiah will overthrow Domitian (see 12:33). But there is also
mention of two wings which had gone over to the last head, who set
themselves up to reign and whose "reign was brief and full of tu-
mult" (12:2, RSV). In the interpretation, these two wings are identified as the ones the Most High has kept for the eagle's end (12:30).
It appears that the vision was originally composed during Domitian's
reign and that the end was expected during that reign. After Domitian's death, the elements concerning the two wings were added. These
probably represent one or more of Domitian's successors as emperor.
In spite of the need to adapt the prediction, the conviction endured
that the end was very near. One of the rhetorical effects of this
powerful vision is the conviction that the deadly enemy of the people,
the Roman empire, had little time remaining to rule the world.

The final passage of this type in *4 Ezra* occurs in the final revelatory dialogue. God informs Ezra that the age is divided into twelve
parts and that ten parts have already passed; that is, that half of the
tenth part has gone by (14:11–12).[25] The revelation is meant to move
the reader to prepare for the nearing end. Such a rhetorical intention is indicated by the ethical exhortation which follows (14:13–18).

The parable about the flame and the cloud, the eagle vision and
the saying about the age's twelve parts all emphasize the nearness of
the end, though they abstain from particular calculations of years,
months and days. A similar passage is found in Revelation 17, the
vision of the harlot sitting upon the scarlet beast. The beast has seven
heads which are interpreted as seven mountains and seven kings.
The allusion is clearly to the Roman empire.[26] Concerning the kings
it is said that "five have fallen, one is, the other has not yet come,
and when he comes he must remain a little while. And the beast,
which was and is not, he himself is both an eighth and one of the
seven and he goes to perdition" (17:10–11). Many interpreters understand the seven kings as seven Roman emperors. Others hold
that the statement is purely symbolic. I have argued elsewhere that
seven Roman emperors are meant and that the sixth is probably
Domitian, during whose reign Revelation was written.[27] But in any

---

[25] See the translation and textual notes in Myers, *I and II Esdras*, 317; see also
Stone, *Fourth Ezra*, 414–24.
[26] See the discussion in Yarbro Collins, *The Combat Myth in the Book of Revelation*,
175.
[27] Adela Yarbro Collins, *Crisis and Catharsis: The Power of the Apocalypse* (Philadelphia: Westminster, 1984) 59–64.

case, the rhetorical intention is clear. The majority of the seven kings have passed away. Only one has not yet come on the scene and his reign will be short. The return of the beast marks the beginning of the final crisis which precedes the end. The end is near; there is little time to lose.

The passages cited so far from the book of Revelation do not give the impression that the author was interested in calculating the time of the end. In a number of other passages, periods of time are mentioned which are variants of Daniel's time, times and a half a time. Some interpreters have concluded from the appearance of these figures in the text that the author was indeed making some temporal calculations.[28] That conclusion is unfounded. It is extremely difficult to correlate the time periods given with each other and even more so with any absolute chronology.

The first passage containing a variant of Daniel's three and a half times is Rev 11:2. It is said that the holy city will be trampled by the nations for forty-two months (three and a half years). This remark seems straightforward enough. From the destruction of Jerusalem until the end of the Gentiles' reign, that is, the end of days, will be forty-two months. The following verse complicates things. God's two witnesses will prophesy for 1,260 days (three and a half years; 11:3). Problems arise in determining who the author believed the two witnesses to be and when he expected their activity to take place. If they are the returned Moses and Elijah,[29] then their activity was in the future from the author's point of view and could not be co-terminous with the three and a half years of the rule of the Gentiles. If they are primarily symbolic figures, then their ministry could coincide with the time of the Gentiles' reign.[30]

In chapter 12, the woman clothed with the sun is to be nourished in the desert for 1,260 days (three and a half years; 12:6) or a time, times and a half a time (12:14). I have argued elsewhere that the woman is a symbolic figure whose story exemplifies the plight of the intended readers of Revelation.[31] If John and some of his audience were refugees from the Jewish war in Palestine, the time of nourish-

---

[28] Russell's remarks seem to imply this conclusion (*The Method and Message of Jewish Apocalyptic*, 187, 195).

[29] The opinion of Bousset (*Die Offenbarung Johannis*, 375) and Charles (*A Critical and Exegetical Commentary on the Revelation of St. John*, 1. 282).

[30] The opinion of Caird (*A Commentary on the Revelation of St. John the Divine*, 134).

[31] Yarbro Collins, *The Combat Myth in the Book of Revelation*, 126–127.

ment in the desert could be a symbolic expression of their exile.[32] Or it could represent, in a general way, the experience of writer and audience as resident aliens in the cities of Asia Minor with precarious social status.[33] In either case, the period of time could be equivalent to the times of the Gentiles, but the major impact of the text is the impression that the time of exile or threat will be limited and short. In 13:5 it is said that the beast was given authority for forty-two months (three and a half years). Because of the fluidity in the image of the beast, it is difficult to determine the significance of that period of time. Does it refer to the duration of the Roman empire as a whole? to the reign of the historical Nero? or to the reign of terror of the eschatological Nero, who is in effect the Antichrist, although the term is not used?[34] If it refers to the reign of the beast as the Antichrist, how does the length of his rule relate to the reign of the Gentiles implied in 11:2?

The problems which arise when one tries to coordinate these periods of time and to relate them to an absolute chronology show that they were not intended to be interpreted in a literal, chronological way. They do not indicate an interest in precise calculation on the part of the author of Revelation. A traditional and therefore authoritative period of time is used to indicate that the time of tribulation just before the end will be limited and brief. The Gentiles will be allowed to dominate the holy city only a short time (11:2). The activity of the two witnesses, which is a time of persecution and death, will be a brief period.

The fate of the two witnesses has often been seen as a reflection of Jesus' fate.[35] The comparison is encouraged by the explicit description of the city where they die as the place where their Lord was crucified (11:8). Given that analogy, it is puzzling that they were

---

[32] On the likelihood of John being a refugee from Palestine, see Yarbro Collins, *Crisis and Catharsis*, 46–49.

[33] See Adela Yarbro Collins, "Insiders and Outsiders in the Book of Revelation and Its Social Context," in Jacob Neusner and Ernest S. Frerichs, eds., *To See Ourselves As Others See Us: Jews, Christians, "Others" in Late Antiquity* (StHu; Atlanta: Scholars Press, 1985) 187–218.

[34] On the development and history of the idea of the Antichrist, see L.J. Lietaert Peerbolte, *The Antecedents of Antichrist: A Traditio-Historical Study of the Earliest Christian Views on Eschatological Opponents* (Leiden: Brill, 1995); Bernard McGinn, *Antichrist: Two Thousand Years of the Human Fascination with Evil* (San Francisco: HarperSanFrancisco, 1994).

[35] E.-B. Allo, *Saint Jean: L'Apocalypse* (EtB 18; 4th ed., Paris: Gabalda, 1933) 155; Caird, *A Commentary on the Revelation of St. John the Divine*, 138.

raised after three and a half days instead of on the third day. The three and a half days makes sense as a telescoped parallel to the three and a half years. Just as the time of testing will be brief (three and a half years), the time between their execution and vindication will be even briefer (three and a half days).

As noted above, the time during which the woman is protected can be seen as a symbol for the time during which the community is threatened. They must be exposed to the threat, but the exposure is for a limited and brief time. Likewise, authority must be given to the beast to test the saints, but that authority is circumscribed by divine decree and fleeting.

One major way in which numbers are used to order time in apocalyptic literature is in calcualtions of the end. In the book of Daniel and related texts, the prophecy of Jeremiah that the exile would last seventy years was reinterpreted to calculate the time from the destruction of Jerusalem to God's final visitation. Most of these calculations reflect the use of seven as an ordering principle. In *4 Ezra* and Revelation one finds imprecise, rhetorical calculations of the end. The interest is not so much in calculating the date of the eschatological turning point, but in persuading the reader that the crisis will indeed occur and that it is coming soon.

Attempts to discern a meaningful pattern in time

The impulse to calculate the time of the end is an important feature of the apocalyptic mentality and plays a role in a number of apocalyptic texts. An even more important way in which numbers are used in apocalyptic literature is in the discernment of meaningful patterns in time, past and future. The discovery of such patterns is a major feature of Jewish apocalyptic texts, especially with regard to the past. Numerical patterns are found in the book of Revelation, one regarding the past and one referring to the future. Such patterns are not a major theme of early Christian apocalyptic literature, although they do occur in a few other texts.

1. *History divided into periods*

a) *Jeremiah's prophecy and sabbatical eschatology*
As indicated above, it is credible that a sort of sabbatical logic influenced the prophecy of Jeremiah that the exile would last seventy

years. In Daniel 9, several major concerns are evident. One is to calculate the time of the end, a concern which was discussed above. Another is to find some meaningful order in events from the crisis of the exile to the present. Such an order is expressed in the description of the period as seventy weeks of years. Its orderliness consists primarily in the use of the number seven as its organizing principle. Seventy is not only a round number, but a multiple of seven. The length of the total period is achieved by multiplying 70 by seven (weeks of years). The use of the word "weeks" indicates that the key idea involved is that significant large blocks of time have the same rhythm and order as the week, a period of time significant for Jews because of the regular celebration of the sabbath.

Little interest is evident in calculating the precise length of epochs within the seventy weeks of years.[36] Rather, the intention seems to be to divide the period in an orderly way and to emphasize the nearness of the end.[37] Assuming that most of Dan 9:24–27 is *ex eventu* prophecy, it is natural that the actual course of events had an impact on how the block of time was divided. On the other hand, there is minimal effort to allude clearly to precisely datable events. It is striking that the units of time at the beginning and at the end are emphasized and that each involves the number seven. Seven "weeks" (49 years) pass at the beginning until the coming of an anointed one. The final period is one "week" (seven years) which comprises the crisis which leads up to the end.

In the *Testament of Levi* 14–18 a brief review of history is given in which the destruction of the temple by the Babylonians is the first major crisis. The text is not an apocalypse, but it contains apocalyptic eschatology. The description of the post-exilic period is somewhat confused (chapters 16–17).[38] It may be that an editor has introduced the confusion. In any case, Levi "predicts" that, after the exile, the people would go astray for "seventy weeks." This period probably designates the time from the exile to the coming of the eschatological

---

[36] Contra Russell, *The Method and Message of Jewish Apocalyptic*, 195–98.

[37] John J. Collins has argued that the primary purpose of Dan 9:24–27 is to show the nearness of the end ("Pseudonymity, Historical Reviews and the Genre of the Revelation of John," *CBQ* 39 [1977] 335); on the details of the passage, see Collins, *Daniel*, 352–58.

[38] The major problem is how to relate 17:10–11 to what precedes. In those verses the fifth and seventh weeks are mentioned. It is unclear whether they relate to the seven jubilees listed in 17:1–9 or to the seventy weeks mentioned in 16:1.

priest (chapter 18). The importance of the number seven and the rhythm of the week is clear in the phrase "seventy weeks."

In chapter 17 a brief history of the priesthood is given. Each priest or priesthood is associated with a jubilee. These are numbered from one to seven (17:2–9). The first jubilee is linked to the first one to be appointed a priest; he shall be great and shall speak to God as to a father (17:2). This first priest could be Levi, Moses, or Aaron.[39] It is probable that the allusion is to the pre-exilic period. After the seventh jubilee, it is said that they shall be taken captive and their land destroyed (17:9). This remark seems to allude to the conquest by the Babylonians. One should probably conclude that the seven jubilees review history prior to the seventy weeks.[40] If that hypothesis is correct, the seventy weeks has not been divided into smaller units and its significance lacks the elaboration given in Daniel 9. Nevertheless, the presence of the analogous seven jubilees shows that the symbolic significance of the seventy weeks was perceived. The rhythm of the week can be extended to weeks of years and jubilees of years as one seeks a way of ordering past experience.

11QMelchizedek posits the same length of time from the exile to the end of days as Daniel 9, 490 years. Instead of formulating the period as seventy weeks of years, the text from Qumran refers to ten jubilees. The use of the jubilee introduces the idea of the repossession of land. In lines 4–7 this traditional idea is applied metaphorically to the return from exile. In the background is the same projection of the rhythm of the week on longer periods of time that we find in Daniel 9. In this case, however, the particular symbolism of the jubilee, involving the canceling of debts, release, liberty and return to the land, has come to the fore.

The period of the jubilee is very prominent in a work which takes its name from it, the book of *Jubilees*.[41] This work is a free paraphrase of Genesis with many additional details. The work as a whole is not an apocalypse, but it contains one, chapter 23.[42] In the prologue, the writing introduces itself as "The Account of the division

---

[39] *T. Levi* 5:2 supports the theory that Levi is the first priest.

[40] This interpretation is more likely than Russell's. He suggests that the final seven years of Daniel 9, the last "week," is reinterpreted in *T. Levi* 17:1–9 as seven jubilees (*The Method and Message of Jewish Apocalyptic*, 199).

[41] As noted above, in the book of *Jubilees*, a jubilee consists of forty-nine years rather than fifty, as in the Pentateuch.

[42] See John J. Collins, "The Jewish Apocalypses," 32–33.

of Days of the Law and the Testimony for Annual Observance according to their Weeks (of years) and their Jubilees throughout all the Years of the World, as the Lord told it to Moses on Mount Sinai . . ."[43] A little further on it is said that the angel of the presence communicated to Moses the divisions of the years beginning with God's creation. These divisions were organized according to jubilees (1:27–2:1). Near the end of the book God says to Moses:

> And after this law I made you know the days of the sabbaths in the wilderness of Sin, which is between Elim and Sinai. And I also related to you the sabbaths of the land on Mount Sinai. And the years of jubilee in the sabbaths of years I related to you. But its year I have not related to you until you enter into the land which you will possess. And the land will keep its sabbaths when they dwell upon it. And they will know the year of jubilee. On account of this I ordained for you the weeks of years, and the years, and the jubilees (as) forty-nine jubilees from the days of Adam until this day and one week and two years. And they are still forty further years to learn the commands of the Lord until they cross over the shore of the land of Canaan, crossing over the Jordan to its western side. And jubilees will pass until Israel is purified from all the sin of fornication, and defilement, and uncleanness, and sin and error. And they will dwell in confidence in all the land. And then it will not have any Satan or any evil (one). And the land will be purified from that time and forever (50:1–5).

In about the middle of this passage, it is said that forty-nine jubilees, one week (seven years) and two years (2,410 years altogether) have passed since the days of Adam. Forty years remained until the people would enter the promised land. Thus, the time between Adam and the gift of the land is fifty jubilees (2,450 years).

The emphasis in this work is clearly on cycles of seven. Cycles of seven years appear in references to the sabbaths of the land and to weeks (of years). As noted above, the period of the jubilee in this writing is forty-nine years (7 × 7) instead of fifty as in the Pentateuch. It is striking that forty-nine jubilees are mentioned in the final chapter, even though the total calculation is actually fifty. From the entrance into Canaan until the end, time will continue to be reckoned in jubilees (50:5). Throughout the retelling of Genesis, dates are given, counting the jubilees and weeks of years since Adam. The book of *Jubilees* manifests a strong interest in ordering meticulously a

---

[43] The translation cited is that of O.S. Wintermute, "Jubilees," in James H. Charlesworth, ed., *The Old Testament Pseudepigrapha* (2 vols.; Garden City, NY: Doubleday, 1983, 1985) 2. 52.

period of Israel's history in periods of jubilees. The logic of this ordering activity seems to be the projection of the regular period of the week onto a large block of time. The week is important because it culminates in the sacred sabbath. This hypothesis is supported by the fact that the book ends with a long passage containing God's commandments for observing the sabbath. This passage follows immediately upon the one quoted above with its emphasis on the ordering of longer periods of time.

A certain sabbatical logic can also be seen in the Enoch literature. It is present in a minor way in The Heavenly Journeys of Enoch or the Book of the Watchers (*1 Enoch* 1–36). The second section of this work (chapters 6–16) relates the narrative of the fall of the angels (based on Genesis 6). Near the time of the flood the fallen angels were bound until the time of their final judgment and punishment at the end of days. According to 10:12, the period of time between their initial and final punishments is seventy generations. This figure does not seem to reflect any interest in chronology or in the number of years in world history. Rather, it is a round number; the fact that it is a multiple of seven is probably not accidental. The number seven plays a major role in this work as a principle of cosmic order, as will be shown below.

The second dream-vision of *1 Enoch* 83–90, the "Animal Apocalypse," is an allegorical history of the world from the creation to the end of days (*1 Enoch* 85–90).[44] In it various animals represent different groups of people. Human beings in the narrative stand for angels. After the account of the destruction of Jerusalem by the Babylonians (89:55–58), the Lord of the Sheep (God) gives his sheep (Israel) to the care of seventy shepherds (angels). The pasturing of the seventy shepherds is divided into four periods. The first lasts twelve "hours" and represents the Babylonian captivity (89:65–72a). The length of the second period can be reconstructed; it is twenty-three "hours" and describes the restoration; it is thus equivalent to the Persian period (89:72b–90:1). The third period is also twenty-three "hours" and describes the domination by the Greeks (90:2–5). The fourth period involves twelve shepherds and extends from the Maccabean revolt until the final judgment (90:6–19).

This apocalypse is roughly contemporary with the book of Daniel,

---

[44] See Patrick A. Tiller, *A Commentary on the Animal Apocalypse of I Enoch* (SBL Early Judaism and its Literature; Atlanta: Scholars Press, 1993).

so any influence of one upon the other is unlikely, especially since they represent quite different points of view. It is likely, however, that this text, like Daniel 9, reflects an attempt to interpret Jeremiah's prophecy of an exile for seventy years.[45] Evidence for this hypothesis lies in the association of the seventy shepherds with the period from the destruction of Jerusalem to the end, the true restoration (see 90:29). The text shows interest in relative chronology, in dividing the time into periods, and in associating the shepherds, group by group, with events in the history of the period. On the other hand, there is little concern for absolute chronology and no attempt to work out a consistent scheme so that an "hour" would represent a particular unit of time. The correspondence between these "hours" and actual time is only approximate, so that the two periods of twenty-three "hours" do represent longer periods than the initial unit of twelve "hours." This correspondence indicates that the end is expected relatively soon, but not immediately.

Even though the number seventy maintains its association with time in the Animal Apocalypse's reinterpretation of Jeremiah's prophecy, the image of seventy shepherds shifts the emphasis to the more synchronic or cosmic idea of the seventy nations and their heavenly counterparts.[46] The sabbatical symbolism inherent in the seventy (years) is not elaborated.

The *Testament of Abraham* is not actually a testament at all, but an apocalypse.[47] The heavenly journey of Abraham and its revelations give the book its apocalyptic character. It has legendary features also and is a highly entertaining story of how Abraham tried to elude Death (this aspect is clearer in recension A, the longer).[48] At one point in the narrative Death reveals his fierce and unclean appearance to Abraham, including his seven fiery heads of dragons (17).

---

[45] So also Russell, (*The Method and Message of Jewish Apocalyptic*, 200) and Tiller, *Animal Apocalypse*, 57.

[46] On the seventy nations and their corresponding angels, see Russell, *The Method and Message of Jewish Apocalyptic*, 201–202, 244–249, 260–261; Tiller, *Animal Apocalypse*, 53–58.

[47] See John J. Collins, "The Jewish Apocalypses," 42 and the literature cited there. See now also Francis Schmidt, *Le Testament grec d'Abraham: Introduction, édition critique des deux recensions grecques, traduction* (TSAJ 11; Tübingen: Mohr [Siebeck], 1986). The work is dated differently by various scholars; the range is from the first century BCE to the second century CE.

[48] Little consensus exists on whether the longer (A) or the shorter (B) recension is prior; see the discussion in Collins, "The Jewish Apocalypses." The remarks made in this essay are based on recension A.

Later, Death explains the heads by referring to the seven ages during which he devastates the world and leads people down to Hades (19). The image of a seven-headed dragon is widespread and traditional.[49] The allegorical interpretation involving seven ages probably reflects an ordering of world-history based on the pattern of the week. Russell goes too far in assuming that each of the seven ages was one thousand years.[50] The text shows no evidence that speculation had begun on the lengths of the ages. The primary impact on the reader is the suggestion that there is a correspondence between "macrotime" and "microtime."

The reference to seven kings in Revelation 17:10–12 was discussed above as an example of an imprecise, rhetorical calculation of the end. It is highly unlikely that the author of Revelation simply was counting Roman emperors from the first to the one reigning in his own time.[51] It is more probable that the seven represent a selection from the number of emperors who had ruled until the author's day. It may well be that the number of emperors selected was calculated so that the total would be seven, because of the symbolic significance of that number. It is noteworthy that mention is made of an eighth which is nevertheless one of the seven. Analogous things are said in contemporary and later literature about the eighth day of the week which is also the first.[52]

The anonymous early Christian epistle attributed to Barnabas shows an interesting development in the use of the number seven to order large blocks of time, namely, the idea of the world-week. The idea is presented and explained with reference to Gen 2:2 and Ps 90:4. God created the world in six days and rested on the seventh; a day with God means a thousand years. The conclusion is that the world will endure for six thousand years. Then Christ will return to judge the wicked and his messianic kingdom of one thousand years will be the true sabbath (*Barn.* 15:3–7). The idea of the world-week also occurs in the long recension (A) of *2 Enoch* (Slavonic Enoch or the Book of the Secrets of Enoch) 33:1–2. In his 1952 edition of *2 Enoch*, A. Vaillant argued that the longer recension is secondary. His opinion

---

[49] Yarbro Collins, *The Combat Myth in the Book of Revelation*, 77, 79.

[50] Russell, *The Method and Message of Jewish Apocalyptic*, 227.

[51] Yarbro Collins, *Crisis and Catharsis*, 58–64.

[52] For example, *Barn.* 15:8–9; see the discussion by H. Riesenfeld, "Sabbat et Jour du Seigneur," in A.J.B. Higgins, ed., *New Testament Essays: Studies in Memory of T.W. Manson* (Manchester: University of Manchester, 1959) 216.

has been followed by most scholars who have written on the subject subsequently.[53] F.I. Andersen, however, has argued that some of the passages in the longer recension could preserve ancient traditions, some of which might well be original, since abbreviation as well as expansion has almost certainly taken place.[54]

The dividing of history into periods is a very prominent feature of Jewish apocalypses, which appears in a few early Christian apocalypses as well. The most frequently occurring pattern in apocalyptic and related literature is the use of seven and its multiples. The use of seven in these works seems to be based on a kind of sabbatical logic in which the order perceived in the week is discovered in significant large blocks of time or even in the entire history of the world.

b) *Four kingdoms or ages*

The use of the number seven in apocalyptic literature is probably connected with the week of seven days, a method of calculating time which had been used by Jews for centuries, but which was not in use among Greeks and Romans during the Hellenistic and early Roman periods.[55] The schema of four kingdoms or ages, on the other hand, was borrowed by the author of Daniel 2, writing in the late third or early second century BCE, from contemporary political oracles.[56] In Daniel 2, the schema has two aspects. One is the image of four metals: gold, silver, bronze, and a mixture of iron and clay. A similar series occurs in Hesiod (*Works and Days* 106–201). The image implies a gradual deterioration, an idea which is emphasized in Hesiod. A new beginning, a return to the golden age, is regularly envisaged when this metaphor is used. The sequence of four kingdoms appears not only in Daniel 2, but also in Roman chronicles, a Sibylline oracle and a Persian text.[57] In each case, a decisive turning point follows the fourth kingdom, sometimes, as in Daniel 2, in the form of a new, eternal kingdom.

The four kingdoms are always actual, historical regimes. The regular

---

[53] Ulrich Fischer, *Eschatologie und Jenseitserwartung im hellenistischen Diasporajudentum*, (BZNW 44; Berlin: de Gruyter, 1978) 37–38; Collins, "The Jewish Apocalypses," 40.

[54] F.I. Andersen, "2 (Slavonic Apocalypse of) Enoch," in Charlesworth, ed., *OTP*, 1. 93–94.

[55] E. Schürer, "Die siebentätige Woche im Gebrauche der christlichen Kirche der ersten Jahrhunderte," *ZNW* 6 (1905) 39–40.

[56] See the discussion in Collins, *Daniel*, 166–70.

[57] See also D. Flusser, "The four empires in the Fourth Sibyl and in the Book of Daniel," *Israel Oriental Studies* 2 (1972) 148–175.

appearance of Media implies that the schema originated in the Near East in a place where the Medes had ruled (thus not Asia Minor, Syria or Palestine). On the other hand, the four are not the same in all cases. The particular kingdoms vary, but their number does not. The reason could simply be the force of tradition. If other reasons played a role, their influence may be evident in the texts.

In Daniel 7 the four kingdoms are associated with four great beasts who came up out of the sea. The association of one or more beasts with the sea is a traditional element with roots in myth.[58] The number four probably derives from Daniel 2. In addition to the weight of tradition, a further rationale for having four beasts or kingdoms is evident in 7:2. The beasts are associated with four winds of heaven. The idea of four winds belongs to speculation on cosmic order and probably involves one wind for each of the four directions.

The "Animal Apocalypse" (*1 Enoch* 83–90) divides the rule of the seventy shepherds into four periods. During the first period the sheep are attacked by lions; the reference is to the Babylonian invasion and captivity. The second period involves the restoration. Only wild boars (the Samaritans) are mentioned, but the Persians presided over the return. Birds of prey attack the sheep during the third period. These seem to be the various successors of Alexander the Great. The new element in the fourth period is the appearance of lambs with horns who resist the birds of prey. The allusion must be to the Maccabeans. There are good reasons for concluding that the four kingdom schema arose in Near Eastern resistance to Hellenistic rule.[59] The four periods in the "Animal Apocalypse" would fit such a framework well. The hated Greeks are successfully resisted by a native leader with divine aid. The success of the indigenous ruler is a prelude to the messianic kingdom.

The four kingdom schema plays a minor role in *4 Ezra* and *2 Baruch*. In *4 Ezra* 11 a single beast is seen rising from the sea, rather than four as in Daniel 7. In 12:11–12 this single beast, an eagle, is identified with the fourth beast of Daniel 7. It is explicitly said that the interpretation given to Ezra is different from the one given to Daniel. These remarks seem to reflect a deliberate adaptation of the old schema to new circumstances. The fourth kingdom is

---

[58] Collins, *Daniel*, 280–94.
[59] See J.W. Swain, "The Theory of the Four Monarchies: Opposition History under the Roman Empire," *Classical Philology* 35 (1940) 1–21.

not Greece, but Rome. The elimination of the first three beasts shows lessened interest in history and chronology in favor of an emphasis on the present. In *2 Baruch* 39 four kingdoms are listed. The remarks on the second and third are vague and indeterminate. The first is clearly Babylon, the one who destroyed Zion. The fourth is the harshest of all; the literary fiction and context of the book as a whole suggests that the fourth kingdom is Rome. As in *4 Ezra*, there is less interest in history and chronology than in Daniel. The maintenance of the four kingdom schema leads the reader to draw an analogy between Babylon and Rome.

In the *Apocalypse of Abraham*, a work roughly contemporary with *4 Ezra* and *2 Baruch*, God reveals to Abraham that his dealings with his people will extend through four "issues," apparently periods of time (chapter 28).[60] During four (or perhaps during three and part of the fourth) of these, God will be angry with them and will punish them. The fourth "issue" will consist of (or perhaps contain a portion equal to) one hundred years, which is evidently one hour of the aeon. The four kingdom schema may be reflected here, but if so, its function is not very clear.[61]

The origin of the four metals is unclear. It may reflect changing technology or it may be purely mythical. In the apocalyptic literature it is overshadowed by the four kingdom schema which has clear historical and political roots. The holding of the number to four, or perhaps even its selection in the first place, may owe something to the cosmic significance of the number (as in four winds, for example.)

c) *Twelve periods*

According to *4 Ezra* 14:11–12, the age is divided into twelve parts. This passage was discussed above as an example of a text whose calculation of the end, though imprecise, evokes the conviction that the time of the end is fixed and relatively near. This text also manifests an interest in ordering time. It divides the "age," probably the period from creation to the messianic age (see 7:26–30), into twelve parts. There is no indication in the context that the twelve parts reflect the twelve patriarchs and the twelve tribes. In vs 10 it is said

---

[60] R. Rubinkiewicz and H.G. Lunt translate "ascents" in "The Apocalypse of Abraham," in Charlesworth, ed., *OTP*, 1. 703. A. Pennington translates "generations" in "The Apocalypse of Abraham," in Sparks, ed., *AOT*, 388; cf. 387, n. 2.

[61] According to *Apoc. Abr.* 29:2, the (present) impious age lasts for twelve "periods" each of which may be equivalent to a symbolic "hour of the age" (29:1).

that the age has lost its youth and the times are growing old. This remark indicates that the age has a beginning and an end, youth and age, just like a human being. The twelve parts should probably be understood as a projection onto the largest unit of time of the twelve months of the year or the twelve hours of the day.

In the eagle vision of *4 Ezra* 11–12, the eagle is described as having twelve wings. As noted above, the twelve wings should be understood as twelve Roman emperors. It is impossible to determine with much probability whom the little opposing wings represent. The references to the two wings that had gone over to the last head (12:2, 29–30) appear to be later modifications, when the empire did not end with Domitian, as was apparently expected. That expectation may have been linked to the theory that the empire would cease after twelve rulers had had their day. The text itself gives no hint about why the number is twelve. Although he was perfectly aware that the empire continued afterward, Suetonius chose to write about the first twelve Caesars. In both cases, the definition of a large block of time may have been based on a smaller one. The twelve Caesars constitute the empire's first (or only) "year" or "day."

In *2 Baruch*, Baruch has a vision of a cloud which pours forth black and bright rain alternately for a total of twelve times. Then he saw an exceedingly violent storm of black waters followed by great lightning over all the earth (chapter 53). The vision is interpreted as an allegory of events in the world (the aeon) from its creation to its consummation (chapter 56). The first, black waters represent the sins of Adam and the fallen angels (56:5–16). The second, bright waters stand for Abraham and those like him (chapter 57). The rest of the twelve waters cover the history of Israel. The black, eleventh waters depict the destruction of Zion by the Babylonians (chapter 67). According to the literary fiction of the book, that event was taking place at the author's time. It is generally agreed by intrepreters of the work that the major event of the author's own time, the destruction of Jerusalem by Rome, is being dealt with by reflecting on the earlier, analogous event. The twelfth, bright waters represent the restoration. It is briefly described as glorious, though not as great as the original kingdom of Israel (chapter 68). The final, very black waters are the eschatological woes, and the lightning is the messianic kingdom (chapters 70–74).

Once again, the text itself gives little indication of why the number twelve was chosen. Besides the twelve periods, the number twelve

also appears in the final element of the vision: twelve rivers ascend
from the sea, surround the lightning and are subject to it (53:11).
That element of the vision is not interpreted. The image is rather
opaque. Charles asks whether the twelve rivers are the Gentiles or
the twelve tribes of Israel.[62] The twelve patriarchs and twelve tribes
are not mentioned in the interpretation of the vision. So, at least for
the author of *2 Baruch* in its present form, the twelve periods have
little to do with the twelve patriarchs and tribes. If the significance
of the number was reflected upon, it was probably in terms of a
world "day" or "year."

The division of history into twelve periods occurs in *Jacob's Ladder*,
a work which is Christian in its present form, but may be a redaction of an older, Jewish work.[63] The writing is an account of a dream-
vision of Jacob, based on Gen 28:10–22. The ladder which Jacob
saw has twelve rungs with a human face on the ends of each rung.
The angel Sariel interprets the dream for Jacob and tells him that
the twelve rungs represent the twelve times of this age. A review of
history in the form of a prediction follows, but it is not related to
the motif of the twelve times. In spite of Jacob's role in the book of
Genesis as the father of the twelve patriarchs, there is no indication
in the text that they have anything to do with the twelve times.
Once again, the most likely explanation is that they represent a world
"day" or "year."

d) *Ten and multiples of ten*

The "Apocalypse of Weeks" (*1 Enoch* 93; 91:12–17) is a formal unit
within the work called the "Letter of Enoch" (*1 Enoch* 91–104). In it
the history of the world is divided into ten periods, each called a
"week." The major events are clear and in chronological order. Nevertheless, there is no interest in absolute chronology, precise dates,
or in calculating periods of time accurately. The periods are of un-
equal length, so the term "week" does not refer to any consistent
unit of time.

The first event mentioned is the birth of Enoch himself, who was
born the seventh in the first "week." The sixth "week" ends with the
destruction of Jerusalem by Babylon. The author apparently sees him-

---

[62] Charles, *APOT*, 2. 510, n. 12.
[63] Yarbro Collins, "The Early Christian Apocalypses," 69; H.G. Lunt, "Ladder
of Jacob," in Charlesworth, ed., *OTP*, 2. 401–11.

self as living near the end of the seventh "week." In it an apostate generation arises, but at its close the eternal plant of righteousness is elected to receive sevenfold instruction concerning God's creation. The plant is evidently an image for the group to which the author belonged. In the eighth "week" the righteous will punish sinners with the sword. In the ninth the world will be destroyed, and judgment on the angels will take place in the tenth, followed by cosmic renewal. After that, there will be many "weeks" without number forever.

The text does not reveal why history is organized into ten "weeks" rather than seven or twelve. The most likely reason is that it is a round number and an important one for any people using a numerical system based on decades. Even though the overall schema is based on ten, the number seven is greatly emphasized within it. Enoch is the seventh of his generation; he is of course the authoritative mediator of the revealed knowledge contained in the book. The author's group lives during the seventh week and they receive sevenfold instruction. The judgment will take place in the seventh part of the tenth week (91:15). It would seem that the sabbatical logic discussed above has influenced the ten "week" schema.

A related motif is the schema of ten generations which occurs in the *Sibylline Oracles*. *Sib. Or.* 4:49–101 divides the period from the flood to the rule of Macedonia into ten generations. *Sib. Or.* 3:156–61 and the Jewish original form of books 1 and 2 of the *Sibylline Oracles* use the same schema. The motif probably has its origin in pagan sibylline oracles in the presentation of political ideologies.[64]

A passage from the Book of the Watchers (*1 Enoch* 1–36) was discussed above in the section on sabbatical eschatology, namely, the remark in 10:12 that the fallen angels were bound for seventy generations. That period of time is also the length between the flood and the final judgment. In chapter 18 Enoch sees a waste and horrible place where seven stars are burning. The angel tells him that they are the stars which transgressed God's commandment in the beginning of their rising, by not coming forth at their appointed times (18:15). They are bound in that place of punishment for ten thousand years (vs 16). The same information is given at 21:1–6. The tradition about the seven stars and that about the fallen angels seem to be independent of one another. At the beginning of chapter 19,

---

[64] See the discussion in John J. Collins, "The Place of the Fourth Sibyl in the Development of the Jewish Sibyllina," *JJS* 25 (1974) 370–72.

the place of punishment of the seven stars is secondarily identified
with the fallen angels' place of punishment before the final judgment. In chapter 21, after Enoch has seen the location where the
seven stars are being punished, he is taken to another place, more
horrible than the first (21:7). This second place is identified as the
prison of the angels where they will be imprisoned forever. It is likely
that these attempts to relate the two traditions are the contribution
of the redactor who joined them at some stage in the composition of
1 Enoch 1–36. No attempt was made to relate the seventy generations to the ten thousand years. The latter figure is a round number,
a multiple of ten (10 × 1,000). The selection of the number is probably related to the importance of ten in the system of counting in
decades.

According to the *Assumption of Moses* (or the *Testament of Moses*),
Moses gave his testament to Joshua in the one hundred twentieth
year of Moses' life, which was the two thousand five hundredth year
from creation (1:2). Near the end, Moses predicts that the final visitation of God would occur two hundred and fifty times after Moses'
death (10:12). On the basis of a comparison of these texts with other
writings which give chronological information, Charles and Russell
infer that the two hundred and fifty "times" are weeks of years, so
that the total number of years from Moses' death to the end is 1,750.[65]
They then add the figures given in 1:2 and 10:12 to get a total of
4,250 years from the creation to the end of the world. They assume
that the basic unit of measurement is a jubilee of fifty years and
conclude that the author considered all of history to equal eighty-five
jubilees.[66]

It should be noted, however, that the *Assumption of Moses* does not
mention the jubilee as a unit of measurement. The text does manifest some interest in chronology. Nevertheless, the concern to find
order, to discover a meaningful pattern in time, seems to be equally
prominent, if not more important. It is surely no accident that there
is a parallel between the 250 times and the 2,500 (250 × 10) years.
The unit of a "time" was evidently chosen to allow the parallel to be
perceived. Further, as an indeterminate period, the "times" could be
reinterpreted, as the need arose, to fix the time of the end.

---

[65] R.H. Charles, *APOT*, 2. 423, n. 12; Russell, *The Method and Message of Jewish
Apocalyptic*, 208, 226.
[66] R.H. Charles, *APOT*, 2. 423, n. 12; Russell, *The Method and Message of Jewish
Apocalyptic*, 199, 226.

The Apocalypse of Weeks, the Book of the Watchers, and the *Assumption of Moses* all show an interest in ordering large blocks of time in some meaningful way. In each case ten or a multiple of ten is used to show the orderliness and rationality in world history.

The division of large blocks of time into periods is a prominent characteristic of apocalyptic literature, especially in Jewish texts. The major reason for dividing time in this way does not seem to be to calculate the precise time of the end or to make chronological measurements. Rather, the primary characteristic of such divisions is the demonstration of a meaningful pattern in time. They show that time is not random, but orderly. The most common method of ordering time is the use of sabbatical eschatology, involving sevens and multiples of seven. This method implies that long periods of time have the same rhythm as the week. Another common principle of order is the number twelve. The use of this figure suggests that large blocks of time have the same rhythm as the day with its twelve hours and the year with its twelve months. Four kingdoms or four ages appear in a number of texts. This motif derives from political oracles of the Hellenistic Near East. It has a primarily historical interest, but the cosmic role of the number four may have played some role in its continued importance if not in its original selection. Finally, the number ten and its multiples occur in a few texts in the ordering of time. Its use seems to reflect the key role of ten in the various numerical systems themselves which are based on decades.

2. *Numerical patterns projected into the future*

Many of the texts discussed in the previous section of this chapter include the future in the periods of history which they enumerate. But what they all have in common is the integration of past, present and future into a grand scheme which makes sense out of time and history and especially of the writers' present situation. A number of other texts involve one or more periods of time, but in the future only. These cases seem to be based on the same kind of logic found in the texts already discussed. They reflect a search for meaningful order in time. They carry that search into speculation on the ideal future.

a) *Sabbatical logic*

In the third revelatory dialogue between Ezra and the angel, the angel reveals what the events of the end-time will be. After the messianic

kingdom, the world will return to primeval silence for seven days
(7:30). A detailed description of the final judgment follows. The day
of judgment will be one without sun or moon or stars (vs 39). Nevertheless, its length can be known. It will last about a week of years
(vs 43). In vss 30 and 43 the number seven appears or is implied. Its
relationship to the week is clear in vs 43. There is no evidence of
speculation on a world-week. The dialogue opens with a long prayer
by Ezra which enumerates and discusses the six days of creation.
The seven days of primeval silence thus may be analogous in some
way to the seven days of creation. In any case, the familiar period of
the week is used to order two periods of crisis in the ideal, eschatological future.

b) *A twelve-part schema*
In a revelatory dialogue of *2 Baruch*, the time of tribulation before
the appearance of the messiah is discussed. Baruch is told that the
time will be divided into twelve parts (27:1). The twelve parts are
enumerated and the woes associated with each one are revealed
(27:2–13). The ordering of the time of woe into twelve portions corresponds to the division of time from Adam to the end into twelve
periods (53–74). The order discovered in the past and present is
projected into the future.

c) *The thousand year reign*
The period of one thousand years appears in the book of Revelation
for the first time in connection with the binding of Satan (20:1–3).
He is bound and confined in a pit for a thousand years. While he is
bound, a judgment, the first resurrection, and the messianic reign
take place (vss 4–6). Then Satan is loosed from his prison (vs 7). He
comes forth to deceive the nations whom he gathers for battle (vs 8).
They are defeated, and then Satan is confined in a place of eternal
punishment (vss 9–10). This passage has a number of elements in
common with the Book of the Watchers (*1 Enoch* 1–36). In both
cases one or more evil angels are confined for a definite period of
time (*1 Enoch* 10:12). This preliminary punishment is followed at the
end of days by a final, absolute and eternal punishment in a different
location. Both books describe the place of preliminary confinement
as underground (*1 Enoch* 10:4–5); the place of eternal punishment is
fiery in both cases (*1 Enoch* 10:6, 13). The myths about the fallen
angels and Satan are attempts to understand evil in the world. The

author of the Book of Watchers described an outbreak of evil in primordial times whose effects lasted into the present. But evil was in some sense controlled. He could speak of the fallen angels as bound. The author of Revelation did not see reality in the same way. His own time had to be characterized as a time when Satan was loose and active on earth (compare 9:1–11 and 12:7–12). Satan's confinement would take place only in the future.

Nothing in the text of Revelation suggests that speculation on a world-week had anything to do with defining the time of Satan's confinement and of the messianic reign as a thousand years.[67] It is doubtful that the period of a thousand years was borrowed from *2 Enoch* 33:1–2, because that passage is found only in the longer recension.[68] The Book of the Watchers has a different period of time for the binding of the fallen angels (*1 Enoch* 10:12; seventy generations). Various considerations probably influenced the approximate determination of the period in the book of Revelation. It had to be long enough to provide the martyrs with an impressive reward.[69] On the other hand, it should not be so long that the final judgment and new creation would be moved into the inconceivable future. Beyond these considerations, the rationale for selecting the number a thousand was probably similar to the one discussed above in the section on "Ten and Multiples of Ten." These numbers had an intrinsic significance as round numbers giving a sense of wholeness or completion, because of their role in a system based on decades.

Another early Christian apocalypse, the *Apocalypse of Paul*, contains a reference to a future period of a thousand years.[70] In chapter 21 it is said that the Lord Jesus Christ will be revealed and will reign over all his saints for a thousand years. It is likely that the motif of a thousand year reign was borrowed from the book of Revelation.

d) *The Messianic age in* 4 Ezra

In the same passage that mentions the seven days of primeval silence (see the section on "Sabbatical Logic" above), it is said that the messiah

---

[67] So also E. Schüssler Fiorenza, "Die tausendjährige Herrschaft der Auferstandenen (Apk 20, 4–6)," *Bib Leb* 13 (1972) 122.

[68] Fiorenza thought such a borrowing possible (ibid., 121); see the discussion above related to notes 53 and 54.

[69] See the discussion of Rev 20:4–6 in Chapter Six below, "The Political Perspective of the Revelation to John."

[70] This is the apocryphal, not the Gnostic Apocalypse of Paul; on its provenance see Yarbro Collins, "The Early Christian Apocalypses," 85–86.

will be revealed and that those who remain will rejoice for four hundred years (*4 Ezra* 7:28). The figure four hundred appears in one of the Arabic manuscripts and in the Georgian version. The Syriac version has thirty; the other Arabic manuscript reads one thousand and one of the Latin manuscripts has three hundred written above. The Armenian and Ethiopic versions have no number at all.[71] The reading four hundred is generally accepted as the original.

The rationale for defining the messianic kingdom as a period of four hundred years is unclear. Gunkel suggested that the number is due to a combination of Ps 90:15 and Gen 15:13.[72] The Psalm text reads, "Make us glad as many days as thou hast afflicted us, and as many years as we have seen evil" (RSV). The Genesis passage refers to the slavery of the descendants of Abram in Egypt for four hundred years; it is described as a time of oppression. Another possibility is that the number four hundred was chosen as a multiple of forty, a traditional round number used in a variety of contexts. For example, the rain which brought about the flood fell for forty days and nights (Gen 7:4); Moses remained on Sinai for forty days and nights (Exod 24:18); the Israelites wandered for forty years in the wilderness (Deut 1:3). Whatever the rationale, it was apparently not powerful enough to prevent later scribes and translators from changing or omitting the number. Some of the changes probably resulted from Christian concern to make the prediction conform to the reality of Jesus' ministry or to the text of Revelation.

The ordering of revelatory experience

Two ways in which numbers are used to order time in apocalyptic literature have been discussed so far in this chapter. The first is the attempt to calculate the time of the end. The second is the effort to discover a meaningful pattern in time, past, present and future. Numbers are also used in a few Jewish apocalypses to indicate that there is a certain orderliness in revelatory experience.

---

[71] On the textual variants, see Myers, *I and II Esdras*, 208, n. 1; Stone, *Fourth Ezra*, 202.

[72] H. Gunkel in E. Kautzsch, ed., *Die Apokryphen und Pseudepigraphen des Alten Testaments* (cited by Myers, *I and II Esdras*, 233); cf. Stone, *Fourth Ezra*, 215.

1. *Periods of seven days*

In the narrative framework of *4 Ezra*, the various revelatory experiences of the seer are clearly separated by references to periods of time. The period of time most commonly mentioned is seven days. On two occasions Ezra is instructed to fast for seven days (5:13, 6:35). The angel's words in the first of these passages make clear that the fast is intended as preparation for the reception of further revelation: ". . . if you pray again, and weep as you do now, and fast for seven days, you shall hear yet greater things than these." On two other occasions, Ezra is commanded to observe a period of seven days in which he will eat no meat and drink no wine, but eat only the flowers of the field (9:23; or plants, 12:51). The two fasts of seven days are followed by revelatory dialogues (5:21–6:34 and 6:35–9:25). The two seven day periods of eating only flowers are followed by visions (9:38–10:59 and 13:1–58).

Like *4 Ezra*, the narrative framework of *2 Baruch* contains several references to periods of time. On four occasions Baruch fasts for seven days (9:2, 12:5, 21:1, 47:2). Each of these fasts prepares for and introduces a revelatory experience. Each of them serves also to separate major sections of the work. The first fast separates the narrative introduction (1–8) and the second section (9:1–12:4). The second fast separates the second from the third section (12:5–20:6). The third fast divides the third from the fourth major section (21–34). The fourth fast separates the fifth section (35–46) from the sixth (47–77). The seventh and last section is the epistle of Baruch (78–86), which is followed by an epilogue.

The seven-day periods of special preparation in *4 Ezra* and *2 Baruch* clearly have a literary function. They help to order the material contained in these two long and complex works. At the root of this literary function seems to be a deeper ordering power. The regular occurrences of seven day periods, especially in *2 Baruch*, seem to express the conviction that human experience of the divine can and must be ordered. The self-revelation of the divine cannot be controlled. Nevertheless, appropriate occasions for revelation can be provided.

2. *Periods of forty days*

In the last section of *4 Ezra*, God speaks to Ezra from a bush (14:1). At the end of the discourse God tells Ezra to instruct the people not to seek him for forty days (vs 23). During that time Ezra was miraculously inspired to dictate all the holy Scriptures which had been lost in the destruction of Jerusalem. Ninety-four books were written by five scribes who were similarly inspired (vss 24, 42–44).

Near the end of Baruch's last revelatory experience in *2 Baruch*, he is told that he will be taken up into heaven after forty days (chapter 76). He is commanded to instruct the people during the forty days, so that they may live and not die at the last time.[73]

Chapters 9–32 of the *Apocalypse of Abraham* are based on the story of Abraham's sacrifice in Genesis 15: In chapter 9, Abraham is given instructions about how to prepare for the sacrifice he is about to make. He is commanded to avoid cooked food and wine and not to anoint himself for forty days. Then he may offer the sacrifice, at which time he will be shown the ages to come and what will befall the wicked and the righteous. He then fasts with the angel Iaoel for forty days and forty nights, after which they arrive at Mount Horeb (12:1–3).

The example from the *Apocalypse of Abraham* is like those in *4 Ezra* and *2 Baruch* which were discussed above. In all three books the seer must prepare himself in some way to receive revelation. The preparation Abraham makes is less rigorous than the fasts of seven days observed by Ezra and Baruch. It is most similar to the periods in which Ezra ate only the flowers and plants of the field. The implication of all of these texts is that there is a certain orderliness in revelatory experience. Divine revelation cannot be controlled, but it can be encouraged and there are orderly and appropriate ways to invite it.

The period of forty days during which Ezra was inspired to dictate the Scriptures is a sign that divine revelation is offered in bountiful ways to particularly favored individuals in special circumstances. The limit of forty days, however, helps to show that the bounty is not unlimited. Even in extraordinary times, the revelation has its boundaries. The gap between the human and the divine can be bridged, but only in a partial manner. In the same way, Baruch, after having received abundant revelation, has only a limited time to hand it on. Ordinary mortals have a chance to hear the mysteries

---

[73] After his heavenly journey through the seven heavens, Enoch is given thirty days to return to earth and instruct his children. Then he is taken up to heaven (*2 Enoch* 36).

from one who has received them directly from heaven, but only for a limited time. Then Baruch departs and people must rely on written texts and the chain of tradition.[74] The limited character of this opportunity is even more evident when the literary fiction of the work is taken into account. Not only is Baruch gone, but he has been gone already for centuries. The real author does not claim to have received revelation from heaven himself in his own time.

The first part of this chapter has been devoted to a study of how numbers are used to order time in apocalyptic literature. The chronicling interest is present as a minor element. It appears in *4 Ezra* 10:45 and *As. Mos.* 1:2. Texts which reflect the impulse to calculate the end in a fairly precise way all seem to be dependent on Jeremiah's prophecy that the restoration would come after seventy years. The only apocalypse in which this impulse is clarly present is the book of Daniel. *4 Ezra* and the book of Revelation engage in some imprecise calculations of the end. The rhetorical effect is the impression that the time of the end is fixed and near. The primary way in which numbers order time in apocalyptic literature is in the expression of meaningful patterns in past, present and future. The numbers which occur most frequently in this activity are seven, four, twelve and ten. The use of seven and twelve seems to derive from the projection of small units of time onto larger ones. Seven reflects the rhythm of the week and twelve the hours of the day or months of the year. The number four derives from historical, political oracles, but may have cosmic overtones. Ten and its multiples owe their prominence apparently to their key role in numerical systems with a base number of ten. Finally, numbers are used in apocalyptic literature to order revelatory experience. Such experiences are mysterious and overwhelming, but they have their own logic. They cannot be controlled, but they may be channeled. In some cases, revelation is limited to a specific length of time. Such limitations remind the reader of the elusive and partial character of human knowledge of the divine.

---

[74] Compare Acts 1:1–11. Stone concludes that the motif of the forty days comes from the Sinai incident (*Fourth Ezra*, 431). This suggestion is plausible for the three works discussed above, since the reception of the law is mentioned in *4 Ezra* 14:30; *2 Baruch* 77:3 and Mount Horeb in *Apoc. Abr.* 12:3.

In the first part of this chapter, the focus was on the role of numbers in the ordering of time. The emphasis was on apocalyptic literature, because of the prominence of the theme in that group of texts. A few pagan texts were mentioned, which were analagous to those being discussed or which may have influenced the corresponding Jewish texts. For the most part, the passages dealt with treated large blocks of time. In the section "The Ordering of Revelatory Experience" above, smaller units of time were included. In the second part of this chapter, numbers as signs of cosmic order will be discussed. Some of the texts included deal with space, with physical reality viewed as an orderly whole, a macrocosmos. Other passages treat heavenly beings who are associated with order in physical reality and among people. Another group of texts reflects the idea of the human being as a microcosmos. Some of these texts deal with the human body, but others treat the stages of human life, human perception and knowledge. Some similarity or overlap exists between passages in this group which describe stages in human life or regular human activities and the texts discussed above in the section on "The Ordering of Revelatory Experience." Few systems of classification can avoid some anomalies or overlapping. The criterion used here to separate these rather similar texts is the following: those texts which present themselves as treating events which occurred in a particular time and place, once and for all, are included in the first part of this chapter. They have to do with time in a way that is history-like. Texts which describe repeatable events are included in the second part of the chapter. They are human in a general and typical way and thus more cosmic than historical or history-like.

The Pythagorean tradition

Mystical speculation based on numbers, reflection on numbers as symbols, and various other activities grouped under the rubric of numerology, or better arithmology, were widespread in the Hellenistic and Roman periods.[75] Indeed, they seem to be universal human

---

[75] See the literature cited by Walter Burkert, *Lore and Science in Ancient Pythagoreanism* (Cambridge, MA: Harvard University, 1972) 466, n. 2; in addition, see Peter Friesenhahn, *Hellenistische Wortzahlenmystik im Neuen Testament* (Leipzig: Teubner, 1935).

phenomena and still exert some influence today.[76] In the Greco-Roman period the best known tradition about the qualities of numbers was the Pythagorean. There has been extensive debate during modern times on the development of Pythagorean tradition, particularly on what is early or late and how much goes back to Pythagoras himself. A veritable search for "the historical Pythagoras" has occurred. Another common question is the extent to which early Pythagoreanism was scientific. These difficult questions were carefully sorted out by Walter Burkert in his relatively recent study.[77]

The best source for early Pythagoreanism is Aristotle. His remarks on the Pythagoreans imply that for them, things are numbers; they consist of numbers. Being identical with things, numbers are bound to space and time. They came into being at a particular point in time; they have magnitude. Evidently, the early Pythagoreans did not distinguish between the incorporeal and the corporeal. For them only the corporeal existed.[78] It is clear from all this that numbers for the early followers of Pythagoras were not human inventions for practical purposes. They were rather independently existing entities with their own peculiar, sometimes powerful characteristics.

According to Aristotle, the Pythagoreans taught that numbers have the elements of the even and the odd. The odd were associated with the limited; the even with the unlimited. The limited is the positive, masculine principle. The unlimited was considered feminine. The odd was considered masculine because, when the odd number was represented by pebbles, there was a pebble "left over" in the middle when the pebbles were divided in half. The even number was feminine, because it had an "empty space" in the middle.[79]

The One had its origin in the forces of limit and unlimited together; therefore it is both odd and even, male and female. It was the world before its further evolution.[80] It was called "mind" (νοῦς) and "substance" (οὐσία).[81] The One became Two when the force of the unlimited penetrated it.[82] Two is associated with "opinion" (δόξα); "three is the number of the whole—beginning, middle and end; four

---

[76] Burkert, *Lore and Science in Ancient Pythagoreanism*, 468–472.
[77] Ibid.; German original: *Weisheit und Wissenschaft. Studien zu Pythagoras, Philolaos und Platon* (EBSK 10; Nürnberg: Carl, 1962).
[78] Burkert, *Ancient Pythagoreanism*, 31–32.
[79] Ibid., 32–34.
[80] Ibid., 36.
[81] Ibid., 467.
[82] Ibid., 36.

is justice—equal times equal. . . ."[83] Nine is also associated with justice, probably for the same reason.[84] Four is also called the whole
nature of numbers because the sum of the first four numbers is equal
to ten, the perfect number. This insight is related to speculation on
the "four group" or "tetractys." When the first four numbers are
laid out in pebbles they form a triangle.[85] Five "is marriage, as the
first combination of odd and even, male and female. . . ."[86] Seven is
"right time" or "opportunity" (καιρός). Seven neither begets nor is
begotten. It is therefore associated with Athena who was born from
Zeus' head and remained a virgin.[87] "Ten is the perfect number,
which comprehends the whole nature of number and determines the
structure of the cosmos, and with it ends the symbolic interpretation
of numbers."[88]

As a philosophical school, the Pythagorean movement drops from
the historian's view in the fourth century BCE. There is evidence,
however, that Pythagorean traditions continued to circulate in connection with a Pythagorean way of life which had affinities with
Orphism and mystery religions.[89] A revival of Pythagorean philosophy
began perhaps as early as the late second century BCE.[90] Participants in this movement are referred to by modern scholars as Neo-
Pythagoreans. The Pythagorean revival is attested in Rome and in
Alexandria in the first century BCE.[91] Later famous Neo-Pythagoreans
include Apollonius of Tyana (Cappadocia) and Moderatus of Gades
(Spain) in the first century CE, Nichomachus of Gerasa (Transjordan)
and Numenius of Apamea (Syria) in the second century CE and
Philostratus (lived in Athens and Rome) in the third.[92] The portrayal
of Apollonius by Philostratus is unusual in its lack of reverence for
the power and significance of numbers.[93]

---

[83] Ibid., 467.
[84] Ibid., 40.
[85] Ibid., 72.
[86] Ibid., 467.
[87] Ibid.
[88] Ibid., 467–468.
[89] E. Zeller, *Die Philosophie der Griechen in ihrer geschichtlichen Entwicklung* (4th ed.; Leipzig: Reisland, 1903) 3/2. 92–97.
[90] Ibid., 103–108.
[91] Ibid., 109–114; J. Dillon, *The Middle Platonists* (London: Duckworth, 1977) 117–121, 126–129.
[92] Zeller, *Die Philosophie der Griechen*, 124–175; on Moderatus, Nicomachus and Numenius, see Dillon, *The Middle Platonists*, 344–383.
[93] Zeller, *Die Philosophie der Griechen*, 172.

M. Terentius Varro (116–28 BCE) was a Roman scholar who apparently participated in the Neo-Pythagorean movement. Toward the end of his life, he published a work called *Hebdomades* or *On Portraits*.[94] A portion of this work is quoted by Aulus Gellius in his *Attic Nights* (3.10). In it Varro discourses on the "excellencies and powers of the number seven."[95] He discusses first of all the various astronomical phenomena which are governed by the number seven; for example, that seven stars form the constellations of the Greater and Lesser Bears and the Pleiades. He also mentions the seven planets and the fact that the moon completes its course in four periods of seven days.

Next Varro describes the various ways in which the number seven governs human life. He believed that the human embryo developed in stages of seven days and that a child born before the seventh month could not survive. According to him, the extreme limit the human body could achieve in height was seven feet. He noted that human teeth appear in the first seven months and fall out within seven years. Varro includes also the idea that the seventh day (and multiples thereof) was a critical day in human illnesses.[96] Finally, those who aim to die by starvation do not meet their end until the seventh day. Besides these two categories of astronomical and human data (which may be due to Aulus Gellius' method of quotation), Varro also mentions various geographical, legendary and personal facts in which the number seven is prominent.

Burkert is surely correct in concluding that the cosmic significance of numbers in Pythagorean number symbolism belongs to pre-logical thought.[97] Kirk and Raven probably went too far in asserting the unity of science and religion in the teaching of Pythagoras.[98] Nevertheless, they provided a credible reconstruction of the practical meaning of numerical symbolism for the Pythagoreans. They perceived the central notions in the Pythagorean way of life to be contemplation (θεωρία), an orderliness found in the arrangement of the universe

---

[94] Dillon, *The Middle Platonists*, 62, 118, n. 1.

[95] The translation cited is from the LCL (3.10.1).

[96] This idea is found also in the pseudo-Hippocratic book περὶ ἑβδομάδων ("On the Number Seven") and in other Hippocratic writings; see W.H. Roscher, *Die Hebdomadenlehren der griechischen Philosophen und Ärtzte* (ASGW.PH 24/6; Leipzig: Teubner, 1906) 62–86.

[97] Burkert, *Ancient Pythagoreanism*, 479–480.

[98] G.S. Kirk and J.E. Raven, *The Presocratic Philosophers* (Cambridge: Cambridge University, 1957) 227–228.

(κόσμος), and purification (κάθαρσις). The logic of the Pythagorean
life-style seems to have been based on the conviction that by contemplating the order in the universe and by conforming one's life to
that order, a person may progressively purify oneself until one es-
capes the cycle of rebirth and attains immortality.[99]

Points of contact between Judaism and Pythagorean tradition

It was noted above that the old Pythagorean school appears to have
died out toward the end of the fourth century BCE. The Pythagorean way of life apparently persisted in small associations in various places around the eastern Mediterranean. In addition, a large
number of pseudonymous Pythagorean writings appeared in the third
and second centuries BCE. These writings are not held to represent
a continuation or a revival of the Pythagorean movement; by Dillon
because they are "sub-philosophical" and by Thesleff because they
were not associated with sects practicing the Pythagorean way of life.[100]
Nevertheless, they attest the continued widespread circulation of
Pythagorean arithmological traditions.[101] There are two quite clear
examples of the interaction of Pythagorean and Jewish tradition,
namely, the writings of Aristobulus and those of Philo.[102]

1. Aristobulus

Evidence exists for the presence of Pythagorean traditions in Alexandria in the third century BCE. Hermippus of Smyrna was apparently a pupil of Callimachus at Alexandria, and wrote at least two
books on Pythagoras in that city.[103] Eudorus of Alexandria was one
of the earliest Neo-Pythagoreans and was active in Alexandria in the

---

[99] Ibid., 228.

[100] Dillon, *The Middle Platonists*, 118–119; H. Thesleff, *An Introduction to the Pythagorean Writings of the Hellenistic Period* (AAAbo.H 24.3; Åbo, Finland: Åbo Akademi, 1961) 104–105.

[101] See the subject index, IX. Mathemata, in H. Thesleff, *The Pythagorean Texts of the Hellenistic Period* (AAAbo.H 30.1; Åbo, Finland: Åbo Akademi, 1965) 248.

[102] Scholars of the eighteenth and nineteenth centuries assumed a close relation-ship between the Essenes and the Pythagoreans because of remarks to that effect in Josephus, Philo and Pliny. Since the discovery of the scrolls at Qumran, scholars are much more cautious and explain the similarities in a more indirect way; see the summary of scholarship in Hengel, *Judaism and Hellenism*, 1. 245.

[103] St. Heibges, "Hermippos, der Kallimacheer," *PW* 8/1 (1912) 845–852.

first century BCE.[104] The pseudonymous Pythagorean works mentioned above and these two writers provide ample support for the hypothesis that Pythagorean arithmology was known in Alexandria in Aristobulus' time, the second century BCE.[105] Even if there were no such external evidence, one would have to conclude from internal evidence that Aristobulus was familiar with Pythagorean traditions.[106] He mentions Pythagoras twice and claims that the philosopher borrowed many things from Moses.[107]

Aristobulus' affinities with the Pythagoreans are most apparent in fragment 5.[108] This fragment is à somewhat loosely connected series of remarks on the sabbath; its institution, its etymological meaning, its symbolic meaning, its cosmic meaning, its ethical significance, and finally, a demonstration by quotation of Greek poets that the Greeks considered the seventh day a holy day. Aristobulus argues that their reverence for the seventh day is derived from the Torah. Near the beginning of fragment 5, he remarks that "the seventh day might be called first also, as the genesis of light in which all things are contemplated."[109] This identification of the seventh with the first day of creation is not understandable purely within Jewish tradition. It makes sense only when the identification or association of the number seven with light is presupposed. This association is Pythagorean. Philolaus

---

[104] Dillon, *The Middle Platonists*, 115–121.

[105] On the date of Aristobulus, see N. Walter, *Der Thoraausleger Aristobulos* (TU 86; Berlin: Akademie, 1964) 13–26; Hengel, *Judaism and Hellenism*, 1. 163–164, 2. 105–107, nn. 373, 378. I have argued elsewhere that Aristobulus' work should be dated to about 155–145 BCE. (Adela Yarbro Collins, "Aristobulus," in Charlesworth, ed., *OTP*, 2. 831–42). Carl R. Holladay dates his activity to the reign of Ptolemy VI Philometor (180–145 BCE); idem, *Fragments from Hellenistic Jewish Authors*, vol. 3, *Aristobulus* (SBLTT 39, Pseudepigrapha Series 13; Atlanta: Scholars Press, 1995).

[106] Walter concluded that Aristobulus drew specific Pythagorean ideas and symbols from a Jewish edition of Pythagorean texts (*Der Thoraausleger Aristobulos*, 151–171). Hengel argued that Aristobulus borrowed the idea of the number seven as a cosmic principle of order from Pythagorean, Platonic and Hippocratic numerical speculation, but that his specific arguments and other symbols derive from an inner-Jewish speculative tradition (*Judaism and Hellenism*, 1. 166–169).

[107] Aristobulus makes the same claim about other Greek philosophers and about some poets. He mentions Pythagoras in fragments 3 (Eusebius *Praep. Ev.* 13.12.1–2 [Mras, 2. 190, ln. 14—191, ln. 7]; Holladay, *Fragments from Jewish Hellenistic Authors*, 3. 150–61) and 4 (*Praep. Ev.* 13.12.3–8 [Mras, 2.191, ln. 8—195, ln. 11; Holladay, 3. 162–75]).

[108] Eusebius, *Praep. Ev.* 13.12.9–16 (Mras, 2.195 ln. 12—197, ln. 16); Holladay, *Fragments from Jewish Hellenistic Authors*, 3. 176–97.

[109] Translation is by the author.

connected seven with mind (νοῦς), harmony of the human body (ὑγίεια), and light (φῶς).[110]

A little further on in fragment 5, Aristobulus says that the observance of the sabbath is "a sign of the sevenfold principle which is established around us, in which we have knowledge of human and divine matters. And indeed all the cosmos of all living beings and growing things revolves in series of sevens." Some scholars have understood this "sevenfold principle" (ἕβδομος λόγος) as one of the faculties of mind or soul, deriving from Platonic or Aristotelian doctrine, and have translated it "seventh reason."[111] Since cosmic phenomena are referred to in the context, it makes more sense to translate the phrase "sevenfold principle" and to understand it as a law of nature. The "divine matters" of which the principle yields knowledge are probably cosmic occurrences guided by God, such as the astronomical data which we find a little later in Varro. The "human matters" very likely are the kinds of observations Varro made about human life: the development of the embryo, the appearance of teeth and so on. Perhaps Aristobulus was familiar with the tradition which originated with Solon,[112] that the life of a man was normally a period of seventy years divided into ten stages of seven years each. These stages were distinguished by significant events which occurred at intervals of seven years, such as the losing of the first teeth at seven years, puberty at fourteen, completion of growth and appearance of beard at twenty-one and so forth.[113] According to Burkert, Solon's poem on the stages of human life was frequently cited in ancient numerological texts, where the treatment of seven was generally the fullest.[114]

Among the early Pythagoreans, the most significant numbers were one, two, four and ten. Philolaus, for example, counted ten heavenly bodies: the central fire, counter-earth, earth, moon, sun, and the five planets.[115] Gradually, the number seven came into greater prominence. One reason for this trend was probably the introduction of Babylonian astrology and ideas about the seven planets into Greece,

---

[110] Walter, *Der Thoraausleger Aristobulos*, 156, 160–62.

[111] Ibid., 68–70.

[112] See A.W. Gomme and T.J. Cadoux, "Solon," in N.G.L. Hammond and H.H. Scullard, eds., *OCD* [2nd ed., 1970] 999–1000.

[113] Fr. 19 Diehl; Roscher, *Die Hebdomadenlehren der griechischen Philosophen and Ärtzte*, 14–17.

[114] Burkert, *Ancient Pythagoreanism*, 470, n. 29.

[115] Ibid., 313.

beginning with the fourth century BCE.[116] Roscher has collected
various texts which show the importance of the number of seven in
the Pythagorean tradition.[117] Thus, in Aristobulus' time there was
probably a well-developed Pythagorean speculative tradition on the
number seven. This tradition had probably been discovered, adopted
and expanded by Jews in Alexandria already before Aristobulus.[118]
The Jews would naturally have been most interested in speculation
on the number seven because of its applicability to interpretations of
the sabbath. The Pythagorean tradition reinforced and helped Jewish thinkers carry further the tendency already present in Gen 1:1–
2:4a, the Priestly account of creation, to understand the sabbath in
cosmic terms.

2. *Philo*

Philo lived in Alexandria not long after the Neo-Pythagorean Eudorus.[119] He was well-versed in Greek literature, especially Plato and
the Stoics. Dillon calls him a fully fledged Middle Platonist.[120] He
was able to become one in part because he believed that Plato was
a follower of Pythagoras and that Pythagoras was a follower of
Moses.[121] Philo's discussions of the properties of numbers show that
he can also be called a Neo-Pythagorean with considerable justifica-
tion.[122] He wrote a work "On Numbers," which unfortunately has
been lost. Karl Staehle, in his dissertation presented in 1929 at the
University of Tübingen, attempted to reconstruct the lost book by
collecting all the passages in which Philo discusses the characteristics
of numbers.[123] Most ancient arithmologies discussed only the numbers from one to ten. A few were devoted to only one number. Philo
apparently devoted most of his attention to the first decade. It is

---

[116] W. Roscher, "Planeten und Planetengötter," in idem, ed., *Ausführliches Lexikon
der griechischen und römischen Mythologie*, 3. 2525–2526.

[117] Roscher, *Die Hebdomadenlehren der griechischen Philosophen and Ärtzte*, 24–43.

[118] In fragment 2, when Aristobulus uses an allegorical method of interpretation,
he is very tentative, explains what he is doing, and seems to be breaking new ground.
In fragment 5, on the contrary, he is elliptical and seems to be using a source, one
which was probably Jewish. On this source, see Walter, *Der Thoraausleger Aristobulos*,
166–171.

[119] Dillon, *The Middle Platonists*, 115, 139–40.

[120] Ibid., 143.

[121] Ibid.

[122] K. Staehle simply called him a "Pythagoreer" in method (*Die Zahlenmystik bei
Philon von Alexandria* [Leipzig: Teubner, 1931] 11).

[123] See the previous note.

clear, however, that he discusssed larger numbers in his book as well, such as seventy and one hundred.[124] These and other larger numbers were included probably because of Philo's interest in the exegesis of Biblical texts.

If Staehle's reconstruction gives a fair impression, the number seven received the longest discussion in Philo's lost book. Seven is discussed in a great variety of works and contexts. The longest passage is in *On the Creation* (90–128). The treatment of the number seven is associated with the remark in Gen 2:2 that God rested on the seventh day after creating the world. Philo declares that the number seven has great dignity and is wondrous both in the incorporeal and intellectual sphere as well as in the visible sphere (111). With regard to the incorporeal sphere he discusses the properties of seven in arithmetic (91–94, 99–100, 106), harmony (95–96, 107–110), geometry (97–98), stereometry (102), and grammar (126). His treatment of the visible realm may be divided into two topics: the macrocosmos and the microcosmos. The discussion of the macrocosmos includes the moon (101) and other astronomical matters (111–116). Aspects of the microcosmos are the seven stages in a man's life (103–105), parts of the soul and body, human perception, vocalization, bodily movements, discharges, embryology, delivery, and days of crisis in illnesses (117–125).

Philo shares a number of ideas with the Pythagoreans. Two is even and feminine; three is odd and masculine.[125] Seven is called "right time" (καιρός).[126] Seven is the only number within the first decade which neither "begets" nor is "begotten." One "begets" all the rest ($1 \times 2 = 2$ etc.) but is not "begotten" by any other number. Four is "begotten" ($2 \times 2 = 4$) and it "begets" ($4 \times 2 = 8$). Eight is "begotten" ($4 \times 2 = 8$) but it does not "beget" another number within the decade (*On the Creation* 99). In another passage he mentions the Pythagoreans' association of seven with Athena because of these qualities (*Allegorical Interpretation* 1.15). Ten is perfect and comprehends all the other numbers.[127]

Philo has many of the same observations as Varro in his *Hebdomades*. They both mention the constellations with seven stars (*On the Creation*

---

[124] Staehle, *Die Zahlenmystik bei Philon von Alexandria*, 7–9.
[125] Ibid., 22, 24.
[126] Ibid., 44.
[127] Ibid., 54–55.

114–115), the seven planets (113), and the seven-day phases of the moon (101). Like Varro, Philo observes that the embryo develops in periods of seven days (*On the Creation* 124), that children born in the seventh month of pregnancy survive (124), and that the seventh day of an illness is critical (125).

The similarities among Philo, Varro and other Pythagorean writers are significant enough to warrant the theory that they incorporated or were influenced by a common source. F.E. Robbins argued that this source was a book on arithmology (by an unknown author), now lost, written no later than the second century BCE. It consisted of an introduction and ten chapters, one on each of the numbers from one to ten. According to Robbins, this book was the common source of Philo, Theon of Smyrna (c. 100 CE), Anatolius (fl. 280 CE), and Lydus (b. 490 CE). It influenced Varro and a number of other writers.[128]

Philo's discussion of the number seven very clearly emphasizes its role in the order of the cosmos. He notes that it plays a role in both the incorporeal and the corporeal spheres (111). He comments on the correspondence between the things of the earth and those of heaven and how the principle of the number seven manifests it (117). In the conclusion of his discourse on seven, he says that Moses impressed the number seven on the minds of those under him by bidding them at intervals of six days to keep a seventh day holy. The purpose of abstaining from work on that day is to devote oneself to philosophy in order to improve one's character and submit to the scrutiny of one's conscience (128). Aristobulus also perceived order in the cosmos expressed in terms of the number seven. In both writers the observance of the sabbath is a way of conforming one's life to the cosmic order. Philo apparently understood this conformity primarily in ethical terms.[129]

Analogous ideas in apocalyptic literature

Cosmic order is an important theme in a number of apocalypses. In the Book of the Watchers (*1 Enoch* 1–36) and the Book of the

---

[128] F.E. Robbins, "Posidonius and the Sources of Pythagorean Arithmology," *CP* 15 (1920) 309–322; idem, "The Tradition of Greek Arithmology," *CP* 16 (1921) 97–123.

[129] Aristobulus probably did also; in a comment on a verse attributed to Homer,

Heavenly Luminaries (*1 Enoch* 72–82), there is marked interest in the topography of various regions of the cosmos, especially heaven and the ends of the earth. In these works physical reality is ordered in certain recurring numerical patterns. Many other works contain motifs which presuppose this way of thinking about the cosmos. A number of the same writings mention heavenly beings in orderly groups who govern the cosmos or humanity. The order in physical reality is reflected by the structure of these groups.

1. *Order in the macrocosmos*

The Book of the Watchers (*1 Enoch* 1–36) emphasizes the orderliness of the world in its introduction (chapters 1–5). The unchanging orbits of the heavenly bodies and the regular sequence of the seasons are held up as examples of the way in which the elements of physical reality conform to God's commandments. Their steadfastness is contrasted with the disobedience of sinners who turn away and ignore the commandments of God. The theme of order is quite explicit here. It is implicit in the third portion of the work, the journeys of Enoch in chapters 17–36.

On his first journey Enoch saw "the storehouses of all the winds" (18:1).[130] These "storehouses" may be related to the gates of heaven mentioned in chapters 34–36. Enoch journeys to the ends of the earth in each of the four directions and sees three gates in each place. Winds are associated explicitly with the north and south gates. In chapter 18 reference is made to the four winds which stretch out the height of heaven. These four winds are called the pillars of heaven (18:3).

At another stage on his first journey, Enoch saw "seven mountains of precious stones" (18:6). Three were towards the east and three towards the south. The seventh, which was in the middle, "reached to heaven, like the throne of the Lord . . ." (vs 8). These seven mountains were viewed again by Enoch on another journey (chapters 24–25). On that occasion he observed fragrant trees encircling the throne-like seventh mountain. One of them was singled out for special mention. Its leaves and flowers and wood never wither. The angel

---

he says that the sevenfold principle helps one leave behind forgetfulness and evil of the soul; fragment 5 (Eusebius *Praep. Ev.* 13.12.15; Holladay, *Fragments from Jewish Hellenistic Authors*, 3. 191).

[130] The translation cited is by M.A. Knibb in H.F.D. Sparks, *AOT*, 206.

Michael explained to Enoch that the high (seventh) mountain is the throne of God, where he will sit when he comes down to visit the earth for good (25:3). The fruit of the tree will be food for the righteous and they will live a long life on earth (25:5–6). The image of a mountain which is the throne of God probably derives from the mythic idea of the cosmic mountain which unites heaven and earth and stands at the center of the world.[131] The proliferation of the cosmic mountain to seven mountains is probably related to a perception like Aristobulus' of a sevenfold principle in reality.

The association of the mountains with precious stones may have been suggested by the traditional association of the seven planets with various precious stones.[132] One of the mountains on the east was vaguely defined as "of coloured stone" (18:7). The second was of pearl. The pearl was associated with the planet Venus. The description of the third mountain on the east seems to be corrupt. The original reading may have been jasper or jacinth.[133] Jasper was linked to the planet Mercury. The three mountains toward the south are characterized as "of red stone" (18:7). The sun was connected with "anthrax," a term designating a precious stone of dark red color, including the carbuncle, garnet, and ruby. Mars was associated with λίθοι πυρροί, stones of a flame-color or yellowish red hue. Red sulphide of arsenic was a stone linked to Jupiter. The seventh mountain, the one in the center, was made of alabaster and sapphire (18:8). Alabaster was associated with the moon and sapphire with the sun. The twelve signs of the zodiac also were associated with precious stones.[134] The sardius, possibly a ruby, was linked to the sign Libra, or The Balance. The sardonyx (partly white, partly deep orange-red) was associated with the Scorpion. Aquarius, or The Water-carrier, was connected with the sapphire and The Fishes with jasper. These associations were known to Philo and Josephus. Perhaps *1 Enoch* 18:6–8 reflects a fusion of the two traditions.

In the first part of this chapter in the section on "Ten and Multiples of Ten," the tradition about the seven stars in the Book of the Watchers was discussed (*1 Enoch* 18:12–16, 21:1–6). Enoch saw them

---

[131] Richard J. Clifford, *The Cosmic Mountain in Canaan and the Old Testament* (HSM 4; Cambridge, MA: Harvard University, 1972); M. Eliade, *Patterns in Comparative Religion* (New York: Sheed & Ward, 1958; reprinted New York: World, 1972) 375.

[132] Roscher, "Planeten und Planetengötter," 2534.

[133] So Charles, *APOT*, 2. 200, n. 7.

[134] Charles, *A Critical and Exegetical Commentary on the Revelation of St. John*, 2. 159, 167.

burning in a waste and horrible place. He was told that they are the
stars which transgressed God's commandment in the beginning of
their rising, by not coming forth at their appointed times (18:15). It
is likely that the reference is to the seven planets, the stars which
seem to wander in comparison with the fixed stars. By the end of
Plato's life, a number of thinkers were beginning to reject the idea
that planets wandered and to discover their uniform movement. By
the first century CE, the idea that "planet" is a misnomer is widespread.[135] It is rather likely that the tradition about the seven stars in
1 Enoch 1–36 orginated in a context where these new scientific ideas
were unknown. The popular designation "planets" was apparently
seized upon as an example of disobedience. The negative portrayal
of the seven stars is a de facto polemic against the reverence for the
planetary gods which was growing already in Plato's time.[136]

In chapters 28–33, Enoch traveled in stages toward the far regions
in the east. One of the sights he saw was the Garden of Righteousness, presumably the Garden of Eden with its tree of wisdom. On
his way to this garden, Enoch saw "seven mountains full of choice
nard and fragrant trees and cinnamon and pepper" (32:1).[137] These
mountains are apparently not identical with the seven mountains of
precious stones.[138] They have a less central and cosmic role than the
seven mentioned earlier, one of which is God's throne. The fact that
the number seven appears here also probably reflects an idea like
that of Aristobulus, of "the sevenfold principle which is established
around us."

The Book of the Heavenly Luminaries (*1 Enoch* 72–82) focuses on
astronomical "laws," such as the movement of the sun during the
twelve months of the year and the resulting changes in the lengths of
days and nights (72:2–37). The importance of these laws is that they
provide the necessary information for establishing the correct calendar (82:4–9). The perception of a fixed order in the macrocosmos is
very clearly implied in the enunciation of these "laws."

Certain numbers appear in the description of the cosmic order.
The sun is associated with six gates in the east in which it rises and
six in the west in which it sets (72:2–3). The sun moves through these

---

[135] Burkert, *Ancient Pythagoreanism*, 325.
[136] Roscher, "Planeten und Planetengötter, 2525–2526.
[137] The translation is cited from Charles, *APOT*, 2. 207; Knibb's translation, in
Sparks, ed., *AOT*, 218, reads "full of fine hard etc.," a probable misprint.
[138] Charles, *APOT*, 2. 207, n. 1.

twelve gates in the course of a year. The reference to twelve "gates" is evidently a circumlocution for the twelve signs of the zodiac.[139] The variation in the strength of the sun's heat at different times of the year is explained by the presence of twelve "gate-openings" (lit. "open gates")[140] in the chariot of the sun, through which the rays proceed (75:4). These doors are opened and closed according to their seasons. There are also twelve winds and each of these has a gate (76).

The twelve winds are associated with the four quarters of the earth: east, west, south and north (76:1–3, 14). The four quarters are characterized on the basis of puns in Hebrew (77:1–3).[141]

The number seven and its double, fourteen, appear prominently. The sun is seven times brighter than the moon (72:37, 73:3). The moon waxes in fourteen days (sometimes fifteen) and wanes in fifteen days. The surface of the moon is divided into fourteen parts, each of which is illuminated or darkened as the moon waxes or wanes (73). Enoch saw seven mountains from which snow comes. He also saw seven great rivers and seven great islands (77:4–8).

The numbers most prominently used to describe the orderly macrocosmos in the Book of the Heavenly Luminaries are seven and twelve. Given the book's clear interest in fixing the calendar it is likely that these numbers are used because of their role in measuring time. The number seven is not particularly emphasized in the discussion of the moon's phases. It appears doubled in the comment that the moon sometimes waxes in fourteen days, but the period of fifteen days is the more common. The reason for its prominence in the book as a whole is probably a theory like that of Aristobulus, that all things are governed by a sevenfold principle. This theory owes something to traditional speculation on the properties of the number seven and something to Jewish calculation of time in weeks of seven days and the observance of the sabbath. In all of the contexts where the number twelve appears, heavenly phenomena are being discussed. It is likely that the number twelve was suggested by the twelve signs of the zodiac or the twelve months of the year.

The Book of the Secrets of Enoch (2 Enoch) has the order of the macrocosmos as one of its major themes. In one passage cosmic order

[139] Ibid., 238, n. 8.
[140] Knibb in Sparks, ed., AOT, 263 and n. 7.
[141] See Charles, APOT, 2. 242.

is associated with the governance of heavenly beings. This passage will be discussed below. In the account of Enoch's journey to the fourth heaven (11–17), order is reflected in the regular and unending movements of the sun and moon. In the description of Enoch's visit to the fourth heaven and elsewhere in the book, certain numbers are used to express the orderliness of reality. Perhaps the most striking motif is the schema of the seven heavens through which Enoch travels. The sun is said to have sevenfold more light than the moon (11:2).[142] The sun rises and sets through six gates in the east and six gates in the west (13–14).[143] These last two ideas are reflected in the book of the Heavenly Luminaries also.[144] According to 2 Enoch, Enoch was three hundred and sixty-five years old when he received his revelations (1:1). He recorded all the revelations he received and thus wrote three hundred and sixty books.

As argued in Chapter Two above, it is unlikely that the idea of the seven heavens in 2 Enoch was derived from the current opinion that there were seven planets. Since the astronomical notions of 2 Enoch do not conform to the most advanced scientific ideas of its time, it is unlikely that the Greek idea of planetary spheres played a role in the picture of the cosmos presupposed in the work. It should be noted, however, that the motif of the seven-day week or the sabbath also seems to have had little influence. This hypothesis is supported by the fact that in the account of creation (24–30), the days of creation are not numbered.

As in the Book of the Heavenly Luminaries, the number twelve (the sum of the gates of the sun) probably derives from the twelve signs of the zodiac or the twelve months of the year. Enoch's age (365) and the number of books he wrote (360) seem to reflect in an approximate way the number of days in the year. This hypothesis is supported by the explicit statement that the year contains three hundred and sixty-four days (16:5).[145]

---

[142] 2 Enoch 11:2, according to the numbering of Andersen in Charlesworth, ed., OTP, 1. 120–21; 2 Enoch 6:3, according to the numbering of A. Pennington in Sparks, ed., AOT, 332.

[143] 2 Enoch 13–14 according to Andersen; 6:6–16 according to Pennington.

[144] On the connections between 2 Enoch and The Book of the Heavenly Luminaries, see Chapter Two above, "The Seven Heavens in Jewish and Christian Apocalypses," the section on 2 Enoch.

[145] Three hundred sixty-four is the correct total of the preceding numbers and is read by some MSS; other MSS read "three hundred sixty-five." See Andersen, in Charlesworth, ed., OTP, 1. 130, n. f and Pennington in Sparks, ed., AOT, 334, n. 20.

In the *Apocalypse of Abraham*, Abraham is taken on a heavenly journey on the wing of a pigeon. He is shown seven firmaments (19). In Babylonian tradition seven was one of the typical numbers of heavens.[146] This Babylonian motif may be the origin of the schema in the *Apocalypse of Abraham*. In any case, the fact that the firmaments described in this work are not curved makes it unlikely that the motif comes from contemporary Greek tradition.

Chapters 2–5 of the *Testament of Levi* constitute a brief apocalypse.[147] It contains a brief journey by Levi through the heavens. There are indications that the text originally referred to three heavens, but that it was modified so that seven heavens are mentioned.[148] A system of three heavens was traditional in Babylon, along with that of seven heavens, and may be reflected in 2 Cor 12:2.[149]

The Greek Apocalypse of Baruch (*3 Baruch*) involves a journey of Baruch through five heavens. The number five in counting the heavens is quite distinctive. A number of scholars have concluded that the work once described seven heavens, but has been abbreviated. J.-C. Picard has argued that the work never mentioned more than five heavens.[150] A weakness in his theory is that he does not explain why five rather than three or seven heavens are enumerated. It is likely that *3 Baruch* presupposes seven heavens, even though only five are described.[151]

In the book of Revelation, certain motifs manifest the preception of order in the macrocosmos, which is expressed in numerical terms. In the opening vision (1:9–3:22), John sees a vision of Christ, who appears as one like a son of man with attributes also of the ancient of days (1:13–14). This being holds seven stars in his right hand (vs 16) and is in the midst of seven lampstands (vs 13). Christ himself interprets the two "mysteries" for John. The seven lampstands are seven congregations and the seven stars are angels of the seven congregations. Most commentators agree that the author of Revelation has taken over a traditional image in mentioning seven stars, and

---

[146] See the discussion of the *Apocalypse of Abraham* in Chapter Two above.

[147] Collins, "The Jewish Apocalypses," 40–41.

[148] Compare the various versions translated by Charles (*APOT*, 2. 304–306) and note his comments.

[149] Jeremias, *Babylonisches im Neuen Testament*, 81; T.H. Gaster, "Heaven," *IDB* 2 (1962) 552. See also the discussion of the *Testament of Levi* and 2 Cor 12 in Chapter Two above.

[150] J.-C. Picard, *Apocalypsis Baruchi Graece* (PVTG 2; Leiden: Brill, 1967) 76–77.

[151] See the discussion of *3 Baruch* in Chapter Two above.

that the image still carries some of its traditional connotations. Franz Boll argued that the seven stars are the constellation of the Little Bear which appears at the pole of heaven and which seems to control the motion of the universe.[152] This hypothesis is supported by a passage in the so-called "Mithras Liturgy," a text brought into prominence by A. Dietrich. A great god appears to his devotee "holding in his right hand a golden shoulder of a young bull: this is the Bear which moves and turns heaven around, moving upward and downward in accordance with the hour."[153] The god holding the Bear, it is implied, is the master of heaven. Further support for this interpretation lies in Suetonius' remark that Augustus had a constellation of seven birthmarks on his chest and stomach, which corresponded exactly to the Great Bear (*Augustus* 80).

Alfred Jeremias suggested that the seven stars constitute the constellation Pleiades. In support of his hypothesis, he noted that the Pleiades disappears for forty days and reappears at the winter solstice. This pattern makes it an appropriate symbol for the messiah.[154] K.H. Rengstorf concluded that the seven stars were originally seven planets.[155] The Roman emperors Hadrian (117–138 CE) and Commodus (180–192) issued coins linking their images with seven stars.[156] The seven stars probably represent the seven planets as a symbol of world dominion. The god Mithras was often linked with the seven planets. Seven stars are arranged in various ways around Mithras on reliefs. One relief includes the busts of seven planetary deities.[157]

It is difficult to choose one of these interpretations as more appropriate than the others. Given the nature of the symbols, it is possible that all three connotations were intended by the author. Even if only

---

[152] F. Boll, *Aus der Offenbarung Johannis: Hellenistische Studien zum Weltbild der Apokalypse* (Stoicheia 1; Leipzig: Teubner, 1914) 21. Charles discusses the idea and mentions Bousset as a supporter of it (*A Critical and Exegetical Commentary on the Revelation of St. John*, 1. 30).

[153] A portion of the Greek text is cited by Charles (*A Critical and Exegetical Commentary on the Revelation of St. John*, 1. 30). The translation cited here is by Marvin W. Meyer (*The "Mithras Liturgy"* [SBLTT 10; Missoula, MT: Scholars Press, 1976] 19).

[154] Jeremias, *Babylonisches im Neuen Testament*, 24, n. 4.

[155] K.H. Rengstorf, "ἑπτά . . .," *TDNT* 2 (1964) 633. Charles did not rule out this possibility (*A Critical and Exegetical Commentary on the Revelation of St. John*, 1. 30).

[156] E. Lohmeyer, *Die Offenbarung des Johannes* (HNT 16; 2nd ed., Tübingen: Mohr [Siebeck], 1953) 18.

[157] Franz Joseph Dölger, *Antike und Christentum: Kultur- und Religionsgeschichtliche Studien* (Münster: Aschendorff, 1934) 4. 64–65. See also the discussion of Mithraic monuments in Chapter Two above, the section "The Seven Planets: Explicit Links."

one was intended, the image may well have evoked the others in the minds of some of the earliest readers as well as in those of some modern scholars. In any case, the image of seven stars reflects the widespread ancient idea that the number seven was important in the ordering of the heavenly world.

In the first of two visions inserted between the sixth and seventh seals, John saw four angels standing at the four corners of the earth, holding back the four winds of the earth (7:1). The earth is apparently envisaged as a square, with each of the four winds proceeding from one of the corners. Both the idea of the four corners of the earth and that of the four winds are related to the conception of the four cardinal points, north, south, east and west. The correspondence of cardinal point, wind, and angel gives the impression of an orderly arrangement of various levels of being in the cosmos.

Another way in which a fourfold orderliness was perceived in reality by many Hellenistic writers was the idea of the four elements: fire, air, water and earth. This Hellenistic motif appears in the visions associated with the seven bowls (Revelation 16).[158] There are indications that the author of Revelation in its present form made use of a source in this portion of his work. The source apparently contained an eschatological reinterpretation of the plagues against Egypt recounted in the book of Exodus. The eschatological plagues are directed against the whole world. The source used a traditional Jewish "four-part comprehensive formula" to indicate that the plagues had such a universal object; they were directed against the earth, the salt waters, the fresh waters and the heaven. The author of this source, however, modified the Jewish formula in such a way that it reflects the Hellenistic motif of the four elements. The first bowl is directed against the earth (16:2); the second and third against salt and fresh waters, respectively (16:3–4); when the fourth bowl is poured upon the sun, people are tortured with fire (vs 8); finally the seventh bowl is poured into the air (vs 17).[159] The author of Revelation in its present form neither suppressed nor emphasized this Hellenistic motif. That he found it harmonious with his own ways of

---

[158] See the discussion of this motif by H.D. Betz, "On the Problem of the Religio-Historical Understanding of Apocalypticism" in Robert W. Funk, ed., *Apocalypticism* (*JTC* 6; New York: Harper & Row, 1969) 134–156.

[159] See the more detailed discussion of these matters in Adela Yarbro Collins, "The History-of-Religions Approach to Apocalypticism and the 'Angel of the Waters' (Rev 16:4–7)," *CBQ* (1977) 374–76.

thinking is implied by his use of expressions like the "angel of the waters" (16:5) and the "angel having authority over fire" (14:18).

The number twelve appears in the vision of the woman and the dragon (Revelation 12), a passage which holds an important position in the structure of the book as a whole: it is the opening vision of the second half of the work.[160] The significance of the woman is grasped only when three levels of meaning are kept in mind. On one level, the woman is Queen of Heaven, described with the characteristics of the Ephesian Artemis, the Syrian Atargatis and the Hellenistic Isis.[161] On another level, the woman is presented as the heavenly Israel, the spouse of God, the mother of the messiah and of his followers.[162] Finally, the narrative depicting the woman's fate seems to typify the conflict of the Jewish and early Christian peoples with Rome in the first centuries BCE and CE. Her story is thus a paradigm of the experience of the earliest readers.[163] An element in her depiction as Queen of Heaven is her crown of twelve stars. The word for "star" (ἀστήρ) used in 12:1 was actually supposed to refer to an individual star, but it was often used for a constellation also, especially for those of the zodiac.[164] In the context, the twelve stars can represent only the zodiac; the zodiac as crown is the only appropriate complement to the sun as garment and the moon as footstool. The traditional background of the seven stars gave the vision of Christ in Revelation 1 connotations of a world ruler. Similarly here, the motif of the zodiac suggests that the heavenly patron or counterpart of the Christians is ruler of heaven.

The image of the zodiac is both spatial and temporal. Its spatial aspect is primary: the twelve constellations which, at one time or another, are visible in the sky at night. Its temporal aspect is based on the movement of the sun through the zodiac and the relationship of each of its constellations to the months of the year. A reference to the twelve months of the year appears in Rev 22:2. In his vision of the heavenly Jerusalem, John saw the tree of life, which bears twelve kinds of fruit, yielding its fruit each month.

Several early Christian apocalypses reflect speculation on the num-

---

[160] Yarbro Collins, *The Combat Myth in the Book of Revelation*, 19–32.
[161] Ibid., 71–76.
[162] Ibid., 134–35.
[163] Ibid., 122–127.
[164] Boll, *Aus der Offenbarung Johannis: Hellenistische Studien zum Weltbild der Apokalypse*, 99, n. 1.

ber of the heavens. In the *Martyrdom and Ascension of Isaiah* 6–11, the schema of seven heavens is very strongly emphasized. In effect, this schema provides the organizing principle for the description of Isaiah's journey. The seventh is the highest and brightest heaven, and there God, Christ and the righteous dead dwell. A body of angels dwells in each of the seven heavens. Any one passing through one of the lower three heavens must give a password to the doorkeeper. This motif becomes prominent in later Gnostic and Jewish mystical literature.[165]

The apostle Paul's mythical journey is described in the *Apocalypse of Paul*. One portion of his journey is associated with the third heaven. This visit and the related revelations are presented as the experiences of Paul mentioned in 2 Cor 12:1–5 (see the introduction and chapters 11 and 19).[166] The third heaven is depicted as the place where sinners are punished and the righteous rewarded. The presentation and description of the various heavens in the *Apocalypse of Paul* are not at all as systematic as those in the *Martyrdom and Ascension of Isaiah*. The third heaven is loosely associated with the revelations given in chapters 11–20. The rest of the journey takes place near and beyond the great Ocean which bears the firmament; that is, Paul travels to mythical regions at the ends of the earth. Evidently, the third heaven is not conceived of as the highest. In chapter 29 it is said that David sings psalms before God in the seventh heaven.

The *Apocalypse of Peter* contains a discourse of Christ before his disciples on the Mount of Olives (1–14) and two vision accounts set "on the holy mountain" (15–17).[167] The first part seems to be an expansive rewriting of the eschatological discourse found in Mark 13 and parallels, and the second is a similar reworking of the account of the Transfiguration (Mark 9:2–8 pars.). At the end of the Ethiopic

---

[165] T.H. Gaster, "Heaven," 552; F.T. Fallon, "The Gnostic Apocalypses," *Semeia* 14 (1979) 136, 138; Anthony J. Saldarini, "Apocalypses and 'Apocalyptic' in Rabbinic Literature and Mysticism," *Semeia* 14 (1979) 192; Ithamar Gruenwald, *Apocalyptic and Merkavah Mysticism* (AGJU 14; Leiden: Brill, 1980) 192–193. See also the discussion of the *Martyrdom and Ascension of Isaiah* in Chapter Two above.

[166] For an introduction, English translation and notes, see Hugo Duensing and Aurelio de Santos Otero, "Apocalypse of Paul," in Wilhelm Schneemelcher, ed., *New Testament Apocrypha*, vol. 2, *Writings relating to the Apostles, Apocalypses and related Subjects* (rev. ed.; Cambridge, UK: James Clarke; Louisville, KY: Westminster/John Knox, 1992; Germ. ed. 1989) 712–48. The work was probably composed in Greek, although the oldest and most complete witness is the Latin translation.

[167] For an introduction, English translation and notes, see C. Detlef Müller, "Apocalypse of Peter," in Schneemelcher, ed., *NTApoc*, 2. 620–38. The work was probably composed in Greek, but the Ethiopic translation is better preserved.

version, Jesus ascends to the second heaven with Moses and Elijah (17). Since this element is not in the Greek version it may not be original. In any case, it is impossible to judge from the information available whether only two heavens were envisaged or more.

Order in the macrocosmos is an important theme in the Book of the Watchers. The numbers four and twelve are mentioned, but seven has by far the most prominent role. The indications are that the emphasis on the number seven is due, at least in part, to a recognition of the significance of the seven planets. In the Book of the Heavenly Luminaries, the perception of order in the cosmos is articulated in astronomical "laws." A major concern of the work is fixing an accurate calendar. The numbers twelve and seven are used most often in describing order in time and space. The interest in the calendar makes it likely that the prominence of these numbers is due primarily to their role in measuring time: the seven days of the week and the twelve months of the year. A number of Jewish and early Christian apocalypses reflect speculation on the number of heavens. *2 Enoch*, the *Apocalypse of Abraham*, the *Testament of Levi* 2–5, the *Martyrdom and Ascension of Isaiah* 6–11, and the *Apocalypse of Paul* presuppose a schema of seven heavens. This schema is Babylonian in origin and has affinities with magic.[168] Originally, the *Testament of Levi* 2–5 seems to have listed three heavens. 2 Corinthians 12 may presuppose a schema of three heavens. In dependence on 2 Cor 12:1–5, the *Apocalypse of Paul* emphasizes the third heaven. Babylonian tradition provides precedents for a schema of three heavens also. *3 Baruch* mentions five heavens, but probably presupposes seven. The *Apocalypse of Peter* mentions the second heaven; it is not clear whether this is the "highest heaven" or the second of three or more. The most striking images in the book of Revelation which express cosmic order are the seven stars in chapter one and the twelve stars in chapter 12. It is likely that these images connoted the seven planets and the zodiac for the earliest readers.

2. *Order in the activity of heavenly beings*

Many of the works which manifest the perception of order in the macrocosmos refer also to groups of heavenly beings with cosmic

---

[168] See Chapter Two above, "The Seven Heavens in Jewish and Christian Apocalypses."

functions. These heavenly beings are usually presented in groups of four, seven, twelve or other numbers which are used elsewhere to describe cosmic order. The Ethiopic version of the Book of the Watchers (*1 Enoch* 1–36) reveals the names and functions of "the holy angels who watch" (20:1–8).[169] In the Greek fragment containing this passage, they are called ἀρχάγγελοι ("archangels").[170] The number seven is mentioned only in the Greek fragment, and it is only in the Greek version that seven angels are actually listed. The Ethiopic version names only six. It is difficult to determine what the original number was. The prominence of the number seven elsewhere in the work supports the hypothesis that the original text listed seven angels. In any case, the number seven, if not original, was introduced in the course of the transmission of the work, and the result is harmonious. The functions of some of these angels are clearly cosmic. According to the Greek version, Uriel rules over the world and Tartarus;[171] Raguel controls the world of the heavenly luminaries, apparently by punishing the disobedient ones.[172] One of Michael's tasks, according to the Greek, was to rule chaos. It was pointed out in the preceding section that the seven stars whose punishment is mentioned in 18:12–16 and 21:1–6 seem to be the seven planets, and that there seems to be an indirect polemic against the widespread reverence of the planets. If the number of seven archangels is original, it is tempting to conclude that the seven archangels are meant as a substitute for the seven planets in Jewish cosmic speculation and piety.

In the Book of Heavenly Luminaries (*1 Enoch* 72–82), Enoch is returned to his home after his journey to the ends of the earth by "those seven holy ones" (81:5). There is no reference to a group of seven angels elsewhere in the work. It is likely that the idea of seven archangels is presupposed here.

Near the end of this work, a strong claim is made for the accuracy of the calendar contained in it and differing calendars are attacked (82:1–9). The calendar of the Book of the Heavenly Luminaries is accurate because it is based on the revelations of Uriel, who has

---

[169] In the Greek fragment from Akhmim (Codex Panopolitanus, the Gizeh Papyrus), they are called Ἄγγελοι τῶν δυνάμεων ("angels of the powers"); see M. Black, ed., *Apocalypsis Henochi Graece* with Albert-Marie Denis, col., *Fragmenta Pseudepigraphorum quae Supersunt Graeca* (Leiden: Brill, 1970) 32 (*1 Enoch* 20:1).

[170] *1 Enoch* 20:7; Black, ed., *Apocalypsis Henochi Graece*, 32.

[171] According to the Ethiopic, Uriel is the angel of thunder and of tremors (20:2).

[172] Compare *1 Enoch* 20:4 with 23:4; see Knibb's notes in Sparks, ed., *AOT*, 208, 212–13.

power over all the heavenly bodies. The text goes on to say that
there are heavenly beings who lead the astral bodies, who see to it
that they maintain their proper courses and movements (vs 10). There
are four leaders who govern the four seasons, twelve leaders who
divide the months, and three hundred sixty who divide the days.
The four leaders who rule over the seasons are also responsible for
the four intercalary days which make up the year of three hundred
sixty-four days (vs 11). The names of some of these and other leaders are given, and two.of the seasons are described in deatil (vss 12–
20). In this passage there is a very close correspondence between the
order in cosmic phenomena and the order among heavenly beings
and in their governing activity. The prominent numbers are those
used in the calculation of time, more precisely, in the calculation of
the year.

The Similitudes of Enoch (*1 Enoch* 37–71) describes "four pres-
ences" around the Lord of Spirits (40). Their names are Michael,
Raphael, Gabriel and Phanuel. The functions attributed to them are
not particularly cosmic. No clear indication is given in the immediate context or in the work as a whole why there are precisely four
of these angels.

As noted in the preceding section, the Book of the Secrets of Enoch
(*2 Enoch*) contains a report of Enoch's journey through the seven
heavens. The order in the macrocosmos as such is emphasized in
Enoch's visit to the fourth heaven (11–17). He sees various kinds of
angels in all the heavens, but it is in the sixth heaven that angels are
organized into groups (19). In that place there are seven angels who
order the world, the stars, the sun and the moon (vss 1–2). These
angels also rule over the seasons and the years, the rivers and the
seas (vs 4). In their midst are seven phoenixes, seven cherubim, and
seven six-winged ones (vs 6). Once again there is a clear correspondence between cosmic order and an orderly arrangement of heavenly
beings.

Several passages in the book of Revelation were also discussed in
the preceding section, as texts which reflected the perception of cosmic order. In one of these (7:1–3), the cosmic order is paralleled by
the organization of certain angels. There is a correspondence between the four corners of the earth, four winds and four angels. The
parallelism suggests that various levels of being in the cosmos are
arranged in an orderly way.

A similar perception may be reflected in a series of passages which are related to one another by the use of the same or analogous images. In the prescript, which is part of the epistolary framework of Revelation,[173] a greeting is given from God, from the seven spirits which are before his throne, and from Jesus Christ (1:4). The message to Sardis is characterized as the words of "the one who has the seven spirits of God and the seven stars" (3:1). In the throne vision, it is said that seven torches burn before the throne and that these are the seven spirits of God (4:5). In chapter five, a vision of the Lamb is recounted. He has seven eyes which are the seven spirits of God sent out into all the earth (5:6). The seven torches before the throne and the seven eyes of the Lamb are both identified with the seven spirits. The two images are also closely associated in Zech 4:2, 10. The seven torches before the throne call to mind the lampstand with seven lamps in Zechariah, that is, the *menorah* of the temple. It is striking that both Philo and Josephus associated the *menorah* with the seven planets.[174] It is interesting to note further that the seven spirits are parallel to the seven stars in 3:1. It was argued in the preceding section that the seven stars would certainly have had the connotation of the seven planets for some of the first readers, even if the association was not intended by the author.

If the author of Revelation thought of the seven spirits as concretely existing entities, it is likely, as Charles argued, that he conceived of them as angels.[175] In any case, the interconnections and external associations of the images imply that the motif of the seven spirits was meant by the author to evoke the idea of the seven planets and its connotations. The connotations of cosmic order and divine power seem to have been taken over and adapted by the author of Revelation for his own purposes.[176]

A number of apocalypses describe heavenly beings in orderly groups

---

[173] Yarbro Collins, *The Combat Myth in the Book of Revelation*, 5–8.

[174] The texts are quoted by Charles, *A Critical and Exegetical Commentary on the Revelation of St. John*, 1. 12, n. 1.

[175] Lohmeyer suggested that they have a symbolic function in Revelation and are not depicted as independenlty existing beings (*Die Offenbarung des Johannes*, 47). Charles discussed the opinion held by a number of scholars that the seven spirits represent the Holy Spirit in seven aspects or have a similar role, so that 1:4 refers to the trinity; he himself concluded that they are seven archangels (*A Critical and Exegetical Commentary on the Revelation of St. John*, 1. 11–12).

[176] The author of Revelation seems to have done the same thing with other elements of pagan religion; see Yarbro Collins, *The Combat Myth in the Book of Revelation*, 83–84, 174–190, and eadem, "The History-of-Religions Approach to Apocalypticism and the 'Angel of the Waters' (Rev 16:4–7)," 379–381.

who govern the cosmos or humanity. The motif of a company of seven
high angels appears in the Book of the Watchers (*1 Enoch* 1–36), the
Book of the Heavenly Luminaries (*1 Enoch* 72–82), the Book of the
Secrets of Enoch (*2 Enoch*) and Revelation. In those cases where there
is any indication of the background for these seven beings, it seems
to be the Hellenistic idea of the seven planets. The Book of the
Heavenly Luminaries emphasizes angels who control the changes from
day to day (360 + 4 angels, who rule over the days of the year),
from season to season (four) and from month to month (twelve).

III. THE USE OF NUMBERS IN THE REVELATION TO JOHN

In the thematic discussion of the ordering power of numbers in the
first two parts of this chapter, a number of passages from Revelation
were discussed. The first theme discussed was the use of numbers in
the ordering of time. No chronicling interest was discovered in Revelation, an interest which is minor in apocalyptic literature in any
case. It was also noted that Revelation manifests no intention of
calculating the time of the end in a definite and precise sense. Like
4 Ezra, however, Revelation does contain a number of imprecise,
rhetorical calculations of the end. The passages in question have related rhetorical points: the time of the end is fixed, even though we
cannot know it (6:11), the end is near (17:10–12), and the time of
the tribulation before the end is limited and will be relatively brief
(11:2–3; 12:6, 14; 13:5). Another theme in Revelation is the perception of meaningful patterns in time. The passage which indicates that
the end is near (17:10–12) also serves to divide history into periods.
The block of time taken into account is the period of the Roman
Empire. That period is itself divided into seven parts, the rule of
seven kings. The use of the number seven can be explained on the
basis of the Jewish tradition of the interpretation of Jeremiah's prophecy that the exile would last seventy years. This tradition has been
called "sabbatical eschatology." In Revelation 20, with its reference
to the binding of Satan for a thousand years and the messianic reign
of a thousand years, a meaningful numerical pattern is projected into
the future. The number ten and some of its multiples occur in several Jewish texts also to order time. Its use is most likely based on its
arithmetical and arithmological significance.

Just as prominent as the use of numbers in the ordering of time
in Revelation is the role of numbers as signs of cosmic order. This

cosmic order is perceived both in physical reality and in the activity of heavenly beings. There is a correspondence between the two, and, as in several Jewish apocalypses, the idea is that heavenly beings govern the cosmos. In the opening vision of Revelation, Christ appears with seven stars in his right hand (1:16). These seven stars are identified as the angels of the seven churches in 1:20, but they surely carry with them connotations of the seven planets and perhaps also of the constellations of the Great or Little Bear and the Pleiades. In a number of related passages with a variety of images seven spirits are mentioned (1:4, 3:1, 4:5, 5:6). The images used would very probably evoke the idea of the seven planets for the earliest readers. The author of Revelation probably conceived of the seven spirits as angels. If so, then a correspondence is implied between the seven planets and seven heavenly beings. Such an idea is suggested also by the parallelism of the motifs in the description of Christ at the beginning of the message of Sardis; he is the one who has the seven spirits of God and the seven stars (3:1).

The correspondence between heavenly being and cosmic element is explicit in 7:1–3. At the four corners of the earth, four angels are seen holding back four winds. The repetition of the number four gives an impression of symmetry and order in reality. Further, the idea that heavenly beings control the winds is expressed. The number four appears indirectly in the plagues of the seven bowls in the motif of the four elements (16). References to the angel of the waters (16:5) and to the angel having authority over fire (14:18) imply that the four elements are also controlled by four angels.

In Revelation 12 a woman is depicted, clothed with the sun, with the moon under her feet, and wearing a crown of twelve stars. These stars allude to the twelve constellations of the zodiac. On one level of meaning, the woman is a heavenly being, the heavenly Israel. So here too heavenly bodies are subordinated to a heavenly being. The number twelve appears again in the final vision of salvation in connection with the tree of life (22:2). It bears twelve kinds of fruit, one each month. The number twelve is here associated with the rhythm of the year.

Gematria

In addition to expressing order in time and cosmos, numbers are used in another distinctive way in the book of Revelation. In 13:18

it is said, "Let the one who has understanding calculate the number of the beast, for it is a number of a human being; and its number is six hundred sixty-six." This passage contains a cryptogram based on the fact that in Greek and Hebrew each letter is also a number; alpha and aleph function also as the numeral one and so forth.[177] Thus any name or ordinary word has a numerical value equal to the sum of the values of its letters. It is quite a simple matter to move from name to sum. On the other hand, it is virtually impossible to move from sum to the name the author of such a cryptogram had in mind, unless one has additional information. As G.B. Caird put it, "A sum has only one correct answer, but an answer may be the answer to many sums."[178]

In Greco-Roman popular culture, such cryptograms functioned as playful riddles or games. A *graffito* at Pompeii reads, "I love the girl whose name is phi mu epsilon (545)."[179] The rabbis called the practice of making and solving such cryptograms *gematria*. They used it primarily to discover edifying meanings in otherwise uninteresting or offensive texts.[180] A variant of the method is the establishing of relations between two different words by pointing out that their sums are identical. This process is called isopsephism and was apparently widely practiced in the ancient world.[181]

The closest parallels to Rev 13:18 occur in the *Sibylline Oracles*. The fifth book is a collection of oracles written in Egypt at the end of the first and the beginning of the second century CE.[182] In this book is a brief chronicle of Roman history which contains a list of Roman rulers from Julius Caesar to Hadrian. Their reigns are characterized briefly and the rulers identified by the numerical value of the first letter of their names (*Sib. Or.* 5.12–51). The identity of each ruler can be inferred from what is said about his reign and from the sequence. Thus, the numerical values given are not the only means

---

[177] For the numerical values of the Greek alphabet see Friesenhahn, *Hellenistische Wortzahlenmystik im Neuen Testament*, 83.
[178] Caird, *A Commentary on the Revelation of St. John the Divine*, 174.
[179] Cited by A. Deissmann, *Light from the Ancient East*; quoted by Caird, *A Commentary on the Revelation of St. John the Divine*, 174.
[180] Caird, *A Commentary on the Revelation of St. John the Divine*, 174.
[181] Charles, *A Critical and Exegetical Commentary on the Revelation of St. John*, 1. 365, n. 1. Friesenhahn believed that this process was used by writers of the New Testament and that it provides an important key to understanding it (*Hellenistische Wortzahlenmystik im Neuen Testament*; especially the last five chapters).
[182] J.J. Collins, "Sibylline Oracles," in Charlesworth, ed., *OTP*, 1. 390.

of recognizing who is meant. The reference to the first letter of the name, instead of the entire name, and the mention of a number, rather than simply a letter, are part of the mysterious style of the work. An oracle allegedly revealing the future does not simply name people; it alludes to them in a veiled manner.

The first two books of the *Sibylline Oracles* constitute a unified collection of oracles. It was originally a Jewish composition, but it contains Christian modifications and additions in its present form. The Christian redaction is definitely later than 70 CE, and it is usually dated to about 150 CE or later.[183] In one of the Christian portions of the work, the birth of the Son of God is "predicted." While he is in the flesh, his name will contain four vowels and two consonants. The whole number of his name is revealed: eight hundred eighty-eight (1. 323–31). The name Jesus is not mentioned, but the knowing reader can make the necessary calculations and determine that it is the name which is meant. The number eight, like six, was ignored by the early Pythagoreans.[184] Perhaps the reason was the lesser value assigned to the even numbers.[185] The number eight did come into prominence in late antiquity and in Christianity.[186] It may well be that the calculation of the number of Jesus' name in this work was suggested by Rev 13:18.

A staggering variety of solutions to the riddle of the 666 in Rev 13:18 has been proposed. As noted above, such cryptograms rely upon prior knowledge on the part of the reader or upon further information provided by the context. Several allusions in Revelation 13 and 17 point to Nero. Therefore, the most likely solution is that 666 is the sum of the name *Nero Caesar* written in Hebrew. Because of the variation in the spelling of *Nero* (with and without a final *n*), this theory can explain the textual variant 616.[187] As in the fifth book of the *Sibylline Oracles*, the use of the numerical value of letters adds a mysterious dimension to the text. The passage in Revelation is even more enticing and powerful because it is more ambiguous. It is

---

[183] Yarbro Collins, "The Early Christian Apocalypses," 97.

[184] Burkert, *Ancient Pythagoreanism*, 431, 467, n. 8, 474.

[185] Ibid., 32–34.

[186] Ibid., 474, n. 53. The number eight was discussed in several passages by Philo (Staehle, *Die Zahlenmystik bei Philon von Alexandria*, 50–52); the negative side of the number is apparent only in his remark that babies born after seven months in the womb are viable, whereas those born after eight are not.

[187] See the discussion in Yarbro Collins, *The Combat Myth in the Book of Revelation*, 174–75.

not as closely tied to a specific historical person. It thus invites adaptation and reinterpretation.

A number of commentators have suggested that 666 appears in
Rev 13:18 at least in part because of its symbolic significance.[188] One
theory is that it symbolizes imperfection or evil because it persist-
ently falls short of the perfect number seven. Against this theory it
must be said that the number six does not function in that way elsewhere in Revelation. The allusions to three and a half times or years
do not particularly support this hypothesis. That time span derives
from Daniel and is thus traditional. The contexts in which it appears
do not particularly suggest a symbolic connotation of imperfection or
evil. Rather, as was suggested above, their import seems to be that
the time of tribulation is of a fixed and limited duration. Further
evidence against this theory is that the number six is called a perfect
number by Philo. His discussions of it show no awareness of a negative aspect.[189] Finally, it is the number seven, not six, which appears
in association with the dragon, who has seven heads and seven dia-
dems (12:3), and with the beast, who also has seven heads (13:1;
17:3, 7, 9). Another theory is that 666 was chosen because it is the
triangular number of 36, which is the triangular number of eight. A
certain equivalency would thus have been felt between eight and 666,
and the beast is "an eighth" (17:11). This theory is enticing, but it
may be based on a mere coincidence.[190]

The prominence of numbers in Revelation

As the first two parts of this chapter have shown, many Jewish
apocalypses and a few Christian ones use numbers rather prominently to express the perception of order in time and in the cosmos.
The most common patterns involve periods of history and multiple
heavens. The book of Revelation has some motifs which are similar
to these basic patterns. Nevertheless, one senses some significant differences in Revelation vis-à-vis other apocalypses.

First of all, numbers are far more prominent in Revelation than
in most other works of the same genre. In the prescript the reader

---

[188] See the summary in Caird, *A Commentary on the Revelation of St. John the Divine*, 176.
[189] Staehle, *Die Zahlenmystik bei Philon von Alexandria*, 32–34.
[190] H. Kraft doubts that the author of Revelation was aware of it (*Die Offenbarung des Johannes* [HNT 16a; Tübingen: Mohr (Siebeck), 1974] 183–184).

hears about the seven congregations and the seven spirits (1:4–5). In the opening vision, the seven congregations are mentioned again and seven golden lampstands, seven stars and seven angels are introduced (1:12, 16, 20). Chapters 2 and 3 are organized as seven messages. The number seven appears later most obviously in the seven seals (5:1–8:1), the seven trumpets (8:2–11:19) and the seven bowls (15–16). The numbers three, four and twelve are also rather prominent.[191] Numbers clearly play a major role in both the form and content of the book.[192] In no other apocalypse of comparable length is this the case.

There is some evidence that the number seven served as a formal element or a principle of composition in both Jewish and Christian circles around the turn of the era. Two major Jewish apocalypses consist of seven sections, *4 Ezra* and *2 Baruch*.[193] The Lord's Prayer contains seven petitions; the gospel of Matthew records seven beatitudes and contains a group of seven parables in chapter 13.[194] Seven functions as a formal principle in the messianic seventeenth psalm of the *Psalms of Solomon* and in certain midrashic works whose sayings go back to the Tannaitic period.[195] A notable difference exists,

---

[191] R. Halver, *Der Mythos im letzten Buch der Bibel* (Hamburg: Reich, 1964) 31–32, 115–118.

[192] On series of seven as an organizing principle in Revelation, see Yarbro Collins, *The Combat Myth in the Book of Revelation*, 13–19.

[193] The seven sections of *4 Ezra* are 3:1–5:20, 5:21–6:34, 6:35–9:25, 9:26–10:59, 11:1–12:51, 13:1–58, 14:1–48. Each of these sections contains a clearly demarcated revelatory experience of Ezra, either a revelatory dialogue or a vision. The demarcation of the parts of *2 Baruch* are not quite as obvious, but the most logical division does lead to a structure of seven parts. First is a narrative introduction (1–8), then a section containing God's promise of revelation and a lament of Baruch; this section is introduced by a fast of seven days (9:1–12:4). The third section is also introduced by a fast of seven days and contains a revelatory dialogue (12:5–20:6). A seven-day fast introduces the fourth section also, which consists of a revelatory dialogue and the related report by Baruch to the people (21–34). The fifth section contains a dream vision and a related report to the people (35–46). The sixth section is introduced by a fast of seven days once again. The fast is followed by a prayer of Baruch for revelation. This prayer is answered first by a revelatory dialogue and then by a vision which follows closely upon the dialogue. The vision is followed by the interpretation of it, Baruch's response, his commission, and finally his report to the people. These elements constitute chapters 47–77. The seventh section is the epistle of Baruch (78–86). Chapter 87 is a kind of epilogue.

[194] Rengstorf, "ἑπτά . . .," 630, n. 25, 632, n. 38. Hans Dieter Betz argues that there are ten beatitudes in the Sermon on the Mount; idem, *The Sermon on the Mount: A Commentary on the Sermon on the Mount, including the Sermon on the Plain (Matthew 5:3–7:27 and Luke 6:20–49)* (Hermeneia; Minneapolis, MN: Fortress, 1995) 105–53.

[195] Rengstorf, "ἑπτά . . .," 633.

however, between the structuring techniques used in these works and in Revelation. In the texts mentioned above, as far as I have been able to determine, the number seven is used only implicitly as a formal principle. The seven parts in each case are not numbered and there is no concern to notify the reader that there are seven parables, sayings, sections, or whatever. In two sections of Revelation, there are seven unnumbered visions.[196] The messages to the seven churches are not numbered. Elsewhere, the series of seven elements are explicitly referred to as seven seals, trumpets and bowls. With each of these series, each unit is numbered, as first, second, and so on up to the seventh. It seems clear then, that for some reason, the author of Revelation was more concerned than other writers to make his readers aware that seven was his organizing principle.

Another distinctive aspect of Revelation is that some of its numerical motifs do not fit neatly into categories that can be established on the basis of the use of numbers in other texts. There is no obvious, defining precedent or illuminating parallel for the selection of seven particular congregations in chapters 1–3. The seven seals, trumpets and bowls do not correspond very closely to the numbered periods of history found in other works. In fact, their relation to ordinary time and space is rather difficult to determine. It seems evident that the number seven in Revelation is symbolic, but its connotations are not immediately apparent.

All of the works discussed in the first two parts of this chapter share the view that reality is ordered and that this order can be perceived and expressed in various numerical operations. Some of the Jewish texts have been influenced directly by neo-Babylonian, Pythagorean and other non-Jewish, Hellenistic arithmological speculation and traditions. Aristobulus' and Philo's works are the clearest examples of such influence. Such direct influence is likely in several other works. The schema of four ages or kingdoms in Daniel 2 and 7 was taken over from Hellenistic political oracles. The seven mountains and seven stars of the Book of the Watchers (*1 Enoch* 18, 21) seem to be modeled on the seven planets. The twelve gates of the sun in the Book of the Heavenly Luminaries (*1 Enoch* 72) and in the Book of the Secrets of Enoch (*2 Enoch* 13–14) reflect the idea of the zodiac. The earliest Greeks were aware of six planets in the

---

[196] The two sections are 12:1–15:4 and 19:11–21:8; see Yarbro Collins, *The Combat Myth in the Book of Revelation*, 13–19.

narrower sense: ἐωσφόρος (Venus as morning star), ἕσπερος (Venus as evening star), φαέθων (Jupiter), φαίνων (Saturn), πυρόεις (Mars), and στίλβων (Mercury).[197] Only later was the identity of morning and evening star discovered. The discovery is attributed to Parmenides by some and to Pythagoras by others.[198] By Plato's time, the Greeks, like the Babylonians, counted seven planets. The old Greek names were replaced by the names of the deities which corresponded to the Babylonian planetary gods. The sun and moon were included with the five mentioned above, so that seven planets (in the wider sense) were recognized. The zodiac originated among the neo-Babylonians around 400 BCE. It was introduced into Egypt in the early Hellenistic period.[199]

The book of Revelation also shows signs of such direct influence. The seven stars (1:16, 20; 2:1, 3:1) and the seven spirits (1:4, 3:1, 4:5, 5:6) reflect the idea of the seven planets. The image of the twelve stars (12:1) is based on the zodiac. These particular motifs in Revelation show that the author of Revelation was aware of certain Hellenistic astral traditions and was able to view them in a positive light and adapt them for his own purposes. The same is true of the Jewish apocalypses mentioned above.[200]

Besides the influence manifested in the borrowing and adapting of such particular motifs, the book of Revelation seems to have been influenced by Hellenistic arithmological tradition in a more general way. As was noted above, the number seven was used in Revelation as a formal principle. Revelation is not unique on that point, but it is distinctive in that the numbering in much of the book is explicit. In two cases, the series of seven is clearly divided into groups of four and three, which are also important numbers in arithmological speculation. The first four seals are grouped by the fact that each involves a horseman (6:1–8); the last three trumpets are designated as three woes (8:13). This kind of explicit numbering, as well as the phenomenon of the impressive prominence of numbers in various ways throughout the book, can be explained in terms of the reverence for numbers characteristic of neo-Pythagorean, Hippocratic and other

---

[197] Roscher, "Planeten und Planetengötter," 2519–2524.
[198] Ibid., 2521–2522; Burkert, *Ancient Pythagoreanism*, 307–308.
[199] Hengel, *Judaism and Hellenism*, 2. 160, n. 834.
[200] In one case, as was noted earlier, there seems to be a polemic against the seven planets, namely, in the motif of the seven stars which are being punished for failing to keep their appointed order (*1 Enoch* 18:16, chapter 21).

forms of speculation on numbers. The author of Revelation was less explicit than Aristobulus and Philo about his understanding of the significance of particular numbers. The role of numbers in his work, however, implies that they had much the same significance for him as for Philo and Aristobulus.

The significance of the number seven

K.H. Rengstorf was surely correct, when he commented that each use of the number seven in Revelation must be interpreted in light of the history of the particular traditions involved and in view of the historical context.[201] The various uses of the number probably share certain connotations, but the precise or primary meanings are likely to vary. Some passages in which the number seven appears have been discussed already. There may well be a variety of reasons for the number of seven kings in Rev 17:10-12, but the most immediate and natural context in which it can be understood is the Jewish tradition of sabbatical eschatology. Both the seven stars (1:16) and the seven spirits (1:4) evoke the Hellenistic motif of the seven planets. Another set of passages, not yet discussed in this chapter, have a different history-of-religions background. The seven heads of the dragon (12:3), and by analogy the seven heads of the beast (13:1; 17:3, 7, 9), is a traditional Semitic mythic motif.[202]

As was noted above, however, some uses of the number seven have no clear history-of-religions background or parallel. The seven congregations, for example, and the seven messages addressed to them have no real parallels. Rengstorf explains the seven seals in terms of the Roman practice of sealing one's last will and testament with seven seals.[203] But this theory is doubtful, since the image of a will or testament is not drawn upon in depicting the scroll with seven seals and its effects.[204] The lack of a clear parallel is especially striking in the cases of the seven trumpets and the seven bowls. The trumpets and bowls recall the plagues against the Egyptians described in the book of Exodus.[205] But in Exodus, ten plagues are depicted. The

---

[201] Rengstorf, "ἑπτά . . .," 632.

[202] Ibid.; see also Yarbro Collins, *The Combat Myth in the Book of Revelation*, 77–79.

[203] Rengstorf, "ἑπτά . . .," 633.

[204] Yarbro Collins, *The Combat Myth in the Book of Revelation*, 22–25.

[205] On the relationship between the plagues of Revelation and those of Exodus, see H.P. Müller, "Die Plagen der Apokalypse," *ZNW* 51 (1960) 272–277.

Apocalypse of Abraham, like Revelation, describes eschatological plagues. But unlike Revelation and like Exodus, the Apocalypse of Abraham lists ten plagues (29–30).

It seems then that the most prominent uses of the number seven—the seven congregations, seals, trumpets and bowls—are precisely the cases in which the reason for the choice of that particular number is least apparent. As was noted in the introduction to this chapter, the commentaries are not particularly helpful on this point. With regard to the choice of seven congregations, Charles simply says that seven was a sacred number. Bousset's explanation is that seven was a holy number.[206] A. Farrer argued that the seven messages and the other series of seven represent the symbolical week and that the seventh element in each case reflects the sabbath.[207] The seventh message contains an element near the end that might be interpreted liturgically. Christ says, "Behold, I stand at the door and knock; if someone hears my voice and opens the door, I will go in to him and will dine with him and he with me" (3:20). The reference to the meal has eucharistic overtones.[208] A heavenly liturgy is presented near the end of each of the series of seven seals, trumpets and bowls.[209] But it is unlikely that the sabbath *per se* was a central constitutive symbol for the author of Revelation. The significant day of the week for him was the Lord's day (1:10), presumably Sunday. The mutual enmity between Christian congregation and synagogue (2:9, 3:9) very likely was based not only on differences in theological perspective but in religious observance as well. The author of Revelation and his addressees had probably ceased to practice or require circumcision and to observe the sabbath. It is apparent that the author was heir to Jewish sabbatical eschatological thought in one case (17:10–12). It may well be that he was aware of the tradition in which Aristobulus and Philo stood, which united the Jewish week of seven days culminating in the sabbath with Hellenistic speculation on the significance of the number seven. The awareness of this tradition may have contributed to the central role of the number seven in Revelation. The cosmic significance of seven would have been emphasized, the role of sabbath deemphasized. If H. Riesenfeld is correct, as seems likely, that the early Christian worship on Sunday evolved gradually out of

---

[206] See note 2 above.
[207] See note 3 above.
[208] So, for example, Caird (*The Revelation of St. John the Divine*, 58).
[209] Yarbro Collins, *The Combat Myth in the Book of Revelation*, 41, 234.

sabbath observance, no unbearable contradiction need have been felt on this score.[210] In some circles, the observance of Sunday as the Lord's day led to an emphasis on the number eight (*Barn.* 15:8–9).

I.T. Beckwith and G.B. Caird argued that these prominent uses of seven in Revelation were symbolic. Both suggested that the symbolic meaning was "completeness." Neither gave reasons for this interpretation, except that Beckwith referred to Hebrew tradition and the Scriptures.[211] These two commentators, and many others who take this position, were probably influenced (directly or indirectly) by the work of J. Hehn.[212] Hehn made a case that for the Babylonians seven was a symbol of fullness and completeness.[213] "Seven gods" is equivalent to "all the gods" and "seven winds" to "all the winds." He then went on to argue that the number seven had the same meaning in many passages of the Bible.[214] This line of argumentation is much more ambitious and less persuasive. Hehn himself admitted that the interpretation does not fit every case.[215] It is plausible enough for certain texts. Seven-fold wrath or vengeance might well be taken as full, complete wrath or vengeance (Gen 4:15, 24; Ps 79:12). But it is not an interpretation which forces itself upon the reader in any particular Biblical text. In many of his examples, Hehn spoke about seven as a symbol of massive intensification or as a small round number.[216] Such interpretations are rather different from the theory that seven represents completeness or fullness. Hehn had prepared for the discrepancy by establishing in the Babylonian examples a category called "seven as an expression of the highest intensification, the highest fullness and power."[217] But there are problems with that category. Compared with the examples of seven as a totality, this usage is rather rare. More seriously, the examples cited do not require this interpretation. Gilgamesh chides Ishtar for making seven and seven pitfalls for the lion. The whale is said to have seven fins and the number of the fins is supposed to be an expression of its

---

[210] H. Riesenfeld, "Sabbat et Jour du Seigneur," in A.J.B. Higgins, ed., *New Testament Essays: Studies in Memory of Thomas Walter Manson* (Manchester: Manchester University, 1959) 210–217.

[211] See note 4 above.

[212] See note 4 above.

[213] Hehn, *Siebenzahl und Sabbat bei den Babyloniern und im Alten Testament*, 4–16.

[214] Ibid., 77–90.

[215] Ibid., 77.

[216] Ibid., 78–79.

[217] Ibid., 16.

character as a terrifying monster. The other passages are analogous to these. They are ambiguous and could easily be explained in a variety of ways. All they show is that seven was a special number. They do not reveal the reason for its special role. The same must be said about the corresponding Biblical passages.[218]

Hehn did not make a compelling case in favor of the theory that the number seven, even only somewhat consistently, symbolizes completeness or fullness in the Bible. Further, there is little in the book of Revelation which supports the validity of the theory for this particular work. When reading "John to the seven congregations which are in Asia" (1:4), the ancient informed reader, like his or her modern counterpart, was quite aware that the congregations listed in 1:11 were not the only ones in Asia at that time. The use of the definite article in 1:4 only points ahead to the selective list of congregations in 1:11. The reason for and the method of selection are not shared with the reader. There is nothing in the text which suggests that a figure of speech like metonymy or synecdoche is being used. It is doubtful that the ancient Babylonian equivalence of seven and totality had an influence here.

It is true that Philo refers to the number seven as "perfection-bringing" (τελεσφόρος) (*On the Creation* 102–103). But Philo does not mean that the number symbolizes or represents perfection, or, even less, that seven objects represent all objects of their class or seven actions all actions of their type. He means something quite different, namely, that reality is ordered and that the order in question expresses itself in patterns of seven. He notes the circumstance that every organic body has seven aspects: three dimensions (length, breadth and depth) plus four limits (point, line, surface and solid). He also cites the theory that a man's life progresses through stages of seven years each. Hehn's, Beckwith's and Caird's theories seem to be rationalizing attempts to make sense for a modern reader out of Revelation's use of the number seven, which has more in common with Philo's logic than with Hehn's theories.

Hehn's interpretation has more internal support in the seven seals, trumpets and bowls than in the passages relating to the seven congregations. He argued that in each case the seven "plagues or woes" are all conceivable plagues which exceed that which can be

---

[218] On the importance of the number seven in Babylonian magic, see Chapter Two above, the section on the *Testament of Levi*.

imagined.[219] Some of the afflictions associated with the seals are general and traditional. Images of war follow the second seal (6:3–4), images of death the fourth seal (vss 7–8), and images of cosmic dissolution the sixth seal (vss 12–17). The use of seven seals could be interpreted as an intensification of the traditional imagery of sealing, of the connotations of mystery and secrecy.[220] The trumpets and bowls affect the earth (8:7, 16:2), the sea (8:8–9, 16:3), the rivers and the fountains of water (8:10–11, 16:4–7), and the sun (8:12, 16:8). These elements express the totality of the cosmos under the rubric of earth and heaven, salt waters and fresh waters.[221] The seven bowls are associated also with the four elements: earth (16:2), water (vss 3–4), fire (vs 8), and air (vs 17).[222] But it is not necessarily the case that the idea of the plagues affecting the whole cosmos is closely linked to the plagues being seven in number. The universal character of the plagues is related to their nature as eschatological events. The ten plagues in the *Apocalypse of Abraham* affect the entire world also (30). The theory that the number seven is used to express intensification is plausible, but the discussion above has already put in question the hypothesis that seven was generally so used.

Since the author of Revelation was alienated from the Judaism of his time to a significant degree[223] and since that alienation probably involved the rejection of the traditional observance of the sabbath, it is unlikely that the prominence of the number seven in Revelation is due solely or even primarily to reverence for the sabbath and speculation on its cosmic role. Along with other traditions, however, the author does seem to have inherited elements of sabbatical eschatology from Judaism. It was noted in the first part of this chapter that several Jewish apocalyptic writers, as well as Aristobulus and Philo, adapted Hellenistic astronomical and arithmological motifs and in-

---

[219] Hehn, *Siebenzahl und Sabbat bei den Babyloniern und im Alten Testament*, 81.

[220] On the traditional connotations of sealing, see Charles, *A Critical and Exegetical Commentary on the Revelation of St. John*, 1. 138.

[221] See the discussion in Yarbro Collins, "The History-of-Religions Approach to Apocalypticism and the 'Angel of the Waters' (Rev 16:4–7)," 374–376.

[222] Ibid.

[223] See the section "The Author as a Jew" in Adela Yarbro Collins, "Persecution and Vengeance in the Book of Revelation," in David Hellholm, ed., *Apocalypticism in the Mediterranean World and the Near East* (Tübingen: Mohr [Siebeck], 1983) and the section "The Temple in Jerusalem" in eadem, "Myth and History in the Book of Revelation: The Problem of its Date," in Baruch Halpern and Jon D. Levenson, eds., *Traditions in Transformation: Turning Points in Biblical Faith* (Winona Lake, IN: Eisenbrauns, 1981).

corporated them in their own work. The author of Revelation was another thinker-writer of this type. The number seven was emphasized because it was generally recognized in the Hellenistic world as having a major cosmic role. By the first century CE, not only Jews, but most people living under the Roman empire, used a seven-day week.[224] The image of the seven planets was a widespread and powerful one and it is reflected in several passages of Revelation, as was noted above. Philo's and Varro's works attest to the importance of the number seven in the eyes of the older contemporaries of the prophet John. They saw it as a principle of order in all aspects of physical reality and human life. Behind the choice of seven congregations, seven seals, seven trumpets and seven bowls is an idea somewhat like that of Aristobulus: "And indeed all the cosmos of all living beings and growing things revolves in series of sevens" (fragment 5).

The significance of the number twelve

In the throne vision of chapter four, twenty-four thrones are depicted around the throne of God. On these thrones sit twenty-four elders, clothed in white garments and wearing golden crowns (4:4). They worship God and cast their crowns before God's throne (4:10–11; see also 11:16–18, 19:4). They fall down before the Lamb, play the harp, sing a song of praise, and offer up the prayers of the saints (5:8–10). Some early commentators and modern ones as well have argued that the twenty-four elders are or symbolize the twelve patriarchs and the twelve apostles.[225] These twenty-four leaders in turn are supposed to represent the church in its totality. This interpretation is untenable for a number of reasons. It is true that the names of the patriarchs are written on the twelve gates of the new Jerusalem (21:12) and the names of the twelve apostles on the twelve foundation stones (21:14). But it is striking that there are twelve gates and foundations, not twenty-four. Neither in Revelation 21 nor elsewhere in the book or in the New Testament are the twelve patriarchs and apostles coordinated to a make a new, composite group.[226] As Charles

---

[224] Schürer, "Die siebentätige Woche im Gebrauche der christlichen Kirche der ersten Jahrhunderte," 18–19.

[225] H.B. Swete took this position (*The Apocalypse of St. John* [London: Macmillan, 1906] 69); Charles lists others of the same opinion (*A Critical and Exegetical Commentary on the Revelation of St. John*, 1. 129–130).

[226] So also Beckwith, *The Apocalypse of John*, 499.

pointed out, the activities of the elders are typical of angels.[227] Their
angelic character makes the link with patriarchs and apostles tenuous.

Charles himself argued that the twenty-four elders are the angelic
representatives of the twenty-four priestly orders (1 Chr 24:7–18).
This theory is not compelling. The activities of the elders are not
particularly priestly. Charles had already demonstrated that offering
the prayers of the saints was an act often ascribed to angels.[228]

The most persuasive theory about the origin of the motif of the
twenty-four elders is the one proposed by Gunkel. He was followed
by Bousset and, to some extent, by Beckwith.[229] Gunkel argued
that the author of Revelation did not simply invent the image of the
twenty-four elders, but that he took over the motif from Babylonian
astrological tradition. In support of this theory he cited a passage
from Diodorus of Sicily (who wrote in the first century BCE). Diodorus
says, "Beyond the circle of the Zodiac [the Chaldaeans] designate
twenty-four other stars, of which one half, they say, are situated in
the northern parts and one half in the southern, and of these those
which are visible they assign to the world of the living, while those
which are invisible they regard as being adjacent to the dead, and so
they call them 'Judges of the Universe'" (2.31.4).[230] The twenty-four
elders seem to be angels modeled on these twenty-four Babylonian
astral deities. The description of these deities as "judges" (δικασταί)
is compatible with the depiction of the elders in Revelation as seated
on thrones (compare the association of thrones and judgment in Dan
7:9–10). Just before describing the twenty-four stars, Diodorus mentions thirty stars which oversee the affairs of earth and the heavens.
These are called "gods of the council" (βουλαῖοι θεοί) by the Babylonians. Being part of a council is rather similar to being an "elder"
(πρεσβύτερος) in connotations. In 2 Enoch 4:1, an angel which rules
the stellar orders is called an elder. The twenty-four astral deities
described by Diodorus may be identical with the twenty-four "elements (στοιχεῖα) of the cosmos" mentioned in a magical papyrus.

---

[227] Charles, *A Critical and Exegetical Commentary on the Revelation of St. John*, 1. 130.
[228] Ibid., 130; besides the texts cited by Charles, see also *3 Baruch* 12, Tob 12:15.
[229] H. Gunkel, *Schöpfung und Chaos in Urzeit und Endzeit* (Göttingen: Vandenhoeck
und Ruprecht, 1895) 308; Bousset, *Offenbarung Johannis*, 290–291; Beckwith, *The
Apocalypse of John*, 498–99.
[230] The translation, slightly modified, is taken from C.H. Oldfather, trans. and
ed., *Diodorus of Sicily* (12 vols.; LCL; Cambridge, MA/London: Harvard University
Press, 1933) 1. 453, 455; the Greek text is given on pp. 452, 454.

These in turn may be related to the twenty-four deities associated with the hours of the day and night.[231]

If these texts are representative of the background against which the twenty-four elders of Revelation must be understood, then the number twelve may very well have played a role in the symbolism of this group of twenty-four. It was not, however, the role traditionally envisaged, namely, that twenty-four was suggested by the combination of the traditions of the twelve patriarchs and the twelve apostles. If the number twelve played a role it was in its astronomical and astrological use. The twelve signs of the zodiac and the twelve hours of the day have influenced the designation of twenty-four astral deities or judges, and thus indirectly, the twenty-four elders.

Between the events following the opening of the sixth seal and the unsealing of the seventh, two visions are inserted (7:1–8 and 7:9–17). The first of these opens with the vision of the four angels at the four corners of the earth, a passage which was discussed above. Then another angel appears and instructs the four angels not to harm earth, sea or trees until the servants of God have been sealed. The number of the sealed is announced, one hundred forty-four thousand sealed. These are twelve thousand from each of the twelve tribes of Israel. A number of issues relating to this passage have been debated; such as, whether 7:1–8 or some part of it is based on a Jewish source, whether the 144,000 is symbolic or meant to be a real, literal, fixed number, and whether it refers to all the faithful or to a special group within the people of God.[232]

I have argued elsewhere that the 144,000 represent an ideal and special group, those who would be prepared to die for their Christian faith and maintain sexual abstinence (compare 14:1–5).[233] The

---

[231] H.G. Gundel, *Weltbild und Astrologie in den griechischen Zauberpapyri* (Munich: Beck, 1968) 56. Boll also makes this connection (*Aus der Offenbarung Johannis: Hellenistische Studien zum Weltbild der Apokalypse*, 35–36).

[232] Bousset argued that the author of Revelation took over Jewish apocalyptic tradition in 7:1–8; he thought it likely but uncertain that a written source was used. He also concluded that the 144,000 were intended to be understood as converted Jews (*Die Offenbarung Johannis*, 330–331, 336–339). Beckwith held that a source was used, but that for the apocalyptist, the 144,000 represented the whole Church (*The Apocalypse of John*, 532–536). Charles concluded that a Jewish or Jewish-Christian source was used in 7:4–8, that the 144,000 were Jews or Jewish-Christians originally, and that for the author of Revelation 144,000 was a purely symbolic number representing the whole Church (*A Critical and Exegetical Commentary on the Revelation of St. John*, 1. 193–194, 199–200).

[233] Yarbro Collins, *Crisis and Catharsis*, 127–31

primary, immediate source of the numerical symbolism is the Jewish tradition of the twelve tribes of Israel. Remarks made in the messages imply that membership in the tribes of Israel is not primarily a matter of birth (2:9, 3:9). The use of the twelve tribes evokes a sense of chosenness; these tribes, this people is chosen from among all peoples. The twelve thousand from each tribe intensifies the impression of chosenness, of exclusiveness. Not every one does or can remain sexually abstinent and die for the faith. But the large numbers used suggest that many will and ought to live such lives and die such a death.

The vision of the woman and the dragon in chapter 12 was discussed in the section "Order in the Macrocosmos" above. The number twelve appears in that vision in the twelve stars with which the woman is crowned (12:1). Since her other attributes are sun and moon, it is highly probable that the twelve stars are the signs of the zodiac. These heavenly adornments characterize the woman as a heavenly being, the queen of heaven. For the author of Revelation she is the heavenly Israel whose destiny foreshadows that of the followers of Jesus, her "seed."

The number twelve appears repeatedly in the last vision of the book of Revelation, the vision of the heavenly Jerusalem.[234] The wall around the city has twelve gates, three on each side (21:12–13). The sides correspond to the four directions. The names of the twelve tribes of the sons of Israel are inscribed on the gates, presumably one name on each gate. This complex of motifs is apparently based on Ezekiel 48:30–34.[235] Two motifs which are distinctive of Revelation 21 in comparison with Ezekiel 48 are the presence of twelve angels on the gates and the construction of each gate from a single pearl. The association of angels with the gates may have been inspired by Isa 62:6, "Upon your walls, O Jerusalem, I have set watchmen," as Charles implied.[236] Or the image may be an adaptation of the cherubim which were placed east of the Garden of Eden to guard the tree of life (Gen 3:24; see also Ezek 28:16). Such an origin would

---

[234] This vision is parallel to the vision of the harlot (the "Babylon appendix") in 17:1–19:10 and may be designated the "Jerusalem appendix" (see Yarbro Collins, *The Combat Myth in the Book of Revelation*, 19). Charles Homer Giblin calls them counterpoised interpretation-scenes; idem, *The Book of Revelation: The Open Book of Prophecy* (GNS 34; Collegeville, MN: Michael Glazier/Liturgical Press, 1991) 159.

[235] These motifs appear also in the *New Jerusalem*, fragments of which have been found in caves 1, 2, 4, 5 and 11 at Qumran.

[236] Charles, *A Critical and Exegetical Commentary on the Revelation of St. John*, 2. 162.

be compatible with the saying in 21:27 that nothing unclean shall enter the city, nor any one who practices abomination or falsehood. Like Eden, the heavenly Jerusalem must be guarded. The new city is assimilated to Eden in that the tree of life is there (22:2). The pearl does not appear in the Old Testament, since it became wide-spread only after Alexander the Great.[237] The notion that the gates of Jerusalem would someday be made each of a single pearl is found also in the rabbinical literature.[238]

The heavenly Jerusalem is made of gold and its wall of jasper. The foundations of the city's walls are made of (or decorated with) precious stones. These images may have been suggested by Isa 54:11–12.[239] Distinctive of Revelation 21 is the numbering of the foundation stones, twelve in all. On the foundation stones are the names of the twelve apostles of the Lamb (vs 14). The numbering and naming of the foundation stones is parallel to the treatment of the gates in vss 12–13. But a further distinctive element of Revelation 21 makes it unlikely that the symbolism of the number twelve is confined to the connotations evoked by the allusions to the twelve tribes and apostles.

This element is the naming of the twelve precious stones, each of which is associated with one of the foundation stones (vss 19–20). There is a correspondence of name between at least eight of the twelve stones mentioned here and the twelve stones which adorned the breastplate of the High Priest (Exod 28:17–20; a similar list of twelve precious stones appears in the description of the splendor of the original man in the LXX of Ezek 28:13). The differences among the three lists may be due to variations in the translation of the original Hebrew.[240] Philo and Josephus interpreted the twelve stones on the breastplate of the High Priest in terms of the twelve signs of the zodiac.[241] Philo is apparently the earliest witness for the associa-tion of twelve colors with the twelve signs of the zodiac.[242] A. Kircher published a list of twelve precious stones which correspond to the

---

[237] See Kraft, *Die Offenbarung des Johannes*, 272.

[238] Charles, *A Critical and Exegetical Commentary on the Revelation of St. John*, 2. 170.

[239] These motifs are also present in the *New Jerusalem*; see n. 235 above.

[240] Charles, *A Critical and Exegetical Commentary on the Revelation of St. John*, 2. 165; Kraft, *Die Offenbarung des Johannes*, 271; Caird, *A Commentary on the Revelation of St. John the Divine*, 274–275.

[241] Charles, *A Critical and Exegetical Commentary on the Revelation of St. John*, 2. 159.

[242] W. Gundel and H.G. Gundel, *Astrologumena: Die astrologische Literatur in der Antike und ihre Geschichte* (Wiesbaden: Steiner, 1966) 181, n. 6.

twelve signs of the zodiac according to Egyptian and Arabic monuments.[243] Kircher's list differs from the one given by Martianus
Capella (fifth century CE) and other sources.[244] But it corresponds
exactly to the list in Revelation 21, except that it is in the reverse
order. W. Gundel and H.G. Gundel expressed the opinion that the
association of particular stones with the signs of the zodiac in Arabic
astrology probably goes back to ancient zodiologia. To support this
hypothesis, they pointed to the similarities between the Arabic traditions and motifs in Philo.[245]

Charles was impressed by the parallel between Kircher's list and
the one in Rev 21:19–20, and by the fact that Philo and Josephus
associated the twelve stones on the High Priest's breastplate with the
signs of the zodiac. He concluded that the twelve precious stones
constituting the foundations of the heavenly Jerusalem were intended
by the author to symbolize the zodiac. But he was struck by the fact
that the stones representing the constellations are listed in Revelation
in the reverse order of the apparent path of the sun through these
signs. Charles concluded from this last observation that the author of
Revelation wanted to show that the heavenly Jerusalem had nothing
to do with the "ethnic" speculations about the city of the gods.[246]

This last conclusion of Charles simply does not follow. If the author
of Revelation wished to show that the heavenly Jerusalem had "nothing
to do" with contemporary and earlier descriptions of the city of the
gods, he certainly could have done so much more clearly. He would
not have used precious stones associated with the zodiac, but other
stones. Or, if the choicest stones were already linked to the signs of
the zodiac or to the planets, he could have used the same order in
which the stones were placed on the High Priest's breastplate. Or,
he could have arranged them in another order which would have
had no correspondence to the usual order associated with the zodiac.

Charles' conclusion that the new Jerusalem had "nothing to do"
with the speculations of non-Jews seems to contradict a previous

---

[243] A. Kircher is cited by Jeremias (*Babylonisches im Neuen Testament*, 68, n. 1) and
Charles (*A Critical and Exegetical Commentary on the Revelation of St. John*, 2. 159, 167).

[244] Cited by Boll (*Aus der Offenbarung Johannis: Hellenistische Studien zum Weltbild der
Apokalypse*, 40, n. 2) and H.G. Gundel ("X. Der Zodiakos in der Astrologie," PW 19
A 2 [1972] 577–579).

[245] W. Gundel and H.G. Gundel, *Astrologumena: Die astrologische Literatur in der Antike
und ihre Geschichte*, 181, n. 6.

[246] Charles, *A Critical and Exegetical Commentary on the Revelation of St. John*, 2. 167–
168.

argument made in discussing 21:10. Following Zimmern, Gunkel and others, he stated that one of the basic notions expressed in the description of the new Jerusalem is the idea of the heavenly city or city of the gods found among many peoples of the ancient world.[247] This notion is related to the correspondence seen by many of these peoples between earthly things and their heavenly prototypes.[248] The signs of the zodiac were perceived as gates of the heavenly city and the Milky Way as the major street. The remark that the holy city came down from heaven (vs 2) would have evoked the idea of the city of the gods for those in the audience familiar with this motif. In this context, the twelve gates would have connoted the twelve portals of heaven, the zodiac. So Charles' earlier argument is credible, that for many readers, the new Jerusalem would be perceived in part at least, as a cosmic, astral city.

As Charles and others have noted, other traditions were also used and Revelation's description departs from the traditions about the heavenly city in certain ways. For example, the signs of the zodiac, through their stones, are linked to the foundations of the city, rather than to the gates. But allusions are not exact quotations, and influence is not manifested only in direct borrowing of unchanged traditional elements. The reversal of the order of the signs of the zodiac does need to be explained. Some dissociation of the new Jerusalem from the cosmic heavenly city is probably intended. Its images are borrowed, but adapted in light of the notion of a new creation. The new Jerusalem is illuminated and gives light, just as the sun and moon give light to the earth. But in the new creation, there will be no more sun and moon. They will be unnecessary because of the illuminating presence of God and the Lamb. Night, darkness and the things they symbolize (evil and ignorance, for example) will be no more. The temporary lights which move and change will be replaced by permanent, unchanging luminaries. Like the sea, sun and moon, the zodiac probably also does not exist in the new creation. Therefore, the order of the signs is not important. If there is no sun, it does not move through the signs in an orderly fashion or in any

---

[247] Ibid., 158–160.

[248] Jeremias, *Babylonisches im Neuen Testament*, 62–69; on the reciprocity of heaven and earth and the rule of regions by designated deities, see Francesca Rochberg-Halton, "Mesopotamian Cosmology," in Norriss S. Hetherington, ed., *Encyclopedia of Cosmology: Historical, Philosophical, and Scientific Foundations of Modern Cosmology* (New York/London: Garland Publishing, 1993) 400–1.

fashion. The reversal of the order reminds the attentive reader that the sun and its repeated journey are no more. The symbolism of light is transferred from sun and moon to God. The symbolism of the zodiac appears in the foundations of the city's wall. Just as the zodiac represents the core or center of the heaven, the reference point in many cases for other other heavenly bodies and movements, so the new Jerusalem is the center of the new cosmos.

The number twelve appears again in this vision in a way that would call to mind the zodiac for the ancient reader. In 22:2 the tree of life is described, which bears twelve kinds of fruit, one in each month. Each of the signs of the zodiac was related to one of the twelve months of the year. In the magical papyri the constellations of the zodiac are called "the twelve rulers over thirty (days)."[249]

The dimensions of the city given in 21:16–17 involve the number twelve once again. The city is depicted as a cube with each side measuring twelve thousand stades. The wall of the city is one hundred forty-four (12 × 12) cubits. These numbers contribute to the strikingly repetitive rhythm of the number twelve in 21:12–21. The reference to twelve tribes calls to mind the ideal, prototypical past; the twelve apostles the idealized recent past. The allusion to the zodiac puts the whole into a cosmic context. The correspondence among the various groups of twelve elements gives a reassuring impression of order, stability and constancy.

In the symbolism of the number twelve in Revelation one finds a traditional Jewish element (the twelve tribes, 7:1–8, 21:12), a traditional Christian element (the twelve apostles, 21:14), and two Hellenistic astral elements (the twenty-four astral deities reflected in the twenty-four elders, 4:4 et al.; the twelve signs of the zodiac, 12:1, 21:19–20 and indirectly, 22:2). The cosmic role of the number twelve has a temporal and spatial aspect. Twelve hours are measured in the day, twelve months in the year. The twelve signs of the zodiac are seen in the sky. These cosmic elements seem to reinforce the sense that God was at work in selecting the twelve tribes and the twelve apostles. The structure of the people of God corresponds to the cosmic order, also created by God. The vision of a new Jerusalem defined in terms of the number twelve gains credence because of its correspondence to other divine acts. As the divine will was revealed in the past and is revealed at present in the cosmos, so will it be in the future.

---

[249] H.G. Gundel, *Weltbild und Astrologie*, 52–53.

IV. CONCLUSION

Numerical symbolism in apocalyptic and related literature creates the impression of order in the physical world and in human experience. Numbers are used to order experience in two basic ways, to discover order in time and in the cosmos. It is widely believed that Jewish apocalyptic literature and some early Christian apocalypses use numbers to calculate the time of the end. Closer examination shows that only a few works, including just one apocalypse (Daniel 7–12), actually attempt to predict the date of the *eschaton*. In a few other cases, numbers are used rhetorically to express the conviction that the time of the end is fixed or near. In most cases, the numbers are used to discern meaningful patterns in time. History, in the sense of the remembered past, the experienced present, and the expected future, is divided into a certain number of periods. The number of periods perceived or the length ascribed to particular periods involves numbers which are significant for the role they play in other aspects of life.

The numbers used naturally have many symbolic connotations. The original reasons for the prominence of these particular numbers are very difficult to discern and probably have little to do with rational explanations based on the observation of nature.[250] There may have been deep psychological factors at work which may still be discerned today.[251] But at many times and places, these original and deeper reasons are forgotten and other, more rational reasons are expressed. At the times when the apocalypses were written, such rational explanations were current for several of the more prominent numbers. Some of these had to do with ancient Jewish ritual practice, others with the observation of sun, moon and stars. For a particular writer or reader one or more or even all of the symbolic connotations may have been conscious. But usually one or two levels of meaning are indicated by the context.

In the ordering of time, the numbers most commonly used are seven, four, twelve and ten. For seven, the meaning closest to the surface and the most likely to have been conscious is the complex of connotations associated with the seven-day week and the sabbath. The rhythm of the week with its sabbatical climax is projected onto larger blocks of time. Seldom is there a clear hint about the reasons

---

[250] Burkert, *Ancient Pythagoreanism*.
[251] See Ludwig Paneth, *Zahlensymbolik im Unbewußstein* (Zürich: Rascher, 1952).

for listing four kingdoms or periods. The evidence there is points to the cosmic role of four in the four directions or four cardinal points. There is no evidence for a direct link between twelve periods of history and the tradition of the twelve tribes. As with the number seven, the twelve hours of the day or the twelve months of the year were smaller patterns which led the writers to discern a pattern in all of history. The texts which speak of ten periods or use a multiple of ten provide few hints about the reasons for these numbers. There is no clear precedent in Jewish cult or tradition. Nothing points to the ten commandments, for example, as a prototype. The most likely reason seems to be the role the number ten played in arithmetic. It is the completion of the first decade, and thus a logical round number. The decade of course is then the foundation for all other numbers.

In the ordering of the cosmos, the numbers most frequently used in apocalyptic literature are seven and twelve. This use of the number seven has no direct link to the Jewish week of seven days or to the sabbath. The most immediate associations are with the Babylonian and then Hellenistic idea of the seven planets. Likewise, the number twelve most often has cosmic associations which have their roots in the notion of the zodiac. These astral motifs indicate the significant degree to which Jewish and Hellenistic culture have interacted in these works. Two non-apocalyptic Jewish writers, Aristobulus and Philo, show an even greater degree of compatibility between the two cultures. Their use of or response to Hellenistic ideas is much more explicit.

The book of Revelation presents a distinctive case. It has much in common with other apocalyptic works from the perspective of numerical symbolism. But Revelation goes beyond other writings of the same genre in the prominence of numerical symbolism. It is by no means as explicit as the texts of Aristobulus and Philo in adapting Hellenistic speculation on numbers. But the role of numbers in Revelation indicates that its author, along with the two Alexandrians, shared with the neo-Pythagoreans and other Greco-Roman groups convictions about the power of numbers to reveal the basic order in all reality.

In his discussion of the role of numbers in Revelation in a book called *Der Mythos im letzten Buch der Bibel*, Rudolf Halver cited Mathias Rissi with approval on the subject.[252] Rissi says that the numbers in the book of Revelation, as well as the eschatological periods of time

---

[252] Halver, *Der Mythos im letzten Buch der Bibel*, 32.

mentioned, do not serve, as in Jewish apocalypses, to calculate the time of the end. Rather, they make visible the will of God and Christ which stands behind and directs all events. They are, as it were, the net in which the Satanic forces are captured, surrounded and confined on all sides. Now, as was shown in the first part of this chapter, it is not the case that the periods of time and numbers in Jewish apocalypses always serve to calculate the end. Their function is usually a symbolic one, helping to create order and meaning in one's perception of history, the world, and life. Rissi's remarks on Revelation, however, are fitting and compatible with the findings of this chapter. The frequent numbering of people, objects and events in Revelation makes the point by repetition that nothing is random or accidental. Everything is measured and counted. There is a divine plan, all is in God's control, and the outcome will be advantageous to those loyal to God's will as revealed in the book. There is a correspondence between the symbolic numbers in the tradition of Israel, the numbers which show the order in the cosmos, and the numbers which are emphasized in early Christian tradition, especially in this work. These correspondences make indirect claims for the reliability of God, God's ultimate control over all reality, and the truth of the Apocalypse. The implication that all is counted and numbered must be very reassuring to those who hope to be among the innumerable multitude (chapter 7).

These symbolic implications were probably at least intuitively intended by the author of Revelation. The difficulties involved in correlating the various visions with ordinary time and space and the numbered entities with one another and in discerning anything like a clear timetable in the book make it likely that the author deliberately wrote in an indirect and symbolic manner. It is credible that the symbolic values of orderliness, stability and security were intended and conscious.

But the process which culminates in the evocation of these values is a long and complex one. I have argued elsewhere that the book of Revelation creates, or at least intensifies, the conflict which its visions ultimately seek to resolve.[253] This theory finds support in a certain psychological dimension of the number seven, the dominant

---

[253] Adela Yarbro Collins, "The Revelation of John: An Apocalyptic Response to a Social Crisis," *Currents in Theology and Mission* 8 (1981) 4–12; see also eadem, *Crisis and Catharsis: The Power of the Apocalypse* (Philadelphia: Westminster, 1984).

number of the book. According to Ludwig Paneth, a Jungian psychologist, the number seven has a qualitatively different character in dreams from smaller primary numbers. Seven and larger primary numbers represent in dreams circumstances which cannot be reduced any further, situations which cannot be resolved, at least not in this world and this life. Such a situation may involve either the inner or the outer factors of a person's life.[254] This connotation of the number seven from the perspective of depth psychology fits in well with major themes of Revelation, for example, the theme of irreconcilable conflict between the kingdom of God and the kingdom of Caesar. The expected persecution cannot be ignored, evaded or overcome in any way except by individual death and cosmic destruction.

The study undertaken in this chapter has shown that the use of numerical symbolism in apocalyptic literature is part of the fundamental human enterprise of creating order in experience and environment and discovering analogies in various realms of experience. The particular numbers used and those of their connotations which become somewhat explicit reveal a good deal about the cultural affinities and purpose of the writers.

---

[254] Paneth, *Zahlensymbolik im Unbewußtstein*, 72–75.

CHAPTER FOUR

THE ORIGIN OF THE DESIGNATION OF JESUS AS "SON OF MAN"

Taking up this well worked problem in New Testament scholarship may seem audacious to some, futile to others. At least one scholar has exulted over his own claim, supported by a few, to have solved the problem;[1] whereas at least one other scholar has declared the problem insoluble.[2] Although the problem is difficult, the elements of a solution are indeed present in the discussion. It is taken up again in this essay because of its importance for research on the historical Jesus and on the emergence of Christology.

TRANSLATION AND INCLUSIVE LANGUAGE

Before addressing the scholarly context in which this topic must be treated, I would like to comment on the problems involved in the translation "Son of Man," particularly the question of gender-inclusive versus gender-exclusive language. Some have chosen to translate the phrase "Child of Humanity." "Son of Man" is an attempt at a literal or formal translation. "Son" is an accurate literal translation, since υἱός means "son" as opposed to "daughter" (θυγάτηρ). "Man" is a more problematic translation. Ἄνθρωπος in Greek, like its Semitic equivalents, is best understood as a generic term meaning

---

[1] Geza Vermes, "The 'Son of Man' Debate," *JSNT* 1 (1978) 28–29. See also Norman Perrin, *A Modern Pilgrimage in New Testament Christology* (Philadelphia: Fortress, 1974) 5. Vermes is followed in large part by Barnabas Lindars, *Jesus Son of Man: A Fresh Examination of the Son of Man Sayings in the Gospels and in the Light of Recent Research* (Grand Rapids: Eerdmans, 1983); C.H. Dodd, *The Founder of Christianity* (New York: Macmillan, 1970) 110–13, 178 n. 25; and T.A. Burkill, *New Light on the Earliest Gospel* (Ithaca, NY: Cornell University Press, 1972) 36, n. 27.

[2] A.J.B. Higgins, "Is the Son of Man Problem Insoluble?" in E.E. Willis and M. Wilcox, eds., *Neotestamentica et Semitica: Studies in Honor of Matthew Black* (Edinburgh: T. & T. Clark, 1969) 70–87. See the review of scholarship on this issue by John R. Donahue, S.J., "Recent Studies on the Origin of 'Son on Man' in the Gospels," in *A Wise and Discerning Heart: Studies Presented to Joseph A. Fitzmyer In Celebration of His Sixty-Fifth Birthday, CBQ* 48 (1986) 484–98.

"human being;" other words designate "male human beings" in those languages. "Son of a human being," however, is infelicitous in English, to put it mildly. "Son of Humanity" is a possible translation, but does not yield very good sense in English. Where, besides in a Gnostic description of emanations in the pleroma, would one expect to encounter the offspring of an abstraction? In any case, the phrase is not really equivalent to the corresponding terms in the other languages.

One could argue that we are dealing here with what is ultimately a Semitic idiom which demands a dynamic, rather than a formal translation. Such a translation, "Human One," for instance, would do justice to the intention of the Semitic idiom and also make sufficiently elegant sense in English. The problem with adopting such a translation in the context of this article is that it prejudges some historical and interpretive issues. It assumes that ὁ υἱὸς τοῦ ἀνθρώπου is an appropriate Greek translation of the Semitic idiom and that it means something like "human one" or "human being." One of the unresolved questions to be addressed in this article is whether the Greek phrase really is equivalent to the Semitic idiom and if not, why not. There is also the question whether the masculine gender of "Son" and the male human being as the normative ἄνθρωπος are important historical meanings which must be taken into account in any attempt at a historical reconstruction of the origin of the phrase in Greek. For these reasons the older translation "Son of Man" will be retained, at least for the time being.

SCHOLARLY CONTEXT

As is well known, Rudolf Bultmann concluded that a few Son of Man sayings were spoken by Jesus; namely, those which distinguished Jesus from a Son of Man figure who was to have a role in the eschatological judgment.[3] This conclusion was disputed by two scholars whose work has been highly influential, Norman Perrin and Philipp Vielhauer.[4] Both of these men argued that none of the Son of Man

---

[3] Rudolf Bultmann, *The History of the Synoptic Tradition* (rev. ed.; New York: Harper & Row, 1968) 112, 122, 128, 151–52.

[4] Philipp Vielhauer, "Gottesreich und Menschensohn in der Verkündigung Jesu," in *Festschrift für Günther Dehn zum 75. Geburtstag am 18. April dargebracht von der Evangelisch-Theologischen Fakultät der Rheinischen Friedrich Wilhelms-Universität zu Bonn* (Neukirchen:

sayings goes back to Jesus. The tradition rather originated as one of several attempts to make sense of the death and vindication of Jesus. According to Vielhauer, the designation of Jesus as Son of Man was the earliest Christology, which arose in connection with the experience of Easter.[5]

Because of the affinities with Daniel 7 and the Similitudes of Enoch, the Synoptic sayings which speak of a future Son of Man are recognized generally as apocalyptic sayings. Bultmann was quite willing to speak of Jesus as an apocalyptist, building as he did upon the work of Johannes Weiss and Albert Schweitzer.[6] Perrin and Vielhauer, on the other hand, wanted to distinguish between Jesus as an eschatological teacher and prophet and the oldest Christian community in Jerusalem as an apocalyptic movement.[7] In the background is a theologically based distinction between eschatology and apocalypticism, a distinction which reflects a bias toward eschatology and against apocalypticism. The tendency is evident in the title of Vielhauer's major article on the subject—"Gottesreich und Menschensohn." In this article he argued that kingdom of God and Son of Man are two totally distinct and separate elements in the history of the Synoptic

---

Kreis Moers, 1957) 51–79, reprinted in idem, *Aufsätze zum Neuen Testament* (ThBü 31; Munich: Kaiser, 1965); idem, "Jesus und der Menschensohn: Zur Diskussion mit Heinz Eduard Tödt und Eduard Schweizer," *ZThK* 60 (1963) 133–77, reprinted in idem, *Aufsätze zum Neuen Testament*; the references in this chapter are to the latter volume for both reprinted articles. Norman Perrin, "Mark XIV. 62: The End Product of a Christian Pesher Tradition?" *NTS* 12 (1965–66) 150–55; idem, "The Son of Man in Ancient Judaism and Primitive Christianity: A Suggestion," *BR* 11 (1966) 17–28; idem, "The Creative Use of the Son of Man Traditions by Mark," *USQR* 23 (1967–68) 357–65; idem, "The Son of Man in the Synoptic Tradition," *BR* 13 (1968) 3–25. These four articles were reprinted in *A Modern Pilgrimage*. See also idem, *Rediscovering the Teaching of Jesus* (New York: Harper & Row, 1967) 154–206. See the discussion of Perrin's work in Donahue, "Recent Studies," 485–86, 494–96. Hans Conzelmann also concluded that none of the Son of Man sayings goes back to Jesus (*An Outline of the Theology of the New Testament* [New York: Harper & Row, 1969] 135–36).

[5] Vielhauer, "Gottesreich und Menschensohn," 90–91.

[6] Rudolf Bultmann, *Theology of the New Testament* (New York: Scribner's Sons, 1951) 4; Johannes Weiss, *Die Predigt Jesu vom Reiche Gottes* (Göttingen: Vandenhoeck & Ruprecht, 1892); ET *Jesus' Proclamation of the Kingdom of God* (trans. and ed. R.H. Hiers and D.L. Holland; Lives of Jesus series; Philadelphia: Fortress, 1971). Albert Schweitzer, *Von Reimarus zu Wrede* (1906); ET, *The Quest of the Historical Jesus: A Critical Study of Its Progress from Reimarus to Wrede* (introduction by James M. Robinson; New York: Macmillan, 1968).

[7] Vielhauer, "Gottesreich und Menschensohn," 87–91; Perrin, *Rediscovering the Teaching of Jesus*, 154–206. See also Norman Perrin and Dennis Duling, *The New Testament: An Introduction* (2nd ed.; New York: Harcourt Brace Jovanovich, 1982) 71–79, 411–12.

tradition. Vielhauer is correct that these two traditional elements are not closely intertwined in the Synoptic tradition. But since the two belong to the same pattern of ideas in roughly contemporary Jewish texts, the claim that they are totally separate in the tradition related to Jesus seems tendentious.[8]

In the meantime, claims are being made that Weiss and Schweitzer have sold us a bill of goods and that Jesus was not even eschatological, let alone apocalyptic.[9] As Marx did to Hegel, Burton Mack is attempting to turn Bultmann on his head. According to Mack, the question is not how the Proclaimer became the Proclaimed, but how the Proclaimed became the Proclaimer![10] Jesus now appears to have been, not an apocalyptic prophet, but a sage, a poet, or a wandering Cynic philosopher, playfully challenging the established order in favor of a return to a simple life close to nature.[11] In a word, there has been a paradigm shift: Jesus is now placed in a wisdom context rather than in a prophetic-apocalyptic one.

The house of the apocalyptic reconstruction of the historical Jesus, however, was not built on sand. It has not been washed away by the new wave of interpretation and some scholars have noted that fact. E.P. Sanders has made recently a well-conceived attempt to reconstruct the historical Jesus as an eschatological prophet.[12] M. Eugene Boring, in an earlier book, had argued that the point of origin of the

---

[8] In Daniel 7 the dominion of the one like a son of man is closely associated with the kingdom of the people of the holy ones of the Most High (vss 13–14, 27). The context suggests that both the dominion of the one like a son of man and the kingdom of the people result from the decree of the Most High, i.e., they are manifestations of the kingdom of God. The kingdom of God is closely associated with the activities of angelic beings in the *Assumption of Moses* 10 and in the *War Scroll* and 11QMelchizedek from Qumran. See below.

[9] Such claims were made at the October 1986 meeting of the Jesus Seminar at the University of Notre Dame and at a session of the Q Seminar at the 1986 Annual Meeting of the Society of Biblical Literature. On the origins, purpose, and early work of the Jesus Seminar, see the journal *Forum*, vols. 1–3 (1985–87).

[10] Remarks made at the October 1986 meeting of the Jesus Seminar (see n. 9). See also Burton L. Mack, "The Kingdom Sayings in Mark," *Forum* 3 (1987). The reference is to Bultmann, *Theology*, 1. 33.

[11] Mack is inclined to present Jesus as a Cynic philosopher. See also Leif E. Vaage, *Galilean Upstarts: Jesus' First Followers according to Q* (Valley Forge, PA: Trinity Press International, 1994) and the review by Adelbert Denaux, *JBL* 115 (1996) 136–38. For Jesus as a sage or poet, see J. Dominic Crossan, *In Parables* (New York: Harper & Row, 1973) and idem, *In Fragments: The Aphorisms of Jesus* (San Francisco: Harper & Row, 1983); James Breech, *The Silence of Jesus: The Authentic Voice of the Historical Man* (Philadelphia: Fortress, 1983).

[12] E.P. Sanders, *Jesus and Judaism* (Philadelphia: Fortress, 1985); idem, *The Historical Figure of Jesus* (London/New York: Allen Lane, The Penguin Press, 1993).

Synoptic Son of Man tradition was Jesus himself.[13] Although neither of these scholars has made a strong case for connecting any particular Son of Man saying with Jesus himself, they are right in resisting the notion that this tradition arose only after Jesus' death.

LINGUISTIC EVIDENCE

A crucial factor in the debate, too often ignored, is the linguistic evidence. The Greek phrase found in the Synoptic tradition is ὁ υἱὸς τοῦ ἀνθρώπου. This phrase in the Greek of the first century CE would normally mean "the son of the man," or "the man's son." It is not an idiom in Greek. Therefore, most scholars have concluded that it is a translation or a mistranslation of a Semitic idiom. Since both nouns in the Greek phrase have the article, one would expect the Semitic original to be two nouns in a construct chain, both nouns being made definite by the definite character of the second. The relevant expressions would thus be בן האדם in Hebrew and בר אנשא or בר נשא in Aramaic. It is notable that the definite forms of these expressions in Hebrew and Aramaic are relatively rare, especially in the earlier material.[14] Therefore, the indefinite forms בן אדם in Hebrew and בר נש in Aramaic have also been studied.

As with other aspects of the Son of Man problem, there has been a heated debate on the linguistic data. The main point of contention has been whether the targumim, the Talmud of the land of Israel, and certain midrashim, such as the *Genesis Rabbah*, are relevant to the interpretation of the synoptic Son of Man sayings. Geza Vermes argues that they are; Joseph A. Fitzmyer argues that they represent later forms of Hebrew and Aramaic and thus cast no light on the languages spoken in the first century in Galilee and Judea.[15] Even if,

---

[13] M. Eugene Boring, *Sayings of the Risen Jesus: Christian Prophecy in the Synoptic Tradition* (SNTSMS; Cambridge: Cambridge University Press, 1982). See also A.J.B. Higgins, *The Son of Man in the Teaching of Jesus* (SNTSMS; Cambridge: Cambridge University Press, 1980).

[14] See the survey of the evidence by Joseph A. Fitzmyer, S.J., "The New Testament Title 'Son of Man' Philologically Considered," in idem, *A Wandering Aramean: Collected Aramaic Essays* (SBLMS; Missoula, MT: Scholars Press, 1979) 145–53.

[15] Geza Vermes, "The Use of בר נש/בר נשא in Jewish Aramaic," Appendix E in Matthew Black, *An Aramaic Approach to the Gospels and Acts* (3rd ed.; Oxford: Clarendon, 1967) 310–30; idem, *Jesus the Jew: A Historian's Reading of the Gospels* (Philadelphia: Fortress, 1973) 160–91; idem, "The 'Son of Man' Debate," 23–25. Joseph A. Fitzmyer, Review of M. Black, *An Aramaic Approach*, 3rd ed., in *CBQ* 30 (1968) 426–27; idem,

for the sake of argument, one allowed the relevance of Vermes' data, it is doubtful that the solution based on it is tenable. This point will be taken up below.

CATEGORIZATION AND ANALYSIS OF SAYINGS

The Synoptic Son of Man sayings have been categorized in various ways. Many scholars follow Bultmann in dividing them into three groups: sayings "which speak of the Son of Man (1) as coming, (2) as suffering death and rising again, and (3) as now at work."[16] Vermes claims that Bultmann's categories are based on subjective exegesis. As a more objective and formal classification, he proposed dividing the sayings into three groups on the basis of their relationship to Dan 7:13; namely, (1) those which cite the passage explicitly, (2) those which allude to it indirectly, and (3) those which have no apparent link with the older text.[17]

Bulmann's categories are indeed somewhat arbitrarily imposed upon the texts. A few of the sayings do not fit neatly into any one of his three groups. For example, the last beatitude in Luke speaks of Christians being ostracized on account of the Son of Man (Luke 6:22–23). Does this mean on account of their loyalty to the earthly Jesus or their hope in the heavenly Son of Man? In Luke 17:22 Jesus tells the disciples that the days are coming when they will desire to see one of the days of the Son of Man and they will not see it. In a post-Easter context does this saying look back to Jesus as the earthly Son of Man whose absence is now mourned, like the saying in Luke 5:35, "Days will come, when the bridegroom is taken away from them"?[18] Or does it look forward to the revelation of the heavenly Son of Man "in the days of the Son of Man" (17:26)?

"The New Testament Title 'Son of Man,'" 149–53; idem, "Another View of the 'Son of Man' Debate," *JSNT* 4 (1979) 58–65. See the review of the debate by Donahue, "Recent Studies," 486–90.

[16] Bultmann, *Theology*, 1. 30. Among those who follow Bultmann in this classification are Vielhauer, "Gottesreich und Menschensohn," 57–58; Perrin, *Modern Pilgrimage*, 60–77; Heinz Eduard Tödt, *Der Menschensohn in der synoptischen Überlieferung* (Gütersloh: Mohn, 1959); ET, *The Son of Man in the Synoptic Tradition* (London: SCM, 1965); references in this chapter are to the German ed.; Higgins, *The Son of Man*, 2; Lindars, *Jesus Son of Man*, vii.

[17] Vermes, *Jesus the Jew*, 177–86.

[18] Translations of NT passages are by the author based on the 26th ed. of the Nestle-Aland text.

Vermes' categories are not entirely satisfactory either, because none of the sayings are exegetical in form. They do not take Scripture as their point of departure. Thus the basis of his classification is somewhat foreign to the literary form of the sayings.

A more satisfactory approach would be to classify the sayings according to their form and function.[19] Such a grouping allows a more objective approach to the history of the tradition, including its origins. There are seventy-four Son of Man sayings in the Synoptic tradition, including the one clearly relevant saying in the *Gospel of Thomas* (86).[20] When the variants of one saying are grouped together, thirty-seven distinct sayings remain.[21] Ten of these are "I-sayings" in which Jesus comments on his coming or on his passion, death, and resurrection.[22] These are all likely to have originated in a post-Easter situation, expressing interpretations of Jesus' life and work as a whole. Three sayings belong to secondary interpretations of a similitude or parable.[23] Although such interpretations may contain early material, their relatively late position in the history of the tradition does not make any of them a good starting point for determining the origin of the Son of Man motif. Four of the Son of Man sayings belong to legendary narratives within the Gospels.[24] This literary form suggests a relatively late composition by an evangelist, earlier editor, or Christian storyteller. The narratives could reflect Jesus' actual teaching in some respects, but they do not provide a good starting point.

---

[19] In fairness to Bultmann, it should be noted that this procedure is the one he followed in his analysis of the texts in *The History of the Synoptic Tradition*; only in his *Theology of the New Testament* did he classify them in the groups mentioned above. Vielhauer and Tödt were apparently the first to use the classification as a structuring principle or heuristic device in the actual exegesis of the texts.

[20] This enumeration differs slightly from that of Günther Schwarz, *Jesus "der Menschensohn": Aramaistische Untersuchungen zu den synoptischen Menschensohnworten Jesu* (BWANT; Stuttgart: Kohlhammer, 1986) 11–12.

[21] Ibid., 12–13; Schwarz's No. 9 should probably be taken as a variant of No. 25. Luke 24:7, which Schwarz lists as a variant of Mark 14:41d/Matt 26:45c, d (his No. 33), should be counted as a separate saying.

[22] "I-saying" is a form-critical category used by Bultmann; see *Synoptic Tradition*, 150–66. The Son of Man sayings which belong to this type of saying are Matt 11:18–19/Luke 7:33–34; Matt 17:9/Mark 9:9; Matt 17:12/Mark 9:12; Matt 17:22/Mark 9:31/Luke 9:44; Luke 19:10; Matt 20:18/Mark 10:33/Luke 18:31; Matt 20:28/Mark 10:45 (cf. Luke 22:27); Matt 26:2; Matt 26:45/Mark 14:41; and Mark 8:31/Luke 9:22.

[23] The secondary interpretations of a similitude or parable are Matt 13:37; Matt 13:41; and Luke 18:8b.

[24] Son of Man sayings which belong to legendary narratives are Matt 16:13; Matt 26:64/Mark 14:62/Luke 22:69; Luke 22:48; and Luke 24:7 (cf. 24:46). Luke 24:7 was classified by Bultmann as an "I-saying" (*Synoptic Tradition*, 152).

LEGAL SAYINGS OR CHURCH RULES

Two of the Son of Man sayings seem to fit best in the formal category of legal sayings or church rules in their present form.[25] Sayings
of this type seem more likely to have originated in post-Easter communities than in the ministry of Jesus. But in the case of these two
sayings, an older form may be reconstructed which is plausible in
the setting of Jesus' teaching.

One of these occurs in the story of the healing of the paralytic
(Mark 2:1–12 and parallels). The healing narrative has been transformed into a controversy dialogue. When Jesus' authority to forgive
the paralytic's sins is questioned, he responds by demonstrating his
authority by healing the man. The function of the healing is explained with Jesus' remark, "that you may know that the Son of
Man has authority to forgive sins on earth" (Mark 2:10 par.).

In its present form this saying refers to Jesus as the Son of Man.
In the context of Mark as a whole it is a Christological title with a
specific range of connotations.[26] It is possible, however, that at an
earlier stage, the Greek term ὁ υἱὸς τοῦ ἀνθρώπου was a translation
or mistranslation of one of the Semitic terms discussed above.[27] In
fact, this is one of the passages discussed by Vermes in his alleged
solution of the Son of Man problem.[28] He claimed that "Son of Man"
is not a title here, but a circumlocution for "I." Such circumlocutions, he argued, were idiomatic, when the context was one of awe,
reserve, or humility.[29] Jesus did not simply say, "I have authority to
forgive sins," because it would have seemed immodest.

Aramaic philologists have agreed that the Semitic terms relevant
to this discussion may have a generic sense, "a human being," or an
indefinite sense, "someone."[30] Vermes' claim that these terms were
also used as a circumlocution for "I" has been disputed.[31] In each of

---

[25] See Bultmann, *Synoptic Tradition*, 130–50.

[26] Perrin, *A Modern Pilgrimage*, 85.

[27] Wellhausen, cited by Bultmann (*Synoptic Tradition*, 15) and Lindars (*Jesus Son of Man*, 44–45 and 201, n. 42), argued for a mistranslation; Lindars himself (44–47) and Higgins (*The Son of Man* 2, 24–25) argued for a translation.

[28] Vermes, *Jesus the Jew*, 180.

[29] Ibid., 163–68.

[30] Vermes, "The Use of בר נש/בר נשא," 311–19; Fitzmyer, "The New Testament Title 'Son of Man,'" 147–48; Vermes, "The 'Son of Man' Debate," 20.

[31] Joachim Jeremias, "Die älteste Schicht der Menschensohn-Logien," *ZNW* 58 (1967) 165 and n. 9; Fitzmyer, Review of M. Black, 426–27; idem, "The New Testament Title 'Son of Man,'" 152–53; idem, "Another View," 58–60. See also

the examples which he brings forward as evidence, the speaker is included in a general statement about human beings.[32] In no case is the speaker set off from other human beings as distinctive in any way.

If Mark 2:10, therefore, represents an older Semitic saying, it would have meant "human beings have authority on earth to forgive sins."[33] Such a saying would not be strikingly novel in a Jewish context. According to Num 15:25, "the priest shall make atonement for all the congregation of the people of Israel, and they shall be forgiven."[34] The Synoptic saying would be novel if it said that even non-priests could forgive sins or that sins could be forgiven without sacrifice. But it does not say any such thing. The attempt to get behind the link between healing and forgiving sins to a more general saying, therefore, runs into a dead end. If the saying is not pure fiction, it originated either in Jesus' activity of forgiving sins authorized by healing or in similar activity of his followers in a post-Easter context. If Jesus claimed special authority in such a context, it is unlikely that he used a generic or indefinite Semitic idiom such as בן אדם or בר נש. The use of ὁ υἱὸς τοῦ ἀνθρώπου in this context is probably secondary and was added for extraneous reasons.

The Synoptic Sayings Source (Q) contained a saying to the effect that "anyone who speaks a word against the Son of Man will be forgiven, but whoever blasphemes the Holy Spirit will not be forgiven" (Matt 12:32/Luke 12:10). Mark has a similar saying, "All sins and blasphemies will be forgiven the sons of men, as many as they commit; but whoever blasphemes against the Holy Spirit will not

---

the criticisms of F.H. Borsch, *The Son of Man in Myth and History* (Philadelphia: Westminster, 1967) 23, n. 4; Carsten Colpe, "υἱὸς τοῦ ἀνθρώπου," *TDNT* 8 (1972) 403–4; John Bowker, "The Son of Man," *JTS* n.s. 28 (1977) 19–48; and Maurice Casey, "The Son of Man Problem," *ZNW* 67 (1976) 147–54; adapted in idem, *Son of Man: The Interpretation and Influence of Daniel 7* (London: SPCK, 1979) 224–40.

[32] The fullest collection of examples is in "The Use of בר נש/בר נשא," 320–27; many of them are given also in *Jesus the Jew*, 163–68. Even in the two parallel examples which Fitzmyer is willing to accept as circumlocutions for "I," the speaker, Cain, is including himself in a general statement which applies to any human being (Fitzmyer, "The New Testament Title 'Son of Man,'" 152–53; idem, "Another View," 58).

[33] Colpe, Casey and Lindars take the saying in Mark 2:10 as originally an example of the indefinite Semitic idiom, but deny that it refers to *any* human being, including the speaker. Colpe claims that the saying refers to Jesus' authority only ("ὁ υἱὸς τοῦ ἀνθρώπου," 430–31); Casey implies that it refers to healers (*Son of Man*, 228–29); Lindars explicitly argues that it applies only to "*some* people who have God's mandate to heal" (*Jesus Son of Man*, 46). Such interpretations are not supported by the Aramaic evidence collected by Vermes.

[34] Translation of passages in the Hebrew Bible are from the *RSV*.

have forgiveness forever" (Mark 3:28–29). A variant in the *Didache* shows that the Markan form is not idiosyncratic (*Did.* 11.7b). It is possible that behind all these variants stands an older traditional saying to the effect that if a human sins against another human, forgiveness is available, but if a human sins against God, it is not (cf. 1 Sam 2:25).[35] It is possible that Jesus spoke such a saying, using the generic or indefinite Semitic idiom, and that it gave rise to the variants. But this reconstruction leaves unanswered the question why someone who handed on the saying made a shift from speaking about humans or men in general to speaking of Jesus as *the* human or the Son of Man. Was the shift due to a mistake in translation? Did some oral performer or scribe simply not know Hebrew or Aramaic very well? Such an explanation is conceivable, but resorting to it seems desperate, tendentious, or both.

WISDOM SAYINGS

The legal sayings or church rules do not take us very far. Another type of saying is more promising, the λόγιον, that is, the wisdom saying, proverb, or aphorism. Two of the Son of Man sayings belong to this type. One of these occurs in a controversy dialogue about Sabbath observance (Mark 2:23–28/Matt 12:1–8/Luke 6:1–5). As Jesus and his disciples pass through the grainfields on a Sabbath, the disciples pluck heads of grain. Some Pharisees ("*the* Pharisees" according to Matthew and Mark), who just happened to be out in the fields, criticize this activity as unlawful. This challenge is in the form of a question in Mark and Luke. Jesus responds with a counter-question, defending the disciples' behavior by quoting Scripture. Stylistically, the dialogue should end there. The formula "And he said

---

[35] Casey assumes that the original saying in Aramaic had two levels of meaning: (1) if a human sins against another human, and (2) if one sins against Jesus. He claims that a shift of meaning occurred when the saying was translated into Greek: the generic article, which had two meanings in Aramaic, was perceived in Greek to have only one meaning, the reference to Jesus. He concludes that the Greek translators translated literalistically because they could not see how to translate the idiom idiomatically (*Son of Man*, 228–31). Lindars' argument is similar (*Jesus Son of Man*, 37). It seems more likely that, if the generic meaning was present, and if the Greek translators understood it (if they did not, what were they doing attempting to translate Aramaic?), they would have translated freely and accurately, rather than literalistically (i.e., they would have used ἄνθρωπον rather than υἱὸς ἀνθρώπου). The hearer or reader would have been expected to infer the allusion to Jesus from the context.

to them," which appears in Mark and Luke, shows that the sayings material has been added to the dialogue.

The addition in Mark reads, "The sabbath came into being for the sake of τὸν ἄνθρωπον and not ὁ ἄνθρωπος for the sake of the sabbath; so ὁ υἱὸς τοῦ ἀνθρώπου is lord even of the sabbath" (Mark 2:27–28).

There are textual problems with this passage and it is not clear whether it is a unity.[36] It is possible that the part containing the reference to ὁ υἱὸς τοῦ ἀνθρώπου is a secondary expansion of an older saying about ὁ ἄνθρωπος and the sabbath. For the sake of argument, let us assume that the entire saying in Mark 2:27–28 was originally part of Mark and that it is a unity. What then is its origin and meaning?

The controversy dialogue itself probably was composed in a post-Easter situation in which followers of Jesus claimed his authority in order to settle disputes over sabbath observance. The Son of Man saying, although attached to the narrative at a relatively late date, could itself be early, even a saying of Jesus.

The remark about the sabbath coming into being is an allusion to Gen 2:2–3. This evocation of the creation story leads to the interpretation of ὁ ἄνθρωπος as the first human being or as a generic term for humanity. Ὁ υἱὸς τοῦ ἀνθρώπου thus means either the son of Adam or the human being in a generic sense. Being lord of the sabbath recalls the divine command in Gen 1:28 that humanity should rule over the earth.

A saying is attested in later rabbinic literature to the effect that "the sabbath was given to you, not you to the sabbath."[37] If the saying in Mark goes back to Jesus, Jesus may have taken a traditional saying like the one attested in rabbinic literature and placed it in the context of creation. If Jesus said something like Mark 2:27–28, using an Aramaic phrase like בר נשׁ, he probably used it in the generic sense. We thus arrive at a point similar to the conclusion of the discussion of the saying about the word spoken against the Son of Man. There is a gap between Jesus's generic use of an Aramaic term and the Gospels' quasi-titular use of a corresponding Greek term. This gap cannot be explained satisfactorily upon linguistic grounds alone.

---

[36] On these issues see Vincent Taylor, *The Gospel According to St. Mark* (2nd ed.; New York: Macmillan, 1966; reprinted Grand Rapids: Baker, 1981) 218–20.

[37] See Bultmann, *Synoptic Tradition*, 108; Taylor, *St. Mark*, 218–19.

150 CHAPTER FOUR

The other aphoristic Son of Man saying reads "Foxes have holes and birds of the air have nests, but ὁ υἱὸς τοῦ ἀνθρώπου has nowhere to lay his head" (Matt 8:20/Luke 9:58). In Q this saying was the concluding pronouncement in a brief biographical narrative, as the agreement between Matthew and Luke shows. The saying apparently was known apart from this narrative, because the setting is artificial and unrealistic. This judgment is supported by the presence of a variant of the saying in the *Gospel of Thomas*, introduced only by the formula, "Jesus said" (86).

The aphorism is probably an adaptation of a widely known proverb. Another adaptation is known from Plutarch's *Life of Tiberius Gracchus*. In a speech supporting his proposed land reform, Tiberius declared, "The wild beasts inhabiting Italy have holes, their places of rest and refuge, but those who fight and die for Italy have no share in it except air and light and are forced to wander unsettled with their wives and children."[38]

The Synoptic adaptation of the proverb gives no hint that it expresses a protest in behalf of the poor. Rather, ὁ υἱὸς τοῦ ἀνθρώπου seems to allude to the human being as such in contrast to the animals. Bultmann suggested that this saying reflects a kind of folk-pessimism, such as one finds in Job and Ecclesiastes. The saying does resonate with passages like "For the thing that I fear comes upon me, and what I dread befalls me. I am not at ease, nor am I quiet; I have no rest; but trouble comes" (Job 3:25–26) and "For the fate of the sons of men and the fate of beasts is the same; as one dies, so dies the other. They all have the same breath, and man has no advantage over the beasts; for all is vanity" (Eccl 3:19). Such folk pessimism could easily be adapted to a philosophically dualistic, apocalyptic or gnostic perspective, in which humanity has no home or rest in this world, but does find such in the heavenly world. Such an adaptation is suggested by the contrast between animals and humanity in the Synoptic saying and by the addition to the saying in Thomas: "But the Son of Man has nowhere to lay his head *and rest*" (86). The saying as spoken by Jesus, if it belongs to the teaching of the historical Jesus, may have already been given such connotations.

In any case, if the saying goes back to Jesus, it most likely referred to human beings in general, or to Jesus' experience as typical of humanity. At some point, the reference to the generic human being

---

[38] The Greek text is given by Bultmann, *Synoptic Tradition*, 98, n. 1.

was transformed into a reference to Jesus as a particular individual who is without an abode for a specific reason: his sense of vocation, a lifestyle which was a prophetic symbolic action, or the result of hostility to his person or work. At the latest, this transformation occurred when the saying was placed in a pronouncement story concerning discipleship, such as the one preserved in Q. In this context, the life of the disciple is to be homeless in imitation of Jesus' life.

As was the case with the legal sayings or church rules and the other aphorism, the form-critical and linguistic lines of inquiry do not explain the shift from the generic to the particular Son of Man.

PROPHETIC AND APOCALYPTIC SAYINGS

Only two closely related formal types of Son of Man sayings remain to be discussed: prophetic and apocalyptic sayings. Sixteen of the Synoptic Son of Man sayings belong in this category, the largest group. Four of these could well have been formulated by the author of the Gospel in which they appear; three by Matthew (16:28; 24:30a; 25:31) and one by Luke (17:22). Another four are older than the Gospels in which they appear, but are probably post-Easter formulations (Matt 10:23; Mark 14:21 par.; Luke 6:22; 21:36). The origin of the remaining eight is ambiguous.

As mentioned earlier, Bultmann argued that some prophetic and apocalyptic Son of Man sayings originated with Jesus; namely, Luke 12:8–9; Mark 8:38 par.; Matt 24:27 par.; and possibly Matt 24:37–39 par. and Matt 24:44 par.[39] In two of these sayings, an apparent distinction is made between Jesus and the Son of Man (Mark 8:38 par. and Luke 12:8–9). Bultmann argued that this distinction is older than the identification of the two in at least one variant of these sayings (Matt 10:32–33). Bultmann concluded that Jesus spoke about an apocalyptic, heavenly Son of Man, but did not identify himself with that being.

Vielhauer discussed a number of apocalyptic Son of Man sayings and concluded that there were no intrinsic reasons to confirm or deny that one or two of them originated with Jesus.[40] But he argued that

---

[39] Bultmann, *Synoptic Tradition*, 122, 128, 151–52.
[40] Matt 24:37–39/Luke 17:26–27 (28–30); Vielhauer, "Gottesreich und Menschensohn," 74, 79 and idem, "Jesus und der Menschensohn," 101. He is tentative in his judgment on Matt 10:23 ("Gottesreich und Menschensohn," 66, 79).

most of them originated in the early Christian communities, including Luke 12:8–9, "everyone who acknowledges me before human
beings, ὁ υἱὸς τοῦ ἀνθρώπου will acknowledge before the angels of
God; but anyone who denies me before human beings will be denied before the angels of God." This saying makes the clearest distinction between the Son of Man and Jesus as distinct beings, yet
links the activities of the two closely together. It had been argued in
the past that followers of Jesus would not have formulated a saying
after Easter which distinguished between the two figures.[41]

Vielhauer demonstrated that this saying probably does not go back
to Jesus. He pointed out that the saying reflects a legal situation in
which followers of Jesus were required to make a statement about
their allegiance to Jesus. Such a social setting is far more plausible
after the crucifixion than before it.[42]

But it does not follow that all the prophetic and apocalyptic sayings about the Son of Man in the Synoptic tradition originated at
the same time or later than this one. There are several sayings which
do not intrinsically identify Jesus with the Son of Man and which
could well express his prophetic message concerning an apocalyptic
heavenly figure who was to have a role in the imminent eschatological
events. These are Matt 24:44 par., which speaks about the Son of
Man coming at an unexpected hour,[43] Matt 24:37–39 par., which
compares the coming of the Son of Man to the flood from which
Noah was saved,[44] and Matt 24:27 par., which compares the coming
of the Son of Man to a flash of lightning which illuminates the sky.[45]

---

[41] Rudolf Otto, *Reich Gottes und Menschensohn*, (1934; 2nd ed.; München: Beck, 1940);
ET, *The Kingdom of God and the Son of Man* (2nd ed.; London: Lutterworth, 1943);
Tödt, *Der Menschensohn in der synoptischen Überlieferung*, 52–53.

[42] Vielhauer, "Gottesreich und Menschensohn," 76–79; idem, "Jesus und der Menschensohn," 102–7. Although his approach is different, Vielhauer cites Käsemann's
analysis of this saying in support of his judgment that it originated in the early Church
(ibid., 102–3). Käsemann classifies it as an early Christian prophetic saying; specifically,
a correlative saying of eschatological judgment ("Sentences of Holy Law in the New
Testament," *New Testament Questions of Today* [Philadelphia: Fortress, 1969] 77–78).

[43] Vielhauer assumes the unity of Matt 24:43–44 par. and insists on a Christological
interpretation of the unit ("Gottesreich und Menschensohn," 73 and n. 79). But the
saying need not be read Christologically, as the variants in the *Gospel of Thomas*
show (21.3 and 103). Bultmann left open the possibility that the saying goes back to
Jesus (*Synoptic Tradition*, 119, 152).

[44] Vielhauer argues that the origin of Matt 24:37–39 par. must be the same as
that of Matt 24:26–27 par. simply because they are "related" ("Gottesreich und
Menschensohn," 74).

[45] Vielhauer argues against the origin of Matt 24:26–27 par. with Jesus. His reasons

THE QUESTION OF ORIGIN

A supporter of the position that none of the Son of Man sayings goes back to Jesus could reply, "Yes, these sayings *could* go back to Jesus, but unless there is some positive reason for attributing them to him, methodologically sound skepticism requires that they be attributed to a post-Easter situation." There are indeed positive reasons for attributing these sayings in some form to Jesus.

The Synoptic Sayings Source (Q), the Gospel of Mark, and the Gospel of John each represent, to some degree at least, traditions independent of one another. In each the motif of a heavenly Son of Man is a significant theme. In each Jesus is identified with this Son of Man. Norman Perrin and Philipp Vielhauer tried to explain this state of affairs by arguing that the identification of Jesus with the Son of Man was the result of an attempt by the followers of Jesus to make sense of his death and their conviction that God had vindicated him. As is well known, Perrin saw Mark 14:62 as a reflection of this theological-exegetical activity, "And Jesus said, 'I am; and you will see the Son of Man seated at the right hand of Power, and coming with the clouds of heaven.'"[46] He argued that this picture resulted from the combination of Ps 110:1, "The Lord says to my lord: 'Sit at my right hand, till I make your enemies your footstool,'" and Dan 7:13, "I saw in the night visions, and behold, with the clouds of heaven there came one like a son of man...."

It is certainly the case that the followers of Jesus played a creative role in the development and handing on of the tradition related to

---

are: (1) the saying is closely related to the warning in the "Synoptic apocalypse" about false messiahs and prophets (Mark 13:21–23 par.). These warnings may rest on Christian experience of messianic pretenders ("Gottesreich und Menschensohn," 75). But an older saying, represented by Matt 24:26–27 par., may be interpreted in the context of later Christian experience in Mark 13:21–23 par.; Vielhauer himself admits the possibility that Jesus may have warned his disciples about pretenders of some sort (ibid.). (2) Matt 24:26–27 par. presupposes the appearance of some who claimed to be the Son of Man and identifies the Messiah with the Son of Man; such presuppositions are incomprehensible in the teaching of Jesus (ibid., 75–76). The form of the saying in Matthew may be read as implying the appearance of false Sons of Man (24:26 may be translated, "Lo, he is in the desert..."). But the variant in Luke does not imply such a meaning (17:23, "Behold, there! Behold, here!..."). Luke may represent the older form of the saying in this regard, which may be interpreted as counterposing an expectation of an apocalyptic revelation of the Son of Man against expectations of an earthly messiah or the claims of messianic pretenders. Such a counterposing is not incomprehensible in the teaching of Jesus (see below).

[46] Perrin, *A Modern Pilgrimage*, 10–22.

Jesus. It is possible that Jesus never mentioned a heavenly Son of Man and that he sometimes used the expression בר נש or an equivalent in a generic or an indefinite sense. It is conceivable that after his death, his followers connected Dan 7:13 with his person and work for the first time, remembering that he used an expression like בר אנש. It is conceivable, but not highly probable. It is more credible that Jesus spoke of a heavenly Son of Man and that, after his death and presuming his exaltation, some of his followers identified him in his exalted state with that being.

A number of scholars have argued that, during and prior to Jesus' lifetime, "Son of Man" was not a title in Jewish circles and that there was no widespread expectation of the coming of a heavenly being called Son of Man.[47] This argument is dubious.

It is well known that the community at Qumran and at least some early Christians believed that the scriptures were written for their benefit and prophesied events which they were experiencing and other events which they expected to occur in the near future.[48] E.P. Sanders has recently restated, in a cogent way, the case for viewing Jesus as an eschatological prophet.[49] If one accepts this case in general outline, it is likely that Jesus understood the Book of Daniel to refer to his own time and to the near future. He need not have been a scribe or a professional interpreter of scripture to have known the major characters and basic contents of the text.

If we conclude that Jesus alluded to Dan 7:13 in his teaching, the shift from the indefinite or generic use of the phrase "son of man" to its definite or quasi-titular use is explained. In Dan 7:13, the phrase is used generically. The seer speaks of one "like a son of man," meaning one "in the form of a man" or one "with the appearance of a man." The noun אנש, the second noun, is indefinite. Therefore, the whole phrase in the Aramaic text is indefinite. In order to refer to that figure, Jesus probably used a definite form as a way of referring to the figure known on the basis of that text. A similar phenomenon

---

[47] Vermes, "The Use of בר נש/בר נשא," 327–28; idem, "The 'Son of Man' Debate," 20, 26–27; Perrin, *A Modern Pilgrimage*, 23–40; idem, *Rediscovering the Teaching of Jesus*, 164–73; idem, "Son of Man," *IDBSup* (1976) 833; Ragnar Leivestad, "Der apokalyptische Menschensohn: Ein theologisches Phantom," *ASTI* 6 (1968) 49–105; idem, "Exit the Apocalyptic Son of Man," *NTS* 22 (1975) 52; Casey, "The Use of the Term 'Son of Man' in the Similitudes of Enoch," *JSJ* 7 (1976) 29, adapted in idem, *Son of Man*, 112; Bowker, "The Son of Man," 26.

[48] See, e.g., the pesharim from Qumran and 1 Cor 10:11.

[49] Sanders, *Jesus and Judaism*.

is evident in a text roughly contemporary with Jesus, the Similitudes of Enoch (*1 Enoch* 37–71).[50] There a heavenly figure similar to the one in Daniel 7 is called "that Son of Man," presumably in reference to the older text which was already known to the audience.

If Jesus had already associated his activity and teaching with the heavenly figure in Dan 7:13, it is more understandable that some of his followers would have identified the two after Jesus' death.

THE HISTORY OF RELIGIONS CONTEXT

There were precedents in Jewish tradition for closely linking an extraordinary human being with a heavenly figure. Ezekiel the tragedian, writing about 200 BCE, described a dream of Moses in his work on the Exodus. Moses sees a great throne on Mount Sinai and a "man" (φώς) seated upon it. This figure beckons Moses. When Moses draws near, the being gives Moses his crown and scepter and instructs him to be seated on the throne. Moses does so and the other figure withdraws.[51] In a document from Qumran, 11QMelchizedek, Melchizedek is described as a counterpart of Belial; in other words, as a heavenly being, spirit or angel. Melchizedek, according to this document, will protect the children of light and judge or punish the wicked. He is thus an eschatological redeemer and judge.[52] This being is presumably the same as the Melchizedek mentioned in Gen 14:18–20, the king of Salem and priest of God Most High. This being is also mentioned in Ps 110:4 as a priest. In Hebrews 7 Melchizedek is described first of all in terms similar to those of Genesis 14. Then it is said, "He is without father or mother or genealogy,

---

[50] In spite of the fact that the Similitudes of Enoch do not appear in the form of *1 Enoch* discovered at Qumran and that in their place another work is found (the Book of the Giants—see Vermes, "The 'Son of Man' Debate," 26–27), the Similitudes of Enoch are still best understood as a Jewish work written between the reign of Herod the Great and the destruction of Jerusalem in 70 CE; see J.C. Greenfield, "Prolegomenon," in Hugo Odeberg, *3 Enoch or the Hebrew Book of Enoch* (New York: Ktav, 1973) xi–xlvii; David Suter, "Weighed in the Balance: The Similitudes of Enoch in Recent Discussion," *Religious Studies Review* 7 (1981) 217–21; John J. Collins, *The Apocalyptic Imagination* (New York: Crossroad, 1984) 142–43.

[51] The Greek text may be found in B. Snell, ed., *Tragicorum Graecorum Fragmenta* (Göttingen: Vandenhoeck & Ruprecht, 1971) 1. 292; an English translation by R.G. Robertson is available in Charlesworth, ed., *OTP*, 2. 811–12.

[52] See the texts, translations, and commentary in Paul Kobelski, *Melchizedek and Melchiresa* (CBQMS 10; Washington, DC: Catholic Biblical Association, 1981).

having neither beginning of days nor end of life, but resembling the
Son of God he continues a priest forever" (Heb 7:3). These remarks
are evidence for a tradition that Melchizedek was a heavenly being
who appeared to Abraham in human form or who became incar-
nate for an extended time.

Philo implies something similar about Moses in his work *On the
Birth of Abel*. In sections 9–10, he says that God sent Moses as a loan
to the earthly sphere, allowed him to dwell therein, and appointed
him as a god. It is said that no one knows his grave. Such language
suggests that Moses was a heavenly being who took on human form
and then returned to heaven.

In the Similitudes of Enoch, it is said that "that Son of Man" was
named, chosen, and hidden before the sun and the constellations
were made. His role is to execute judgment "on that day" (*1 Enoch*
48–49). Later in the document (70–71), Enoch is identified with "that
Son of Man." The pattern of ideas behind this identification in the
present form of the work could be as follows. There was a preexist-
ent, heavenly being, known from Daniel 7, who was to have an
eschatological role. Enoch began as an ordinary human being. Instead of dying like other humans, he was exalted to heaven and
identified with (merged with or replaced) that heavenly being. Enoch
then would exercise the predetermined eschatological role. Alternatively, the logic may be that Enoch himself was the heavenly, pre-
existent being, who became human, or took human form for a time,
and then returned to heaven. The identity of the heavenly Son of
Man as Enoch has been revealed only to the elect.

CONCLUSION

The conclusion seems warranted then that the ultimate origin of the
designation of Jesus as "Son of Man" is in the teaching of Jesus
himself. Jesus closely associated, but probably did not identify, himself with that heavenly being. The proximate origin of the designation is thus in the reflection of some of Jesus's followers upon his
death who were convinced of his vindication.

In the traditions which link an extraordinary human being with a
heavenly figure, the point seems to be bridging the gap between the
human and the divine, between the earthly and the heavenly. The
best known examples of extraordinary humans in these traditions are

male, presumably because men were perceived, conciously or uncon-
ciously, as the normative human beings. Thus, how כבר אנש in Dan
7:13 and ὁ υἱὸς τοῦ ἀνθρώπου in the Gospels should be translated
depends on the aim of the translator. If the aim is historical accuracy, כבר אנש in Dan 7:13 should be translated "one who had the
appearance of a man" and ὁ υἱὸς τοῦ ἀνθρώπου should be translated
"that Man."[53] Such a choice would seem appropriate for scholarly
studies and study Bibles for a general audience. The lectionary is a
special case. Through the lectionary the Word of God is proclaimed
as a living voice in the intention of the Church. The translation of
Scripture used in liturgy shapes the self-understanding of boys and
girls, men and women. Such a translation should foster equity and
mutuality in gender roles. Therefore, if the aim is to serve the process by which an ancient text becomes living Word for the worshipping community and to foster equity, כבר אנש in Dan 7:13 should be
translated something like "one who had a human appearance" and
ὁ υἱὸς τοῦ ἀνθρώπου in the Gospels and Acts should be translated
"the Human One," or "that Human One." Such a translation is in
line with the primary intention of the tradition in which these texts
stand, to overcome the division between the human and the divine,
the material and the spiritual.

What significance does this study of Son of Man traditions have
for a contemporary understanding of the historical Jesus? First of all,
such a study gives specific content to the affirmation that Jesus was
fully human. It demonstrates how Jesus was fully conditioned by the
culture and thought-world of his time. It reminds us to let Jesus be
a stranger to us and not to cast an image of him in our own cultural
likeness and theological preference. But we need not stop there and
forget him as utterly foreign to our categories of thought and concerns. We can struggle to appreciate the particularity of his teaching
in its circumstances, the options chosen, the options rejected, and
attempt to discern the intention, the function, and the effects of his
teaching about that Son of Man.

Belief in and hope for the future activity of a heavenly being appear
to some moderns and post-moderns as a failure to work with the
realities of politics and history, or as the wishful thinking of the
powerless. Such is a hasty judgment based on modern preferences. It

---

[53] Or "like a son of man" and "the Son of Man" for the sake of continuity with
religious and scholarly tradition.

is important to note that the Son of Man is in fact a powerful political symbol. This figure is not a fantasy cut off from the real world,
but a symbol of a specific way of being, living, and hoping embod-
ied by Jesus and his followers. The Son of Man is an alternative to
other symbols of authority, such as the Roman emperor and his agents,
the heirs of Herod the Great, and the messianic pretenders who
attempted to overthrow Roman rule by force. Jesus' teaching in this
regard was similar to that of the book of Daniel, the Qumran community, the *Assumption of Moses*, certain teachers and prophets described by Josephus, and the book of Revelation.[54] None of these
advocated violence. Yet none was content with accommodation to
the status quo. All called for resistance to the current unjust order
by creating an alternative symbolic universe which sustained an alternative way of life.

---

[54] See Chapter Six below, "The Political Perspective of the Revelation to John."

CHAPTER FIVE

THE "SON OF MAN" TRADITION AND THE
BOOK OF REVELATION

The book of Revelation contains several sayings which allude to Daniel 7:13[1] and two which are variants of sayings in the Synoptic tradition which, in one or more forms, refer to the Son of Man (ὁ υἱὸς τοῦ ἀνθρώπου).[2] The purpose of this chapter is to clarify how these sayings relate to Daniel 7 and the Synoptic tradition. These clarifications, it is hoped, will contribute to the understanding of an early form of Christology and how this Christology was indebted to Jewish tradition.

The main conclusions are 1) that the tradition regarding the Son of Man in the book of Revelation reflects a stage of the development of that tradition which is older than the Synoptic Gospels and the Synoptic Sayings Source (Q) and 2) that the book of Revelation expresses an angelic Christology which is best understood in the context of the Jewish motif of the principal angel.

I. THE PROPHETIC SAYING OF REV 1:7

The book of Revelation begins with a prologue in the third person, which characterizes the book as a revelation (ἀποκάλυψις) and as words of prophecy (1:1–3). This prologue is followed by an epistolary introduction (1:4–6). In 1:9 the vision account proper begins. Between the epistolary introduction and the vision account are two prophetic sayings. One is spoken anonymously (vs 7) and one is attributed to God (vs 8).

The anonymous saying of 1:7 alludes both to Dan 7:13 and to Zech 12:10–14. Apparently, the only other first century text which conflates these two passages from older Scripture is Matt 24:30. Zech

---

[1] Rev 1:7a, 1:13, and 14:14.
[2] Rev 3:3b/16:15a is related to Matt 24:43–44/Luke 12:39–40 and Rev 3:5c is related to Matt 10:32/Luke 12:8.

12:10 is quoted as Scripture in John 19:37.[3] The texts are laid out below for comparison.[4]

Matt 24:30
καὶ τότε φανήσεται τὸ σημεῖον
τοῦ υἱοῦ τοῦ ἀνθρώπου ἐν οὐρανῷ,
καὶ τότε
κόψονται πᾶσαι αἱ φυλαὶ
τῆς γῆς καὶ
ὄψονται τὸν υἱὸν τοῦ ἀνθρώπου
ἐρχόμενον ἐπὶ τῶν νεφελῶν τοῦ οὐρανοῦ
μετὰ δυνάμεως καὶ δόξης πολλῆς.

ἐν οὐρανῷ] τοῦ ἐν οὐρανοῖς D

Rev 1:7
ἰδοὺ ἔρχεται μετὰ τῶν νεφελῶν,
καὶ ὄψεται αὐτὸν πᾶς ὀφθαλμός
καὶ οἵτινες αὐτὸν ἐξεκέντησαν,
καὶ κόψονται ἐπ' αὐτὸν πᾶσαι αἱ
φυλαὶ τῆς γῆς.

μετά] ἐπὶ C pc
ὄψεται] ὄψονται ‭א‬ al.

John 19:37
ὄψονται εἰς ὃν ἐξεκέντησαν.

Zech 12:10, 12, 14 LXX[B]
καὶ ἐκχεῶ ἐπὶ τὸν οἶκον Δαυιδ καὶ ἐπὶ
τοὺς κατοικοῦντας Ιερουσαλημ πνεῦμα
χάριτος καὶ οἰκτιρμοῦ, καὶ ἐπιβλέψονται
πρός με ἀνθ' ὧν κατωρχήσαντο, καὶ
κόψονται ἐπ' αὐτὸν κοπετὸν ὡς ἐπ'
ἀγαπητῷ καὶ ὀδυνηθήσονται ὀδύνην
ὡς ἐπὶ τῷ πρωτοτόκῳ
... καὶ κόψεται ἡ γῆ
κατὰ φυλὰς φυλάς ...
πᾶσαι αἱ ὑπολελειμμέναι φυλαί ...

MT
וְשָׁפַכְתִּי עַל־בֵּית דָּוִיד וְעַל יוֹשֵׁב
יְרוּשָׁלַם רוּחַ חֵן וְתַחֲנוּנִים וְהִבִּיטוּ
אֵלַי אֵת אֲשֶׁר־דָּקָרוּ וְסָפְדוּ עָלָיו
כְּמִסְפֵּד עַל־הַיָּחִיד וְהָמֵר עָלָיו
כְּהָמֵר עַל־הַבְּכוֹר
... וְסָפְדָה הָאָרֶץ
מִשְׁפָּחוֹת מִשְׁפָּחוֹת ...
כֹּל הַמִּשְׁפָּחוֹת הַנִּשְׁאָרוֹת ...

ἀνθ' ὧν κατωρχ.] εἰς ὃν ἐξεκέντησαν Lucian Theod.—ἐπ' αὐτόν] αὐτόν
Aq. Symm. Theod.

Dan 7:13a LXX
ἐθεώρουν ἐν ὁράματι τῆς
νυκτὸς καὶ ἰδοὺ ἐπὶ τῶν
νεφελῶν τοῦ οὐρανοῦ ὡς
υἱὸς ἀνθρώπου ἤρχετο

Theodotion
ἐθεώρουν ἐν ὁράματι τῆς
νυκτὸς καὶ ἰδοὺ μετὰ τῶν
νεφελῶν τοῦ οὐρανοῦ ὡς
υἱὸς ἀνθρώπου ἐρχόμενος

MT
חָזֵה הֲוֵית בְּחֶזְוֵי
לֵילְיָא וַאֲרוּ
עִם־עֲנָנֵי שְׁמַיָּא
כְּבַר אֱנָשׁ אָתֵה
הֲוָה

μετά] ἐπὶ Q.
ἐρχόμενος] add. ἦν A.

---

[3] See also *Barn.* 7:9–10.
[4] The table of texts which follows is based on that of Krister Stendahl, *The School of St. Matthew* (ASNU 20; Lund: Gleerup, 1954) 212–13.

Relation to Daniel 7:13

The first question to be addressed is how Rev 1:7 relates to the texts of Daniel 7:13. It is well known that the book of Revelation never explicitly quotes Scripture. It is equally well known that it is permeated with the language, forms and ideas of older Scripture, especially the prophets. In spite of the lack of explicit quotation (that is, with a formula), many scholars have believed it possible to discern what text or texts of Scripture the author was using. R.H. Charles concluded that the author translated directly from the Hebrew or Aramaic of the Biblical text, although he was sometimes influenced by the Old Greek and by another, later Greek version. This later Greek version was a revision of the Old Greek,[5] according to Charles, which was later revised and incorporated into his version by Theodotion.[6] H.B. Swete concluded that the author of Revelation "generally availed himself of the Alexandrian version of the Old Testament."[7] L.P. Trudinger has argued that a substantial number of quotations and allusions in Revelation have their closest affinity with the Palestinian Aramaic Targumim.[8]

With regard to Rev 1:7, Charles concluded that the author of Revelation used a Semitic text of Dan 7:13 similar to the text used by Theodotion in translating his version. Charles argued further that he translated directly from the Hebrew of Zech 12:10, 12.[9] Bousset simply noted that the preposition μετά of Rev 1:7 agrees with the reading of the Massoretic text[10] and of Theodotion.[11] Grelot, following Montgomery, linked Rev 1:7 to Theodotion because of the μετά.[12]

---

[5] Hereafter, OG.

[6] R.H. Charles, *A Critical and Exegetical Commentary on the Revelation of St. John* (ICC; New York, 1920) 1. lxvi–lxxxi.

[7] H.B. Swete, *The Apocalypse of St. John* (3rd ed.; London, 1909, reprinted, 1917) clv.

[8] L.P. Trudinger, "Some Observations Concerning the Text of the Old Testament in the Book of Revelation," *JTS* 17 (1966) 82–88. Although he points out that Rev 1:7b reads against the OG, he does not find any particular affinity between Rev 1:7 and the Palestinian Targumim (85, n. 3 and 86, n. 1). The article by H.M. Parker ("The Scripture of the Author of the Revelation of John," *The Iliff Review* 37 [1980] 35–51) is concerned with the implicit canon of the Apocalypse, not with the text or version of the Old Scripture used by the author.

[9] Charles, *The Revelation of St. John*, 17–18.

[10] Hereafter, MT.

[11] W. Bousset, *Die Offenbarung Johannis* (KEK 16; rev. ed.; Göttingen, 1906, reprinted, 1966) 189.

[12] P. Grelot, "Les versions grecques de Daniel," *Bib* 47 (1966) 386; J.A. Montgomery, *A Critical and Exegetical Commentary on the Book of Daniel* (ICC; Edinburgh, 1927, reprinted, 1979) 304.

Swete concluded that in Rev 1:7 the author made use of a collection of prophetic testimonies in Greek.[13]

Recent text-critical discoveries and studies have changed the scholarly view of the text of the Jewish Bible in comparison to the time of Charles and Swete. Although Swete acknowledged that the author of Revelation may have used a text of the OG different from that which is found in the surviving manuscripts,[14] too often earlier scholars neglected to distinguish between the original OG and the mixed textual witnesses which reflect modifications made by Origen in his attempt to reconstruct the Septuagint.[15] Further, it was too often assumed that the *Vorlage* of the OG was identical to the Hebrew and Aramaic of the MT.[16]

Recent discoveries which contribute to our knowledge of the text of the Jewish Bible in the first century CE are the Biblical manuscripts from Qumran (and elsewhere in the Judean wilderness) and Papyrus 967, which contains OG versions of Esther, Ezekiel, and Daniel.[17] The Qumran manuscripts at times provide evidence for a different Hebrew or Aramaic text from the MT. Pap. 967 is a witness to the OG which may antedate Origen. At least it is non-Hexaplaric.[18]

A study which has had great impact on current thinking about the history of the Greek version is D. Barthélemy's analysis of the Greek Scroll of the Minor Prophets which was discovered in Wadi Khabra in 1952.[19] The manuscript has been dated to the second half of the first century BCE. Barthélemy has persuaded many schol-

[13] Swete, *The Apocalypse of St. John*, 9–10.

[14] Ibid., clv.

[15] See Sharon Pace Jeansonne, *The Old Greek Translation of Daniel 7–12*, (CBQMS 19; Washington, DC: CBA, 1984) 2.

[16] Ibid., 2–3.

[17] In Pap. 967 the order of episodes is different from that in the MT. P.-M. Bogaert has argued that the order in Pap. 967 is secondary ("Relecture et refonte historicisante du Livre de Daniel attestées par la première version grecque [papyrus 967]," in *Études sur le judaïsme hellénistique* [LD 119; Paris, 1984] 197–224).

[18] Angelo Geissen, *Der Septuaginta-Text des Buches Daniel Kap. 5–12, zusammen mit Susanna, Bel et Draco sowie Esther Kap. 1,1a–2, 15 nach dem Kölner Teil des Papyrus 967* (PTA 5; Bonn: Habelt, 1968) 18.

[19] D. Barthélemy, "Redecouverte d'un chainon manquant de l'histoire de las Septante," *RB* 60 (1953) 18–29; see also his *Les devanciers d'Aquila* (VTSup 10; Leiden: Brill, 1963). Subsequent investigation has led to the conclusion that the scroll was actually found at Nahal Hever in 1953. See now the definitive publication of this manuscript by Emanuel Tov, with the collaboration of R.A. Kraft and a contribution by P.J. Parsons, *The Greek Minor Prophets Scroll from Nahal Hever (8HevXIIgr)* (DJD 8; Oxford: Clarendon, 1990).

ars that this manuscript represents a revision of the OG in order to bring it more into line with the MT or its prototype. This recension is an early example of the enterprise reflected in the recensions attributed to Theodotion and Aquila, which went further in the direction of literalness of translation and consistency in translating a particular Hebrew or Aramaic word with a particular Greek word. The consensus now appears to be that the works attributed to Theodotion, Aquila and their predecessors should be called recensions rather than versions, because they seem to have been revisions of the OG rather than fresh translations.[20]

These recent studies reopen the question what the original reading(s) of Dan 7:13 were and with what reading or readings the author of Revelation may have been familiar. The major witnesses are given below for comparison.

MT Biblia Hebraica Stuttgartensia 1967/77 (Aramaic)

חָזֵה הֲוֵית בְּחֶזְוֵי לֵילְיָא
וַאֲרוּ עִם־עֲנָנֵי שְׁמַיָּא
כְּבַר אֱנָשׁ אָתֵה הֲוָה
וְעַד־עַתִּיק יוֹמַיָּא מְטָה
וּקְדָמוֹהִי הַקְרְבוּהִי

OG
Ziegler 1954[21]
ἐθεώρουν ἐν ὁράματι τῆς νυκτὸς καὶ ἰδοὺ ἐπὶ τῶν νεφελῶν
τοῦ οὐρανοῦ ὡς υἱὸς ἀνθρώπου ἤρχετο, καὶ ἕως παλαιοῦ
ἡμερῶν παρῆν, καὶ οἱ παρεστηκότες προσήγαγον αὐτόν.

Codex Chisianus (MS 88; Chigi MS.; 9th/11th CE; Origen's
Hexaplaric recension) and Syh (the Syro-Hexaplar; early 7th CE)[22]
ἐθεώρουν ἐν ὁράματι τῆς νυκτὸς καὶ ἰδοὺ ἐπὶ τῶν νεφελῶν
τοῦ οὐρανοῦ ὡς υἱὸς ἀνθρώπου ἤρχετο, καὶ ὡς παλαιὸς
ἡμερῶν παρῆν, καὶ οἱ παρεστηκότες παρῆσαν αὐτῷ.

Kölner Teil des Papyrus 967 (2nd–early 3rd CE)[23]
ἐθεώρουν ἐν ὁράματι τῆς νυκτὸς καὶ ἰδοὺ ἐπὶ τῶν νεφελῶν
τοῦ οὐρανοῦ ἤρχετο ὡς υἱὸς ἀνθρώπου καὶ ὡς παλαιὸς
ἡμερῶ(ν) παρῆν καὶ οἱ παρεστηκότες προσήγαγον αὐτῷ.

[20] Pace Jeansonne, *The Old Greek Translation of Daniel 7–12*, 19–23.
[21] Text cited is Ziegler's critical edition of the Old Greek (o´) from Joseph Ziegler, *Susanna·Daniel·Bel et Draco* (Septuaginta: Vetus Testamentum Graecum 16.2; Göttingen: Vandenhoeck & Ruprecht, 1954) 169–70.
[22] This reading is reconstructed from Ziegler's apparatus. It is also the reading printed by Alfred Rahlfs, *Septuaginta* (7th ed.; Stuttgart: Württembergische Bibelanstalt, 1935) 2. 914 as the reading for the Old Greek (𝔊).
[23] This reading is taken from Geissen, *Der Septuaginta-Text*, 108.

THEODOTION[24]
ἐθεώρουν ἐν ὁράματι τῆς νυκτὸς καὶ ἰδοὺ μετὰ τῶν νεφελῶν
τοῦ οὐρανοῦ ὡς υἱὸς ἀνθρώπου ἐρχόμενος καὶ ἕως τοῦ
παλαιοῦ τῶν ἡμερῶν ἔφθασε καὶ προσήχθη αὐτῷ.

Of the portion of Dan 7:13 which is employed in Rev 1:7a, the only
word of the MT which is disputed is the preposition עִם. It is possible that it was in the *Vorlage* of the OG. If it was, the translator
may have misread עַל for עִם. Another possibility is that the translator
used ἐπί to translate עִם in an attempt to render the sense. The use
of prepositions in the OG of Daniel is not standardized and ἐπί is
the most common preposition. It is unlikely, as some have argued,
that the translator's choice of ἐπί was theologically motivated. It is
also possible that the *Vorlage* of the OG was different from the MT.[25]

Attention may now be turned to the relation of Rev 1:7a to Dan
7:13. Notable is the fact that Rev 1:7a differs from the MT and all
the Greek forms of the text in the order of words. In Rev 1:7a, the
verb follows immediately after ἰδού. In the other texts, the verb comes
later in the clause, after the prepositional phrase regarding clouds.
The Aramaic of the MT has as a verbal form a participle (אָתֵה) with
the perfect tense of the finite verb (הֲוָה). The OG translates this verbal
phrase with the simple imperfect (ἤρχετο). In Theodotion the participle only is used (ἐρχόμενος).[26] Rev 1:7a differs from all the other
texts in having the present finite verb (ἔρχεται). These two differences
are most likely due to the author's free citing of Old Scripture by
way of adapting it to his own concerns and to the context of his
work. The placement of the verb ἔρχεται before the phrase about
the clouds tends to emphasize the verbal action. The use of the past
tense in Dan 7:13 is due to the context: the relating of events in a
vision seen in the past. The new context in Rev 1:7a is a prophetic
saying or oracle. In such a shift from vision to oracle, a shift from past
to future tense would be expected. Here the present is used to express
a vivid, realistic confidence in the speedy fulfillment of the oracle.[27]

The use of μετά rather than ἐπί may be an indication of what text
of Daniel was known to the author of Revelation. Those who argue

---

[24] Text cited is Ziegler's critical edition of Theodotion (θ′) from Ziegler, *Susanna·
Daniel·Bel et Draco*, 169–70.
[25] On these points, see Pace Jeansonne, *The Old Greek Translation of Daniel 7–12*,
65, 109–14.
[26] Alexandrinus and the minuscules 106 and 584 add ἦν.
[27] See BDF, § 323.

that the author of Revelation was quoting or alluding to Scripture from memory are probably correct.[28] Charles envisioned the author writing with a number of manuscripts at his disposal.[29] Recent studies have tended to view the author as an itinerant charismatic leader or prophet.[30] This view makes it unlikely that the author carried scrolls with him. If one assumes, however, that the use of μετά is not simply an oral variant of the tradition, but accurately reflects the text remembered by the author, it follows that in this case, he was not dependent on the OG. Either he himself translated a remembered Aramaic text or he recalled a Greek recension closer to the MT than to the OG.

One of the most significant differences between Rev 1:7a and the various forms of Dan 7:13, as well as the allusion to the Daniel verse in Matt 24:30, is that the allusion in Revelation lacks any explicit reference to the figure described as "one like a son of man" in Daniel and as "the Son of Man" in Matthew. This point will be discussed below.[31]

Relation to Zech 12:10–14

The MT of Zech 12:10 reads "and they [the house of David and the inhabitants of Jerusalem] will look at me whom they pierced."[32] The OG reads "and they will look at me because they treated (me) despitefully."[33] Apparently, the translator of the OG misread דקרו as רקדו.[34] The OG follows the MT or its prototype closely in translating והביטו with ἐπιβλέψονται. The OG follows the MT also in having a first person singular object of the looking.

---

[28] For example, L.A. Vos, *The Synoptic Traditions in the Apocalypse* (Kampen: 1965) 52.

[29] Charles, *The Revelation of St. John*, 1. lxv, lxxxiii.

[30] See Adela Yarbro Collins, *Crisis and Catharsis: The Power of the Apocalypse* (Philadelphia: Westminster, 1984) 34–49 and the literature discussed there.

[31] Traugott Holtz (*Die Christologie der Apokalypse des Johannes* [TU 85; Berlin: 1962] 135–36) tried to explain the lack of the title "Son of Man" in Rev 1:7 as deliberate, because in the book of Revelation, the title was reserved for the expression of the relationship of Christ to the community. This argument fails to take into account the fact that the *title* "Son of Man" does not occur in the messages (chapters 2–3) either.

[32] See the Hebrew text given above.

[33] See the Greek text given above and labeled as LXX[B].

[34] So, for example, argues D.J. Moo, *The Old Testament in the Gospel Passion Narratives* (Sheffield: 1983) 210.

The MT continues, "and they will mourn over him (vs 10) . . .
The land will mourn, family by family, separately (vs 12) . . . All the
surviving families (shall mourn), each family separately and their wives
separately (vs 14)."[35] The OG rendering of this portion of vs 10 is
very similar in meaning to the Hebrew. In both there is a shift from
looking at "me" to mourning over "him." As does הָאָרֶץ, ἡ γῆ can
mean "the land," as in the land of Israel, or "the earth" in vs 12.
The word used (φυλή) to translate מִשְׁפָּחָה has much the same meaning, at least by the Hellenistic period.[36]

The allusion to Zech 12:10 in Rev 1:7b differs considerably in
wording from both the MT and the OG. Instead of referring at first
to a specific group of people, the house of David and the inhabitants
of Jersusalem, the text of Revelation says that "every eye will see
him." Not only is the subject different, but the verb is simply "will
see" (ὄψεται), rather than "will look at" (ἐπιβλέψονται or the equivalent). The change in subject is due to the author's adaptation of the
Scripture for his own purposes. The reference to "every eye" makes
the appearance of the one coming with the clouds an event of universal significance. The difference in the verb may be due to paraphrase of the original.

Rev 1:7b continues "including those who pierced him." In this
allusion to Zech 12:10, Revelation differs from both the MT and the
OG in having the third person rather than the first person singular
object. This change may have been made in order to render the
sense of Zech 12:10, under the assumption that the prophetic, oracular
"I" is the voice of Christ.[37] Revelation agrees with the MT, however,
against the OG, in having a verb meaning "pierced" (ἐξεκέντησαν).
Swete suggested that this non-Septuagintal reading was current in
Palestine at the time the Fourth Gospel was written, since it appears
also in Theodotion.[38] This agreement could be explained either by
the author's knowledge of the prototype of the MT or of a Greek
recension which had corrected the error in the OG on this point.

In the beginning of the next clause of Rev 1:7b, Revelation is
very close to both the MT and the OG; in fact, the wording is

---

[35] See the Hebrew text given above.
[36] See LSJ, 1961.
[37] Compare Moo, *The Old Testament in the Gospel Passion Narratives*, 211.
[38] H.B. Swete, *An Introduction to the Old Testament in Greek* (2nd ed., rev. by R.R.
Ottley; Cambridge: 1914) 398. See also Moo, *The Old Testament in the Gospel Passion
Narratives*, 210–11.

identical to the OG: καὶ κόψονται ἐπ' αὐτόν. The subject of the clause, however, which comes at the end, is quite different: πᾶσαι αἱ φυλαὶ τῆς γῆς. This expression may be seen simply as a paraphrase of the more elaborated subject of the MT and OG and translated "all the tribes of the land." Alternatively, and this seems more likely in light of the phrase "every eye will see him," it may be seen as a universalizing adaptation and translated "all the tribes of the earth."

Relation to Mt 24:30

Matthew and Revelation agree in the universalizing subject of the mourning: πᾶσαι αἱ φυλαὶ τῆς γῆς. They also agree in using a form of the verb ὄψομαι, rather than ἐπιβλέψομαι or another verb close to והביטו in meaning. Very significant also, as noted above, is the fact that these two passages are the only two of the first century which conflate Dan 7:13 and Zech 12:10–14.[39]

A number of differences are noteworthy as well. Only Matthew links the mourning of all the tribes of the earth with the appearance of the sign of the Son of Man.[40] Indeed, only Matthew explicitly mentions the Son of Man. Matthew has ἐρχόμενον rather than ἔρχεται and ἐπὶ τῶν νεφελῶν rather than μετά.

As noted above, Swete explained the similarity between Rev 1:7 and Matt 24:30 in terms of their common dependence on a collection of prophetic testimonies.[41] In this suggestion, Swete may have been dependent on the thesis of J. Rendel Harris that there was a widely used "testimony-book" in the early church, made up of quotations from the Jewish Bible.[42] C.H. Dodd effectively refuted the hypothesis of the testimony-book in his work, *According to the Scriptures: The Substructure of New Testament Theology*.[43] Dodd explained the repeated use

---

[39] The same conflation is found also in Justin Martyr, *Dialogue* 14.8; cf. *Dialogue* 64.7 and *First Apology* 52.11. See Barnabas Lindars, *New Testament Apologetic: The Doctrinal Significance of the Old Testament Quotations* (London: SCM, 1961) 127; Vos, *The Synoptic Traditions in the Apocalypse*, 62.

[40] *Didache* 16.6 may refer to the same or a similar tradition.

[41] Swete, *The Apocalypse of St. John*, 9.

[42] For a summary of Harris' thesis and a discussion of responses to it, see D.M. Smith, Jr., "The Use of the Old Testament in the New," in J.M. Efird, ed., *The Use of the Old Testament in the New and Other Essays: Studies in Honor of W.F. Stinespring* (Durham, NC: Duke University Press, 1972) 25–30. Alternatively, Swete may have been influenced by one of Harris' predecessors, such as E. Hatch (see Stendahl, *The School of St. Matthew*, 208–209).

[43] Smith, "The Use of the OT," 27–29.

of the same and neighboring texts from the older Scripture in early
Christian writings in terms of an oral consensus about which older
texts were significant in expressing the Christian message.[44]

At the time Dodd wrote, the Dead Sea Scrolls were becoming
known. Krister Stendahl suggested that the formula-quotations in
Matthew should be understood as analogous to the use of old Scripture in the *Pesher on Habakkuk* discovered at Qumran.[45] He suggested
that the peculiarities of the text reflected in these quotations were
due to the fact that members of the school made their own translations which were interpretive and actualizing.[46] Stendahl rejected the
hypothesis of a collection or book of testimonies.[47] He argued that
the "methods of the synagogue in dealing with the texts of the O.T.,
both in liturgical reading and in teaching, account for most of the
features that Harris wanted to explain by his Book of Testimonies."[48]
With regard to the relation of Matt 24:30 and Rev 1:7, he concluded that the combination of Zechariah 12 and Daniel 7 must
have been "a common matter, either understood as a *verbum Christi*
or as belonging to the church's basic teaching in Christology."[49]

Seven years after Stendahl's book was published, that is, in 1961,
Lindars' book *New Testament Apologetic* appeared. He attempted to flesh
out Dodd's picture of the early Christian use of Scripture and to
pursue the analogy with Qumran pointed out by Stendahl. Lindars
argued that the early Christian use of the Bible was fundamentally
apologetic and that the church's apologetic needs changed over time.
The earliest concerns were to demonstrate that Jesus was the Messiah and that he had been raised from the dead. Soon followed the
need to explain Jesus's ignominious death. In this "passion apologetic," the book of Zechariah played a prominent role. He argued
further that the use of Zechariah in the Gospel of John better represented the older passion apologetic, than its use in Matthew.[50]

On the issue of the relations between Rev 1:7, Matt 24:30, and

---

[44] Smith says that Dodd's book appeared in 1957 (ibid., 27). This seems to be
incorrect, since in 1954 it is cited by Stendahl with a publication date of 1952 (*The
School of St. Matthew*, 52, n. 1 and 225).

[45] Stendahl, *The School of St. Matthew*, 183–202; for a summary, see Smith, "The
Use of the OT," 44–45.

[46] Stendahl, *The School of St. Matthew*, 200–201.

[47] Ibid., 214.

[48] Ibid., 217.

[49] Ibid., 214.

[50] See the summary in Smith, "The Use of the OT," 31–34.

John 19:37, Lindars claimed that Stendahl went too far in minimizing the verbal agreements among the three versions. He did so, according to Lindars, to avoid the conclusion that there was a written testimony-book in the early days of the church. Lindars thinks it probably better to imagine a living apologetic tradition, oral rather than written, in which the practical usefulness of the abbreviated text helped to preserve its identity.[51]

The verbal similarities among these three passages led Lindars to conclude that behind Matt 24:30, Rev 1:7, and John 19:37 is a common original text, not quite the same as the standard LXX text, abbreviated for its apologetic purpose before its later employment in Christian apocalyptic:

καὶ ὄψονται εἰς ὃν ἐξεκέντησαν
καὶ κόψονται ἐπ' αὐτὸν πᾶσαι αἱ φυλαὶ τῆς γῆς.[52]

Lindars comments that the original context in Zechariah describes the restoration of Jerusalem after devastating warfare, and then, when the new life of the city begins, the inhabitants are expected to "look upon me whom they have pierced." The sight will evoke mourning in liturgical order. The very obscurity of the text is the apologist's opportunity to demonstrate the correct meaning: the apologetic point is that the Messiah was bound to be "pierced," that is, crucified.[53]

Lindars argued further that the brief form of the quotation then came into the Christian apocalyptic tradition by way of the identification of the moment of vindication with the Parousia, the revealing of the Son of Man. Then the unbelievers will have good cause to mourn (Rev 1:7). This version of the text contains a deliberate modification: the distinguishing of all the tribes and the ones who pierced him. The modification is due to the placement of the passage in an apocalyptic framework. The Son of Man will come in judgment to vindicate the righteous and condemn the wicked, namely, those who crucified him.[54] According to Lindars, Matt 24:30 has much the same motive. The Gospel of John "retains the strict reference to the Passion."[55]

---

[51] Lindars, *New Testament Apologetic*, 127. In support of this view, Lindars cited the false ascription to Hosea of the very free precis of Zechariah 12 in Justin's *First Apology* (52.11), when he alludes to it in *Dial.* 14.8, as another sign that it belongs to living tradition.

[52] Lindars, *New Testament Apologetic*, 123–24.

[53] Ibid., 124–25.

[54] Ibid., 125–26.

[55] Ibid., 126.

In his treatment of the problem, Louis Vos argued against those who had argued for independent use of older Scripture by the authors of Matthew and Revelation.[56] He follows one of Stendahl's suggestions, namely, that the combination of the two older passages goes back to a *verbum Christi*. He thus concludes that the author of Revelation in this passage is dependent on an aspect of the *logion* tradition which, in this case, is uniquely shared with Matthew.[57]

Norman Perrin accepted Lindars' overall thesis. He also accepted Lindars' reconstruction of the common source of Rev 1:7, Matt 24:30, and John 19:37 (see the reconstructed Greek text above) with one reservation. Perrin argued that the text (oral or written) probably opened with καὶ ἐπιβλέψομαι rather than with καὶ ὄψονται.[58] He saw this text as a selection from some Greek version of Zechariah. The ἐπιβλέψονται of the source was then, according to Perrin, changed in the formation of the Christian pesher through a play on words with κόψονται. This original form of the pesher Perrin found in John 19:37. Perrin agreed with Lindars in concluding that Rev 1:7 represents the second stage in the development of this pesher tradition and in seeing the combination of Zechariah 12 with Dan 7:13 as characteristic of this stage. Perrin added the idea that the word ἰδού was added at this stage as a further play on words: ἰδού is connected with ὄψομαι. The ἰδού then became ὄψονται in Mark 13:26. He argued that the addition in Matt 24:30 of the quotation from Zechariah 12 to the saying taken from Mark 13:26 supports his thesis about the evolution of the word-play: the addition makes explicit what was implicit in the ὄψονται of Mark 13:26.[59]

The attempt to reconstruct a source common to all three passages is very precarious, since there is not a single word common to all three. All three share the root ὄψονται, but Revelation has the third person singular, whereas Matthew and John have the plural. Revelation and John both have ἐξεκέντησαν, but the verb is lacking in Matthew. The similarities in wording, form and function are greatest

---

[56] Vos, *The Synoptic Traditions in the Apocalypse*, 63, 67–71.
[57] Ibid., 71.
[58] Norman Perrin, "Mark 14:62: The End Product of a Christian Pesher Tradition?" *NTS* 12 (1965–66) 150–55; reprinted with a postscript in idem, *A Modern Pilgrimage in New Testament Christology* (Philadelphia: Fortress, 1974) 10–22; the discussion above relates to p. 14 in the reprinted form of the article.
[59] Ibid., 15.

between Matthew and Revelation.[60] The similarities warrant the conclusion that there is a connection between the two texts. The lack of close similarities in wording precludes the conclusion of literary dependence of one upon the other and any attempt to reconstruct a common source. The most defensible conclusion is that the conflation of Zechariah 12 and Dan 7:13 was known to both of the authors, but not as a saying with fixed wording. The variants ἐπί/ μετά may simply be oral variants, or they may reflect familiarity with different recensions of Daniel.

The argument of Lindars and Perrin that the conflation of Zechariah 12 and Dan 7:13 in Matthew and Revelation represents a second stage in the development of this particular tradition fits in well with the hypothesis that Jesus himself was perhaps eschatological, but non- or even anti-apocalyptic, and that certain groups in the early church apocalypticized older non-apocalyptic traditions. The community which produced and used the Synoptic Sayings Source (Q) and the milieu of the gospel of Mark are so presented by Perrin in his *The New Testament: An Introduction*.[61] It is at least equally plausible that Matthew and Revelation represent the oldest recoverable form of this tradition. Philipp Vielhauer suggested that the earliest Christology was an articulation of an experience of the resurrection conceived in terms of the crucified Jesus's exaltation and identification with the heavenly being described as "like a son of man" in Daniel 7:13.[62] According to Daniel 7, this heavenly figure was to be given "dominion and glory and kingdom, that all peoples, nations, and languages should serve him" (vs 14, RSV). The use of the peshermethod at Qumran was combined with eschatological expectation. Eschatologically minded Christians, especially if their expectations involved political and cosmic elements, would naturally expect this awarding of dominion to involve public events with social implications. Such Christians, reading Zechariah 12, would connect the

---

[60] Vos has made this case in greatest detail (*The Synoptic Traditions in the Apocalypse*, 60–71).

[61] Norman Perrin and Dennis Duling, *The New Testament: An Introduction* (2nd ed.; New York: Harcourt, Brace, Jovanovich, 1982) 424–25; in general, contrast chapters 3, 4 and 8 with chapter 13. This point of view also characterized the first edition of this work (1974) and Perrin's *Rediscovering the Teaching of Jesus* (New York, 1967).

[62] Philipp Vielhauer, "Gottesreich und Menschensohn in der Verkündigung Jesu," in idem, *Aufsätze zum Neuen Testament* (TB, NT 31; Munich: Kaiser, 1965) 90–91.

mourning of the tribes, and their looking at or seeing the one whom they had pierced, with the revelation of the dominion of the human-like figure of Daniel 7. Rather than preserving the original use of Zechariah 12, then, John 19:37 may be seen as a re-interpretation of the significance of that passage for Christian faith. Rather than a prophecy of a future event with a cosmic or apocalyptic character, Zechariah 12 is presented as already fulfilled in the death of Jesus. Such a re-interpretation is consistent with the present-oriented es-chatology of the gospel of John[63] and with the statement of Jesus in John 18:36: "My kingship is not of this world" (RSV). The parousia of Jesus seems to be re-interpreted in John 14:18–24 in terms of the Father's and Jesus' coming to and dwelling in those who keep Jesus' word(s).[64] In John 19:37 a passage which other Christians had used to point to the parousia (Zechariah 12) was used in close connection with a symbolic portrayal of the present significance of the death of Jesus: the blood and water which flow from his side symbolize bap-tism and eucharist which have their salvific power through the sav-ing death of Jesus.[65]

The fact that Rev 1:7 does not use the phrase ὁ υἱὸς τοῦ ἀνθρώπου is an indication of the antiquity of the tradition which it shares with Matt 24:30. This point will be discussed below.

II. THE EPIPHANY OF ONE LIKE A SON OF MAN

In Rev 1:9–3:22, an epiphany of one like a son of man is described, who dictates to John, the author of Revelation, seven messages for "the seven congregations which are in Asia" (1:11; cf. 1:4). The designation "one like a son of man" in an early Christian context suggests to the reader that the risen Christ is meant. But the des-cription of the figure includes also some characteristics ascribed else-where to angels and some elsewhere attributed to God. The reader's assumption that the figure in the epiphany is the risen Christ is

---

[63] See Raymond E. Brown *The Gospel According to John (i–xii)* (AB 29; Garden City, NY: Doubleday, 1966) CXVII.

[64] See Ernst Haenchen, *John 2: A Commentary on the Gospel of John Chapters 7–21* (Hermeneia; Philadelphia: Fortress, 1984) 126.

[65] So Haenchen, *John 2*, 201; another interpretation is that the water (and blood) symbolizes the gift of the Spirit made possible by Jesus' death (see Raymond E. Brown, *The Gospel According to John (xiii–xxi)* (AB 29A; Garden City, NY: Doubleday, 1970) 949–51.

confirmed when he says "I became dead and behold! I am living forever and ever" (1:18).

Angelic attributes

In terms of form and content, Rev 1:9–3:22 seems to have been modeled on Dan 10:2–12:4. Both passages describe the epiphany of a heavenly being to a human visionary. In both, the seer identifies himself by name and gives the time and place of the experience. In both texts, the visionary says that he looked and then gives a description of the heavenly being. Following the description, both passages relate that the seer is overwhelmed by the apparition and falls to the ground senseless. The heavenly being then comforts or strengthens the seer. After this exchange, the heavenly being conveys to the seer a long verbal revelation which is associated with a book.[66]

Significant similarities occur in the descriptions of the heavenly revealer-figures. The figure in Revelation is described as dressed in a robe reaching to the feet (ἐνδεδυμένον ποδήρη—1:13). In the MT the figure of Daniel 10 is depicted as לָבוּשׁ בַּדִּים (verse 5). The OG renders this description as ἐνδεδυμένος βύσσινα, Theodotion as ἐνδεδυμένος βαδδιν. The same Hebrew phrase appears, however, in the MT of Ezek 9:2, which is translated as ἐνδεδυκὼς ποδήρη in the OG. The author of Revelation may have known the prototype of the MT of Dan 10:5 and translated it similarly to the way the phrase is translated in the OG of Ezek 9:2; he may have known a Greek recension which read something like ἐνδεδυμένον ποδήρη in Dan 10:5; or the OG of Ezek 9:2 (cf. vss 3, 11) may have been an influence on this aspect of Rev 1:13.

The heavenly figure of Revelation 1 is also described as girded on the breast with a golden girdle (περιεζωσμένον πρὸς τοῖς μαστοῖς ζώνην χρυσᾶν—vs 13). The figure in Daniel 10 is depicted as girded around the loins with gold of Uphaz. The MT reads חֲגֻרִים בְּכֶתֶם אוּפָז (vs 5). Theodotion reads similarly: ἡ ὀσφὺς αὐτοῦ περιεζωσμένη ἐν χρυσίῳ Ωφαζ. According to the OG, his loins were girded with linen. Here Revelation is closer to the MT and Theodotion.[67] In Rev 15:6 the

---

[66] In Daniel, the book is the heavenly book of truth (10:21); in Revelation it is the book which John is to write (1:11, 19).

[67] According to the OG of Ezekiel 9:2, the angel who marked the faithful in Jerusalem wore a sapphire girdle around his loins (cf. vs 11 OG).

seven angels with the seven plagues are described as girded around their breasts with golden girdles (περιεζωσμένοι περὶ τὰ στήθη ζώνας χρυσᾶς).

The heavenly figure in Revelation 1 is said to have eyes like a flame of fire (οἱ ὀφθαλμοὶ αὐτοῦ ὡς φλὸξ πυρός—vs 14).[68] The being in Daniel 10 has eyes like torches or flames of fire (וְעֵינָיו כְּלַפִּידֵי אֵשׁ—verse 6). The OG and Theodotion read (οἱ ὀφθαλμοὶ αὐτοῦ ὡσεὶ λαμπάδες πυρός. Φλόξ is a possible translation of לפיד, but Revelation differs from the MT in having the singular.

According to Rev 1:15, the feet of the heavenly being were like "χαλκολιβάνῳ, as in a furnace of burnished brass,"[69] or "as when it is smelted (or 'refined') in the furnace."[70] Χαλκολίβανον is the name of a metal or alloy, the exact nature of which is unknown, since the word does not appear independently of Rev 1:15 and 2:18.[71] It means something like *"gold ore, or fine brass or bronze."*[72] The figure in Daniel 10 has arms and legs like the appearance[73] of burnished bronze (MT—וּזְרֹעֹתָיו וּמַרְגְּלֹתָיו כְּעֵין נְחֹשֶׁת קָלָל). The OG reads οἱ βραχίονες αὐτοῦ καὶ οἱ πόδες ὡσεὶ χαλκὸς ἐξαστράπτων; Theodotion, οἱ βραχίονες αὐτοῦ καὶ τὰ σκέλη ὡς ὅρασις χαλκοῦ στίλβοντος. The passage in Revelation is closest to the OG and is most probably a free citation or paraphrase of it or a similar Greek recension.[74]

The voice of the figure in Revelation 1 is like the sound of many waters (ἡ φωνὴ αὐτοῦ ὡς φωνὴ ὑδάτων πολλῶν—vs 15). In Daniel 10, the sound of the words of the heavenly figure is said to be like the sound of a multitude (MT: וְקוֹל דְּבָרָיו כְּקוֹל הָמוֹן—vs 6). The OG reads φωνὴ λαλιᾶς αὐτοῦ ὡσεὶ φωνὴ θορύβου; Theodotion, ἡ φωνὴ τῶν λόγων αὐτοῦ ὡς φωνὴ ὄχλου. In this passage in Revelation, Ezek 1:24 or 43:2 has had an influence, as well as Dan 10:6. In Ezek 1:24, the wings of the four living creatures make the sound of many waters (MT: כְּקוֹל מַיִם רַבִּים). The OG reads ὡς φωνὴν ὕδατος πολλοῦ. According to Ezek 43:2, the sound of the coming of the glory of God

---

[68] The same attribute is associated with Christ as Son of God in Rev 2:18 and as the Word of God in 19:12.

[69] So Hort and Swete, cited by Charles, *The Revelation of St. John*, 1. 29.

[70] So Charles, ibid.

[71] See BAGD, 875.

[72] Ibid.

[73] Or "gleam, sparkle"; see BDB, 744–45.

[74] In Ezek 1:7, the soles of the feet of the four living creatures are said to sparkle like the appearance of burnished bronze (MT—וְנֹצְצִים כְּעֵין נְחֹשֶׁת קָלָל). The OG reads σπινθῆρες ὡς ἐξαστράπτων χαλκός.

was like the sound of many waters (the MT has the same phrase as in 1:24). The OG differs from the MT in 43:2.

In Rev 1:16, the face of the heavenly being is said to shine like the sun (ἡ ὄψις αὐτοῦ ὡς ὁ ἥλιος φαίνει ἐν τῇ δυνάμει αὐτοῦ). Although the wording of Revelation here may have been influenced by Judg 5:31, the description corresponds to that of the figure in Daniel 10 whose face was like the appearance of lightning (MT: וּפָנָיו כְּמַרְאֵה בָרָק—vs 6). The OG and Theodotion read τὸ πρόσωπον αὐτοῦ ὡσεὶ ὅρασις ἀστραπῆς).

The similarities between Rev 1:12–16 and Dan 10:5–6, as well as the analogies between their respective contexts, suggest that the "one like a son of man" in Revelation 1 is an angelic figure.[75] This impression is reinforced by the association of some of these attributes with angels elsewhere in the book of Revelation. The reappearance of the golden girdle around the breast in 15:6 was mentioned above. Angels are not explicitly associated with the voice or sound of many waters, but the song of the 144,000 is so described (14:2). This group may be humans exalted to angelic status. The heavenly hymn of 19:6–8 is likened to a voice or sound of many waters (vs 6). The mighty angel of 10:1 has a face like the sun. Significantly, "one like a son of man" (ὅμοιον υἱὸν ἀνθρώπου in both passages) is closely associated with angels, if not identified as an angel, in 14:14–20.

The fact that "one like a son of man" in Revelation 1 is described with angelic attributes is not surprising in light of the angelic character of the figure in Dan 7:13 to whom allusion is made with that phrase. A convincing case has been made that the "one who was ancient of days" and the "one like a son of man" of Daniel 7 are Jewish adaptations of Canaanite mythic traditions concerning El and Baal.[76] In their present context, that is, from the point of view of the

---

[75] Christopher Rowland has explored the angelic elements of the description of Christ in Revelation 1; "The Vision of the Risen Christ in Rev. i. 13ff.: The Debt of an Early Christology to an Aspect of Jewish Angelology," *JTS* n.s. 31 (1980) 1–11; idem, *The Open Heaven: A Study of Apocalyptic in Judaism and Early Christianity* (New York: Crossroad, 1982) 100–101, 103. See also R. Bauckham, "The Worship of Jesus in Apocalyptic Christianity," *NTS* 27 (1981) 322–341.

[76] J.A. Emerton, "The Origin of the Son of Man Imagery," *JTS* 9 (1958) 225–42; A. Bentzen, *Daniel* (HAT 19; Tübingen: Mohr [Siebeck], 1952) 59–61; C. Colpe, "ὁ υἱὸς τοῦ ἀνθρώπου," *TDNT* 8 (1972) 415–19; F.M. Cross, *Canaanite Myth and Hebrew Epic* (Cambridge, MA: Harvard University Press, 1973) 16–17; John Day, *God's Conflict with the Dragon and the Sea* (UCOP 35; Cambridge: Cambridge University Press, 1985) 157–67; John J. Collins, *Daniel: A Commentary on the Book of Daniel* (Hermeneia; Minneapolis, MN: Fortress, 1993) 280–94.

composition of the book of Daniel between 164–167 BCE, the ancient of days is a representation of God and the one like a son of man is the angelic patron of Israel, namely, Michael.[77]

It is likely that the author of the book of Revelation understood the one like a son of man of Dan 7:13 as an angel. Since the author was familiar with Jewish apocalyptic traditions, it is likely that he knew traditions like those preserved in the *Testament of Moses* and in the sectarian documents from Qumran. In the *Testament of Moses* 10, the manifestation of the kingdom of God is closely associated with the consecration or appointment of an angel as chief who avenges the people of God against their enemies.[78] In the *War Scroll* from Qumran, the victory of God is described in terms of the establishment of the kingdom or dominion of Michael in heaven and of the people of Israel on earth (1QM 17:7–8). 11QMelchizedek is an eschatological midrash[79] or a *Pesher on the Periods of History*.[80] In it the Melchizedek who is mentioned in Genesis 14 and Psalm 110 is reinterpreted as an angelic being, the counterpart of Belial, who will exercise judgment and bring salvation in the end time. There is evidence that this Melchizedek was identified with Michael by the community at Qumran.[81]

Although it is likely that the author of Revelation understood the "one like a son of man" in Dan 7:13 as an angel, it is not necessarily the case that he identified him with Michael. In Daniel 8, after he saw the vision of a ram and a he-goat, the seer sought to understand it. Then he saw before him one with the appearance of a man (MT: כְּמַרְאֵה־גָּבֶר—vs 15). The OG reads ὡς ὅρασις ἀνθρώπου; Theodotion, ὡς ὅρασις ἀνδρός. This being is identified in the next verse as Gabriel. The seer's reaction (vss 17–18) is similar to that

---

[77] N. Schmidt was the first in recent times to propose this view; idem, "The Son of Man in the Book of Daniel," *JBL* 19 (1900) 26. Others who have held this view include T.K. Cheyne, W.E. Barnes, G.H. Box, F. Stier, J.A. Emerton, U. Müller, J.J. Collins, and J. Day. For bibliographical references and discussion of the issues, see Day, *God's Conflict*, 167–77; Collins, *Daniel*, 299–310.

[78] See the translation of R.H. Charles, revised by J.P.M. Sweet under the title *Assumption of Moses* in H.F.D. Sparks, ed.,*The Apocryphal Old Testament* (Oxford: Clarendon, 1984) 612–13; cf. the translation by J. Priest in James H. Charlesworth, ed., *The Old Testament Pseudepigrapha* (Garden City, NY: Doubleday, 1983) 1. 931–32.

[79] So Geza Vermes, *The Dead Sea Scrolls in English* (4th ed.; London/New York: Penguin, 1995) 360.

[80] Following J.T. Milik, so Paul Kobelski, *Melchizedek and Melchiresa* (CBQMS 10; Washington, DC: CBA, 1981) 50–51.

[81] Ibid., 71–74.

described in 10:9, 15. The designation of this being as a "man," especially in the reading of the OG (ἀνθρώπου), may have suggested to the author of Revelation that the "one like a son of man" in Dan 7:13 is the same as the revealing angel in Daniel 8. The similarity of the revealing function of the angel and the seer's response to him in chapter 8 to the corresponding parts of chapter 10 may have suggested to our author that the angels of chapters 8 and 10 were the same, namely, Gabriel.[82] The relationship of Gabriel to Christ for the author of Revelation will be discussed below. If our author identified the "one like a son of man" in Dan 7:13 with the revealing angel of Daniel 10, this identification explains why elements from Dan 7:13 and Dan 10:5–6 are conflated to describe the heavenly being of Rev 1:12–16.

Divine attributes

The most obviously divine attribute, at least from the point of view of the probable original meaning of Dan 7:9, is the statement "his head and hair were white like white wool, like snow" (ἡ δὲ κεφαλὴ αὐτοῦ καὶ αἱ τρίχες λευκαὶ ὡς ἔριον λευκὸν ὡς χιών—Rev 1:14). The MT of Dan 7:9 says that the garment of the ancient of days was white as snow and that the hair of his head was like pure wool (לבוּשׁהּ כִּתְלַג חִוָּר וּשְׂעַר רֵאשֵׁהּ כַּעֲמַר נְקֵא).[83] Rev 1:14 may reflect a Jewish apocalyptic tradition, based on Dan 7:9 ultimately, but varying in wording. *1 Enoch* 46:1 mentions a "head of days" and says that "his head was white like wool."[84] The *Apocalypse of Abraham* says that the hair of the head of Iaoel was like snow.[85]

---

[82] Some modern scholars have made this identification; namely, Z. Zevit, "The Structure and Individual Elements of Daniel VII," *ZAW* 80 (1968) 385–96; J. Fossum, "The Name of God and the Angel of the Lord," (D. Theol. dissertation, University of Utrecht, 1982) 92 (cited by Segal; see next reference); Fossum's dissertation has appeared in the meantime as idem, *The Name of God and the Angel of the Lord* (WUNT 36; Tübingen: Mohr [Siebeck], 1985); and A. Segal, *Two Powers in Heaven* (SJLA 25; Leiden: Brill, 1977) 201, n. 54.

[83] According to Ziegler, the original readings of both the OG and Theodotion were equivalent to the MT (*Susanna·Daniel·Bel et Draco*, 168). In Rahlfs' edition, the text of 𝔊 lacked the λευκήν modifying "snow" and had a λευκόν modifying "wool" (*Septuaginta*, 2. 913). Ziegler seems to think that the text of Revelation influenced the readings of Pap. 967 and 88-Syh; see his apparatus to oʹ on 7:9.

[84] Translation by M.A. Knibb in Sparks, ed., *AOT*, 227. Cf. *1 Enoch* 71:10, which says that the head of days' head was white and pure like wool.

[85] *Apoc. Abr.* 11:2 (*OTP* 1. 694).

Certain literary echoes in Rev 1:10, 12–13 may also be hints that the heavenly figure of 1:12–16 has divine status. In vs 10 the seer says "I heard behind me a great voice like a trumpet" (ἤκουσα ὀπίσω μου φωνὴν μεγάλην ὡς σάλπιγγος). This passage seems to be an echo of Ezek 3:12 which links the glory of God with the prophet's hearing the sound of a great earthquake behind him (MT: וָאֶשְׁמַע אַחֲרַי קוֹל רַעַשׁ גָּדוֹל). The OG reads καὶ ἤκουσα κατόπισθέν μου φωνὴν σεισμοῦ μεγάλου. Rev 1:10 also echoes Exod 19:16. The great sound or voice like a trumpet of Rev 1:10 (see the Greek text above) recalls the theophany on Mount Sinai which involved sounds or voices (MT: קֹלֹת) and a very powerful sound (blast) of a trumpet (MT: וְקֹל שֹׁפָר חָזָק מְאֹד). The OG reads ... φωναὶ ... φωνὴ τῆς σάλπιγγος ἤχει μέγα (cf. also Exod 20:18 OG). Finally, the "one like a son of man" in Rev 1:12–13 is depicted in the midst of seven golden lampstands. These lampstands echo the description of the menorah in Exod 25:31–40, especially vss 35 and 31. In this passage and others, the menorah is a symbol of the divine presence.[86]

James Charlesworth has suggested that καὶ ἐπέστρεψα βλέπειν τὴν φωνὴν ἥτις ἐλάλει μετ' ἐμοῦ (Rev 1:12a) should be translated literally, "And I turned around to see the Voice who spoke with me. . . ."[87] He has argued further that this "Voice" should be understood as a heavenly being; namely, a "hypostatic creature," related to the Bath Qol known from rabbinic literature.[88] It is more likely that the peculiarity of the reference to seeing a voice in verse 12a is to be explained in literary terms. The use of the word "voice" here may be seen as synecdoche, the part, "voice," being used to stand for the whole, "the one like a son of man" described in the following verses. Such a figure of speech fits well with the style of the apocalyptic genre, since visionary and auditory experiences are often presented as mysterious, vague, or partial; in a word, dreamlike. At first the seer has only the sound or voice to go by, and thus refers to his experience as such.

---

[86] C.L. Meyers, *IDBSup*, 586–87. The menorah also appears in Zech 4:2, 11. There the seven lamps are interpreted as the seven eyes of God. This tradition seems to be behind Rev 1:4, 3:1, 4:5, and 5:6, where the seven eyes of God are attributes of the Lamb.

[87] J.H. Charlesworth, "The Jewish Roots of Christology: The Discovery of the Hypostatic Voice," *SJT* 39 (1986) 20–23.

[88] Ibid., 22–25.

The relation of the angelic and divine attributes

How is the interpreter to explain the juxtaposition of angelic and divine attributes in the description of the heavenly being in Rev 1:12–16? Most Christian readers downplay or ignore the angelic elements. They see no problem in the risen Christ being described as divine. Traditional Christians connect this attribution of divinity with the doctrine of the incarnation. More historically minded Christian readers understand it in terms of the divinity of the exalted Christ and link this passage with others like Rom 1:3–4, Phil 2:6–11, and Acts 2:32–36. Some scholars have tried to explain this state of affairs textually, proposing a hypothesis about the relation of Revelation 1 and Daniel 7.

In his critical edition of the Septuagint, Rahlfs followed MS 88 and Syh in reading ὡς παλαιὸς ἡμερῶν in Dan 7:13. J.A. Montgomery, however, had suggested that this reading is an ancient error for ἕως παλαιοῦ ἡμερῶν, but a pre-Christian error, as the citation of it in Rev 1:14 shows. He rejected W. Bousset's suggestion that the reading reflected a Septuagintal notion of a pre-existent Messiah, convinced that the reading was accidental.[89] He reasoned that ἕως was misread as ὡς and that this error resulted in the correction of παλαιοῦ to παλαιὸς. The result of the compounded error was the transformation of the "one like a son of man" into the ancient of days.[90] Since Rev 1:14 seems to identify the two figures, Montgomery assumed that the author of Revelation read the error, namely, ὡς παλαιός in his text. In his critical edition of the OG of Daniel, J. Ziegler followed Montgomery's suggestion and printed ἕως παλαιοῦ ἡμερῶν as the reading of οʹ.[91]

In preparing his critical edition of the OG of Daniel, Ziegler was unable to make use of the portion of Pap. 967 which contains Dan 7:13. This manuscript read ὡς παλαιὸς ἡμερῶ(ν).[92] J. Lust argued that this reading is the original OG reading and that the text of Rahlfs did not need to be corrected on this point.[93] He argued further that

---

[89] Montgomery, *Daniel*, 304. See also his "Anent Dr. Rendel Harris's 'Testimonies,'" *Expositor* 22 (1921) 214–17.

[90] See the citation of the argument from "Anent," 214 by J. Lust, "Daniel 7,13 and the Septuagint," *ETL* 54 (1978) 62–63.

[91] This reading is supported by Justin, Tertullian, Cyprian et al.

[92] See the Greek text cited above as Kölner Teil des Papyrus 967.

[93] Lust, "Daniel 7,13," 63.

the intention of the OG was to identify the "one like a son of man" and the "ancient of days." In this intention, according to Lust, the translator was following a Hebrew *Vorlage*, which was prior to the Aramaic text preserved in the MT. The identity of the two figures in Daniel 7 is supported, in his opinion, by the similarities between the son of man in Dan 7:13 and the human figure (God) on the throne in Ezek 1:26, which was the inspiration of vs 13.[94]

Although he apparently had not seen the reading of Dan 7:13 in Pap. 967, F.F. Bruce took a position similar to Lust's in some respects.[95] Bruce argued that the editor of the OG version intended ὡς παλαιὸς ἡμερῶν παρῆν to convey a definite meaning. He listed the following possibilities:

> 1. "as (when [ὡς taken temporally]) the Ancient of Days arrived, then (καί) the bystanders were present beside him."
> 2. "[as (when) the Ancient of Days arrived,] then (καί) the bystanders presented him," that is, presented the "one like a son of man" to the Ancient of Days.
> 3. "[the one like a son of man appeared] as (the) Ancient of Days."[96]

Bruce found support for (3) in the book of Revelation in which the opening vision records the appearance of "one like a son of man," but whose description is based on the vision of the ancient of days (hair white like wool). Bruce admitted, however, that, since the only witnesses to the OG of Daniel are of Christian provenance, the possibility of Christian influence on this particular rendering of Dan 7:13 cannot be ruled out.[97]

Sharon Pace Jeansonne followed Ziegler in arguing that ἕως in 7:13 was corrupted in the transmission of the OG to ὡς because of the preceding ὡς (υἱὸς ἀνθρώπου) and the immediately preceding καί. The genitive παλαιοῦ would have been "hyper-corrected" to the nominative παλαιός in order for the phrase to be grammatically "correct."[98] She argued further that the reading in 88-Syh, παρῆσαν αὐτῷ (later in vs 13), is a secondary corruption of the original OG προσήγαγον αὐτόν attested in the 88-Syh margin and in Justin. The secondary substitution of πάρειμι for προσάγω was prompted by the

[94] Ibid., 64–69.
[95] F.F. Bruce, "The Oldest Greek Version of Daniel," in H.A. Brongers et al., eds., *Instruction and Interpretation* (OTS 20; Leiden: Brill, 1977) 22–40; see the comment by Lust, "Daniel 7,13," 62, n. 2.
[96] Bruce, "The Oldest Greek Version," 25.
[97] Ibid., 26.
[98] Pace Jeansonne, *The Old Greek Translation of Daniel 7–12*, 97–98.

preceding use of πάρειμι (παρῆν). Once προσήγαγον was altered to παρῆσαν, the corruption of αὐτόν to αὐτῷ follows from sense.⁹⁹ According to Pace Jeansonne, the differences between the OG of Dan 7:13 and the MT and other Greek recensions are due, not to the theological tendency of the translator of the OG, but to secondary scribal errors in the course of the transmission of the OG.

Pace discusses another passage in Daniel in which she argues a similar case. She concludes that the original OG reading in 7:6 was πετεινοῦ (agreeing with Ziegler). In the course of the transmission of the OG, a scribe read πετεινόν instead of πετεινοῦ. Perceiving the form as verbal rather than adjectival, this scribe must have assumed that the initial *epsilon* had mistakenly been omitted. Therefore, he "hyper-corrected" πετεινόν to ἐπέτεινον.¹⁰⁰

This type of argument is convincing both for Dan 7:6 and 7:13. It is better to explain variants as mechanical errors when such an explanation is credible. The reading ὡς παλαιὸς ἡμερῶν is most likely a secondary scribal error rather than a deliberate change by the translator of the OG. As Montgomery suggested, this error may be very ancient. Pap. 967 provides evidence that the error occurred in the second century or earlier. As an inadvertant error, it may have been made by a Jewish scribe as easily as by a Christian scribe. It is possible that, once this reading was in circulation, a theological meaning was attached to it. It is not necessarily the case that Christians were the first or the only ones to find theological meaning in the reading ὡς παλαιὸς ἡμερῶν. Before discussing this possibility, it would be well to review the reading in context as it appears in Pap. 967:

ἐθεώρουν ἐν ὁράματι τῆς νυκτὸς καὶ ἰδοὺ ἐπὶ τῶν νεφελῶν
τοῦ οὐρανοῦ ἤρχετο ὡς υἱὸς ἀνθρώπου καὶ ὡς παλαιὸς
ἡμερῶ(ν) παρῆν καὶ οἱ παρεστηκότες προσήγαγον αὐτῷ.

The passage may be translated:

I was observing in a vision of the night and behold! Upon the clouds of heaven there came one like a son of man, and as (the)¹⁰¹ ancient of days he came, and the bystanders approached him.¹⁰²

---

⁹⁹ Ibid., 98.
¹⁰⁰ Ibid., 93. Rahlfs printed ἐπέτεινον in his edition of 𝕲 (*Septuaginta*, 2. 912).
¹⁰¹ According to Pace Jeansonne, "the OG does not consistently translate the construct chain which has the *nomen rectum* in the emphatic state with the article." She also points out that the OG may have been influenced by the previous reference to the ancient of days in the poetic section of vs 9, which does not have the article (*The Old Greek Translation of Daniel 7–12*, 98–99).
¹⁰² According to LSJ, προσάγω was used at times apparently intransitively, meaning

Ms. 88 (supported by Syh) agrees with Pap. 967 with two exceptions. It has the verb ἤρχετο after ἀνθρώπου rather than before ὡς υἱὸς. Instead of προσήγαγον αὐτῷ, it reads παῆσαν αὐτῷ. The meaning of the two forms is basically the same.[103] The last clause of Dan 7:13 in MS 88 should be translated, "and the bystanders came to him."[104]

The question arises how those who used these manuscripts understood Dan 7:13 in the form in which it appears there. The possibility is worth considering that this form of the text played a role in the controversy over two powers in heaven. Alan Segal has pointed out that the subject of the two powers is introduced in the *Mekhilta* of R. Simeon b. Yohai, Bashalah 15, as an exegetical comment on the two statements made about Yahweh in Exod 15:3.[105] The exegesis notes and explains the repetition of the name YHWH. "YHWH is a man of war" describes YHWH's manifestation at the Red Sea as a young warrior. "YHWH is his name" refers to the manifestation of YHWH at Sinai as old man, showing mercy. The same God is present in both manifestations, even though they look different. The proof-text is Dan 7:9–10, which describes a heavenly enthronement scene involving two manifestations. The "thrones" of vs 9 is interpreted as two thrones. This interpretation relates to the appearance later in the text of one like a son of man. The context suggests that the exegesis implies that God may be manifested either as a young man (one like a son of man) or as an old man (the ancient of days).[106] That the one like a son of man is young and merciful, the

---

"approach." The person approached may appear in the dative case (here, αὐτῷ; see LSJ, 1499).

[103] Unless καὶ οἱ παρεστηκότες προσήγαγον αὐτῷ is to be translated "and the bystanders presented (him) [the one like a son of man] to him [the ancient of days]."

[104] Another possibility is Bruce's translation, "And the bystanders were present beside him" ("The Oldest Greek Version," 25).

[105] The criticism of S. Cohen (review in *AJS* 10 [1985] 114–117) that the exegesis of Exod 15:3 is entirely theoretical and bears no relation to actual heretics has been shown to be mistaken by J. Fossum (*The Name of God and the Angel of the Lord*, 228–29). The Samaritan *Malef* 3:5 contains traditions of mediation attached to Exod 15:3: "The Glory too seemed to be saying: 'O congregation, keep yourself from me, for is there not before me a mighty deed? I slew, I oppressed, I destroyed, I made alive; and with you, I did all this when I was at the sea and showed you every wonder and made you cross with great marvels by the mighty power of God.'" This tradition may not be an old one, but it is an actual heretical one. The Samaritans, of course, did not canonize the book of Daniel, which was so important to the Christian interpretation. I am grateful to Alan Segal for this reference.

[106] Segal, *Two Powers in Heaven*, 35. Segal suggests that the reading ὡς παλαιὸς

ostensible point of the exegesis, is not evident from Dan 7:9–10. Therefore, Segal concludes that the latter text was probably as important for the "heresy" as it was to the defense against it. Since the text of the *Mekhilta* cited above appears to be a fairly late summation of a considerable amount of argumentation over time, it is probably not the earliest version of the tradition; it is rather an epitome.[107]

Another version of this tradition is found in the *Mekhilta* of R. Ismael, Bahodesh 5, Shirta 4.[108] This text uses Dan 7:10 to demonstrate that Daniel 7 does not describe two powers in heaven: a fiery stream . . . came forth from *him* (singular).[109]

The Babylonian Talmud, *Hag.* 14a, describes a debate between R. Akiba and R. Yosi the Galilean on how to explain the seeming contradiction between Dan 7:9a (thrones) and 7:9b (his throne). Akiba said, "One (throne) for Him, and one for David." Yosi said, ". . . one for justice and one for grace." The anecdote ends with the remark that Akiba accepted Yosi's interpretation.[110] Segal concluded that the controversy over the messianic reading of Dan 7:9–10 probably occurred during Akiba's time; the revision in terms of mercy and justice probably derives from the time of his students.[111]

Segal concludes that rabbinic opposition to theories about two powers in heaven can be dated as early as the second century and suspects that it was even earlier. According to Segal, the rabbis opposed the ideas that (1) a principal angel may be seen as God's primary or sole helper and as sharing in God's divinity; (2) a human being could ascend and become one with this figure, as Enoch, Moses or Elijah had.[112]

The prototypes of the MT and of Theodotion and the earliest recoverable form of the OG as reconstructed by Ziegler may be read as revealing that, alongside God (the ancient of days), there is a primary angel or there will be an exalted messiah (the one like a son of man). This point of view apparently was opposed by certain rabbis

---

ἡμερῶν may have been created as a defense against a form of the "heresy" of the two powers (ibid., 201–202).

[107] Ibid., 36.

[108] Ibid., 37–38.

[109] Ibid., 40.

[110] Ibid., 47. In the next interpretation in *b. Hagigah*, Eleazar b. Azariah states that the two thrones are actually a throne and a footrest, referring to Isa 66:1 (ibid., n. 21).

[111] Ibid., 49.

[112] Ibid., 180.

in the second century CE, who argued exegetically that the ancient
of days and the one like a son of man were two different manifestations of the one and only God. Greek-speaking Jews of this persuasion would have welcomed the reading of Pap. 967 and MS 88-Syh
as support for their point of view. Such readers would probably have
taken verses 9–12 and verses 13–14 as parallel accounts of the same
event. The appearance of the one like a son of man and the establishment of his kingdom is a description from a different point of
view of the same complex of events portrayed earlier in terms of the
session of the ancient of days with his court in judgment and the
destruction of the four beasts. What is characteristic of this point of
view is its close association of both figures with God as manifestations of him.

The question arises how the opponents of the point of view described above would have understood the reading ὡς παλαιὸς ἡμερῶν,
if it were current among them, or if they were confronted with it in
a debate. Jews of a "two powers" persuasion may have responded
with the argument that neither the ancient of days nor the one like
a son of man is God himself. The two descriptions should be interpreted rather as variant manifestations of the principal angel, a hypostasis who is God's agent in anthropomorphic form.[113]

If the form of Dan 7:13 known to the author of Revelation read
ὡς παλαιὸς ἡμερῶν, how did he understand this phrase in context
and in relation to Christ? It is likely that the author of Revelation
interpreted *both* the ancient of days *and* the one like a son of man as
hypostatic manifestations of God. In other words, the ancient of days
is not actually God, but a distinguishable manifestation of God as a
high angel. The ancient of days and the one like a son of man from
this point of view are angelic beings, and thus creatures, but creatures of a special kind.[114]

For the author of Revelation, God could be described as seated
on his heavenly throne. He is so described in chapter 4. Since this

---

[113] This hypothesis is supported by the interpretation of Dan 7:9–10 implied by
the *Visions of Ezekiel*, an early Merkavah text. The text seems to identify the ancient
of days with the heavenly prince of the third heaven; see Ithamar Gruenwald, *Apocalyptic and Merkavah Mysticism* (AGJU 14; Leiden: Brill, 1980) 140.

[114] Although the world-view of the author of Revelation is different, there is an
analogy between this reconstruction of his understanding of the relation of the principal angel to God and Philo's notion of the relation of the Logos to God. See the
discussion in Segal, *Two Powers in Heaven*, 161–81.

passage draws on Isaiah 6 and Ezekiel 1, those passages were probably understood as descriptions, however inadequate, of God. Other passages, such as those which refer to the מלאך יהוה and apparently Dan 7:9–10, were interpreted as descriptions of the principal angel. In Rev 3:21 the risen Christ says that he has conquered and sat with his father on his throne. The vision of Dan 7:9–10 may have been understood by the author of Revelation as a prophecy of that event. These verses depict the exaltation of Christ (and his identification with the angelic ancient of days), whereas vss 13–14 predict his second coming (cf. Rev 1:7). Thus the two figures of Daniel 7 represent for the author of Revelation the same being, namely Christ exalted to the status of the principal angel.

It was suggested earlier that the author of Revelation probably identified the one like a son of man in Daniel 7 with the revealing angel of chapter 10, whom he interpreted as Gabriel.[115] This identification is not incompatible with understanding the one like a son of man as the principal angel. Gabriel appears in some texts as simply one of several important angels or archangels. Often, however, one of these angels is depicted as the chief or principal angel and this is sometimes Gabriel.[116] J. Daniélou gathered considerable evidence that traditions linking Gabriel and Michael with the name of God were incorporated into Christian writings, often with the titles transferred to Christ.[117] In chapter 8 of the *Pistis Sophia*, the risen Christ says that he appeared to his mother Mary in the form (τύπος) of Gabriel.[118] Although this conclusion must be tentative, the evidence suggests that the author of Revelation considered Gabriel to be God's principal angel and the risen Christ to be identified with Gabriel.

---

[115] Gabriel is explicitly named as the revealing angel in Dan 8:16 and 9:21. J. Comblin points out that John identifies the "man" of Daniel 10 with the Son of Man of Daniel 7 and draws out the implication that the Son of Man is the envoy of God not only at the final judgment, but also in the present as revealer and instructor; *Le Christ dans l'Apocalypse* (BT; Paris, 1965) 63.

[116] Segal, *Two Powers in Heaven*, 187.

[117] Cited by Segal, ibid., 200.

[118] See the Coptic text in Carl Schmidt, *Pistis Sophia* (Coptica 2; Copenhagen, 1925); a German translation may be found in C. Schmidt and W.C. Till, *Koptisch-gnostische Schriften I* (2nd ed.; rev. W.C. Till; GCS 45; Berlin: 1954) 8. English translations have been provided by G.R.S. Mead, *Pistis Sophia* (2nd ed.; London: 1921) and Violet MacDermot, *Pistis Sophia* (NHS 9; Leiden: Brill, 1978).

III. A SARDIAN THREAT AND A PROMISE TO THE CONQUEROR

The body of the message to Sardis contains a prophetic admonition
to "remember therefore how you received and heard, and keep (that
which you received and heard), and repent" (Rev 3:3a). This admonition is followed by a threat, "If then you do not awake, I will
come like a thief, and you shall surely not know at what hour I shall
come upon you" (3:3b). The formulation of the threat has been identified as a direct use of a saying of Jesus by Louis Vos and by M.E.
Boring.[119] This saying is similar to a saying of Q which was adapted
by Matthew and Luke (Matt 24:43–44 and Luke 12:39–40). In the
Synoptic variants of the saying, the coming of the thief is compared
with the coming of the Son of Man. The variants of the saying,
however, which were known to Paul and to the author of 2 Peter
compare the coming of the thief to the coming of the Day of the
Lord (1 Thess 5:2, 2 Pet 3:10).[120] The statement "I will come/am
coming" of Rev 3:3 and 16:15 may be a variant of the form of the
saying "The day of the Lord is coming/will come." It is a short step,
especially in an oral context, from "the Day of the Lord is coming"
to "the Lord is coming" to (in an oracular, prophetic/apocalyptic
context) "I am coming" (Christ speaking). Thus, the similarity between Rev 3:3/16:15 and Matt 24:43–44/Luke 12:39–40 is not necessarily evidence that the author of Revelation knew a form of this
saying which mentioned the Son of Man.

Also in the message to Sardis, the following promise is given to
the conqueror: "The conqueror will be clothed thus in white garments and I will surely not blot his name out of the book of life and
I will confess his name before my father and before his angels" (Rev
3:5). The verse actually contains three promises. The last one is similar
to a Synoptic saying. The closest parallels are laid out below.[121]

---

[119] Vos, *The Synoptic Traditions in the Apocalypse*, 75–85; M.E. Boring, "The Apocalypse
as Christian Prophecy," cited by David Aune, *Prophecy in Early Christianity and the
Ancient Mediterranean World* (Grand Rapids, MI: Eerdmans, 1983) 421, n. 80. The
saying is used again in Rev 16:15; on the latter passage, see Aune, 283–84 and Vos,
ibid.

[120] In a variant of the saying attested by the *Gospel of Thomas*, the coming of the
thief is compared to the temptations of "the world" (21.3; cf. 103).

[121] See also Matt 16:27, Mark 8:38, Luke 9:26, 2 Tim 2:12b, *2 Clem.* 3:2. The remark in Rev 3:8 that "you did not deny my name" is in a different message, namely
the one to Philadelphia; nevertheless, it may be evidence that the author of Revelation knew the double form of this saying which mentioned acknowledging in one
clause and denying in the other (so Vos, *The Synoptic Traditions in the Apocalypse*, 94).

Rev 3:5c	Matt 10:32–33	Luke 12:8–9
καὶ ὁμολογήσω τὸ ὄνομα αὐτοῦ ἐνώπιον τοῦ πατρός μου καὶ ἐνώπιον τῶν ἀγγέλων αὐτοῦ.	πᾶς οὖν ὅστις ὁμολογήσει ἐν ἐμοὶ ἔμπροσθεν τῶν ἀνθρώπων, ὁμολογήσω κἀγὼ ἐν αὐτῷ ἔμπροσθεν τοῦ πατρός μου τοῦ ἐν [τοῖς] οὐρανοῖς· ὅστις δ' ἂν ἀρνήσηταί με ἔμπροσθεν τῶν ἀνθρώπων ἀρνήσομαι κἀγὼ αὐτὸν ἔμπροσθεν τοῦ πατρός μου τοῦ ἐν [τοῖς] οὐρανοῖς.	πᾶς ὃς ἂν ὁμολογήσῃ ἐν ἐμοι ἔμπροσθεν τῶν ἀνθρώπων, καὶ ὁ υἱὸς τοῦ ἀνθρώπου ὁμολογήσει ἐν αὐτῷ ἔμπροσθεν τῶν ἀγγέλων τοῦ θεοῦ· ὁ δὲ ἀρνησάμενός με ἐνώπιον τῶν ἀνθρώπων ἀπαρνηθήσεται ἐνώπιον τῶν ἀγγέλων τοῦ θεοῦ.

Literary dependence of Rev 3:5c upon Matt 10:32 or Luke 12:8 or vice versa is ruled out by the lack of close similarity in wording. The only word which all three accounts have in common is the root of ὁμολογεῖν.[122] The lack of close verbal similarities between Rev 3:5c and the two passages cited above from Matthew and Luke also rules out the possibility that Revelation is here dependent on the form of the saying in Q. The wording of the saying in Matthew and Luke suggests that it has been translated from Aramaic. Ἐν αὐτῷ and ἔμπροσθεν have been pointed out as semitisms, possibly reflecting Aramaic.[123]

An important aspect of the debate on the original form of this saying has been the question whether the form "I will acknowledge/deny" or the form "the Son of Man will acknowledge/deny/be ashamed" is original. Bultmann argued that the form "the Son of Man will acknowledge" is the older form. He concluded that behind the variants was an authentic saying of the historical Jesus, in which he referred to a coming, apocalyptic Son of Man from whom he distinguished himself, but with whom he linked his teaching and activity.[124] H.E. Tödt followed Bultmann in this conclusion.[125] Philipp Vielhauer agreed with Bultmann that the form of the saying with

[122] So also Vos, *The Synoptic Traditions in the Apocalypse*, 87–89.
[123] Ibid., 90.
[124] Rudolf Bultmann, *The History of the Synoptic Tradition* (rev. ed.; New York: Harper & Row, 1968) 112, 128, 151–52.
[125] H.E. Tödt, *Der Menschensohn in der synoptischen Überlieferung* (Gütersloh: 1959)

the Son of Man is the older form, but did not agree that the saying
originated with the historical Jesus.[126] Vos argued that the form of
the saying in Revelation is the original form, mainly because it has
both "before my/the Father" and "before the/his angels."[127]

Norman Perrin argued that behind Luke 12:8–9 is an authentic
saying of the historical Jesus, namely, "Every one who acknowledges
me before men, he will be acknowledged before the angels of God."
He accepted this saying as authentic because it contains a "double
Aramaism" and because it "is a saying on the basis of which all
other variants found in the tradition are readily explicable."[128] The
earliest form was the one using the passive in the apodosis as a circumlocution for the activity of God. As the tradition developed, an
increasingly Christological emphasis led to the ascription of God's
activity to Jesus. This happened in two ways. In one group of variants, "I" was used for the subject of the action in the apodosis. In
another group, "the Son of Man" was used. The result was the double
tradition we now find in Luke 12:8–9 par.[129] This argument suggests
that Matt 10:32 and Rev 3:5c are related variants of a saying of
Jesus which had been transformed in a post-Easter situation.

Vielhauer had argued that Luke 12:8–9 was probably not a saying
of Jesus, because it presupposed a forensic situation. A situation in
which followers of Jesus would be asked to acknowledge him in a
court-setting is more likely to have occurred after Jesus' death than
before.[130] The same observation must be made about Perrin's reconstruction of the earliest form of the saying. Ὁμολογεῖν is a term
commonly used of testimony in court.[131] Even if the term includes
the metaphorical meaning, such meaning is most understandable if
the literal meaning were a real possibility. It seems best, therefore, to
consider the earliest form of the saying, as reconstructed by Perrin,
to have originated in a post-Easter situation. The earthly courts faced
by Christians are placed in the perspective of the heavenly court in

---

50–56. See also the ET, *The Son of Man in the Synoptic Tradition* (London: 1965);
references in this chapter are to the German.

[126] Vielhauer, "Gottesreich und Menschensohn," 76–79.

[127] Vos, *The Synoptic Traditions in the Apocalypse*, 91–92. Both audiences appear also
Luke 9:26; cf. Matt 16:27a, Mark 8:38b.

[128] Perrin, *A Modern Pilgrimage*, 35–36. The argument is presented in more detail
in idem, *Rediscovering the Teaching of Jesus* (New York: Harper & Row, 1967) 185–91.

[129] Perrin, *Rediscovering*, 189.

[130] See n. 126 above.

[131] O. Michel, "ὁμολογέω, κτλ.," *TDNT* 5 (1967) 200–202.

which God passes judgment. It would have been a short step from that simple perspective to a conception of the heavenly court in which the risen Christ served as the advocate (παράκλητος) of his faithful followers.[132] The forms of the saying which mention the Son of Man connect this conception with Daniel 7 and identify Jesus as heavenly παράκλητος with the one like a son of man. The sayings without reference to the Son of Man do not make this connection (at least not intrinsically). Thus Matt 10:32 and Rev 3:5c (at least prior to their incorporation into Matthew and Revelation) are as close to 1 John 2:1 in their basic conception of the heavenly court as they are to Luke 12:8–9.[133]

This discussion suggests that one should not assume that the author of Revelation was familiar with a form of the saying in 3:5c which referred to the Son of Man. "I" in Rev 3:5c does not necessarily refer to the risen Christ as Son of Man.

The vision of harvest and vintage

Between the seven trumpets (Rev 8:2–11:19) and the seven bowls (15:5–16:21) a series of visions is related, beginning with the woman clothed with the sun (chapter 12) and concluding with the conquerors singing the song of Moses in a heavenly setting (15:2–4). The fifth vision in this series[134] consists of the appearance of three angels, one by one, each with a verbal message (14:6–11). To this vision is appended an editorial comment (vs 12) and two beatitudes, one spoken by a voice from heaven, the other by the Spirit (vs 13). The sixth vision is of a symbolic harvest and vintage carried out by "one like a son of man" and three (other) angels. It is generally agreed that this vision was inspired in large part by an oracle in Joel[135] (4:13; 3:13 RSV) which uses the images of harvest and vintage for divine judgment upon the nations on the Day of the Lord (cf. 4:12 and 14). That the symbolic vision in Revelation has to do with judgment is

---

[132] On the notion of the παράκλητος in early Judaism and early Christianity, see J. Fossum, "Jewish-Christian Christology and Jewish Mysticism," *VC* 37 (1983) 275.

[133] The notion of an angelic παράκλητος was an important one at Qumran; see Otto Betz, *Der Paraklet* (Leiden: Brill, 1963).

[134] For the enumeration of the visions, see Adela Yarbro Collins, *The Combat Myth in the Book of Revelation* (HDR 9; Missoula, MT: Scholars Press, 1976) 13–19.

[135] See, e.g., Charles, *The Revelation of St. John*, 2. 22–24.

supported by the way in which the vision of vintage shifts into battle imagery (vs 20).[136]

Whether or to what degree the vision is dependent on Synoptic tradition is a debatable point. Charles believed that vss 15–17 were an interpolation, so naturally he did not consider parallels in Matthew to be significant for the relation of the (original form of the) book of Revelation to Matthew.[137] Bousset denied any connection to the Synoptics.[138] Although he did not claim literary dependence, Austin Farrer wrote that in this vision "St. John comes very close to a central image of the synoptic tradition, and we should be wise to interpret him by St. Mark and St. Matthew."[139] G.B. Caird takes a position on this issue similar to Farrer's. He argued that "Any Christian at the end of the first century would without a moment's hesitation recognize that the coming of the Son of Man with his angel reapers meant the gathering of God's people into the kingdom."[140]

Louis Vos placed Rev 14:14–19 in his section "The Apocalyptist's Indirect Employment of the Sayings of Jesus."[141] He argued that it is "important to recognize and discern the many contributions which Gospel traditions make to this pericope, both in terms of the expressed allusions, and in terms of the underlying formative thought."[142] He recognizes Dan 7:13 as the ultimate source of the expression ὅμοιον υἱὸν ἀνθρώπου. He doubts, however, that the apocalyptist was directly dependent on Dan 7:13 for this expression, holding rather that the Gospel tradition was its immediate source.[143] The evidence for this conclusion is (1) that the son of man is portrayed as sitting in Rev 14:14, as in Mark 14:62/Matt 26:64, a portrayal different from Dan 7:13; (2) the son of man in Rev 14:14 is associated with a single cloud, as in Luke 21:27; this motif differs from the plural "clouds" in Dan 7:13; (3) the son of man of Rev 14:14 is portrayed as having authority and power to judge; this power and authority is symbolized by the crown and the sickle. These elements are not

---

[136] Cf. *1 Enoch* 100:3.

[137] Charles, *The Revelation of St. John*, 2. 18–19; cf. 1. lxxxiii–lxxxvi.

[138] Bousset, *Die Offenbarung Johannis*, 389.

[139] A. Farrer, *A Rebirth of Images: The Making of St. John's Apocalypse* (Glasgow: 1949; reprinted Albany: 1986) 151.

[140] G.B. Caird, *A Commentary on the Revelation of St. John the Divine* (New York: Harper & Row, 1966) 194.

[141] Vos, *The Synoptic Traditions in the Apocalypse*, x.

[142] Ibid., 145.

[143] Ibid., 146.

reminiscent of Dan 7:13 or Joel 4:13, but they are similar to the statement that Christ will come with "power and great glory" (Matt 24:30 par.). (4) The activity of the son of man, harvest and vintage, is symbolic of the judgment at the end of time, the gathering of the saved and the lost. Joel 4:13 uses the harvest as an image for judgment, but it is not the final judgment. (5) The final judgment is portrayed as a harvest in the sayings of Jesus; the similarities between Rev 14:14–19 and the parable of the tares, together with its explanation, are particularly close. (6) There is no instance in Jewish literature of angels' playing a role similar to the one in both the Synoptic sayings and Rev 14:14b. (7) The command which the angel coming from the temple gives to the son of man is related to the statement of Jesus in the Synoptic apocalypse that only the Father, not even the Son, knows the time of the end; the angel in Rev 14:15 is an agent of God, informing the son of man (= the Son) that the time has arrived; (8) The two-fold ingathering is explained by the Synoptic tradition that there will be a great separation between the elect and the non-elect; Joel 4:13 probably refers to a vintage only; (9) the angel who has power over fire (Rev 14:18) is reminiscent of the fire into which the weeds/sons of the evil one are thrown in the parable of the tares.[144]

In spite of its apparent strength, Vos's argument is not compelling. The similarities between Rev 14:14–20 and various Synoptic sayings can be explained without the assumption that this passage is dependent either on one or more of the Gospels or on any specific saying used by a Gospel. Vos's arguments will be examined one by one.

The portrayal of the son of man as sitting in Rev 14:14 does not necessarily derive from Mark 14:62 par. Although Vos is correct in remarking that the son of man is not portrayed as sitting in Daniel 7 or *4 Ezra* 13, he is so portrayed in the Similitudes of Enoch (*1 Enoch* 37–71). J.T. Milik has argued that the Similitudes is a Christian work of the second or third century CE.[145] Milik's thesis has been severely criticized.[146] Most scholars now agree that the work is Jewish and to be dated to the first century CE. The latest datable

---

[144] Ibid., 146–52.

[145] J.T. Milik, "Problèmes de la Littérature Hénochique à la Lumière des Fragments Araméens de Qumrân," *HTR* 64 (1971); idem, *The Books of Enoch* (Oxford: 1976).

[146] D.W. Suter, "Weighed in the Balance: The Similitudes of Enoch in Recent Discussion," *Religious Studies Review* 7 (1981) 217–21.

historical allusions in the work are the references to the invasion of
Palestine by the Parthians in 40 BCE (56:5–7) and to Herod's use of
the waters of Callirhoe (67:7–9). Thus the Similitudes should be dated
to the early first century CE.[147] In this work, the Son of Man is
portrayed as sitting on the throne of his glory (*1 Enoch* 69:27).[148] It is
explicitly said that he is seated on the throne for the purpose of
judgment (*1 Enoch* 69:27).[149] Although literary dependence of Revelation on the Similitudes of Enoch may not be demonstrable, it is
likely that the author of Revelation was familiar with the apocalyptic
traditions reflected in that text.[150]

Vos himself admits that the parallel between Rev 14:14 and Luke
21:27 (a single cloud) does not prove a connection between the two
texts.[151] The author of Revelation may have employed the singular
simply in order to convey a more vivid picture (cf. 10:1).

The crown of Rev 14:14 can readily be explained as a visual
representation of the statement in Dan 7:13 that the one like a son
of man was given "dominion and glory and kingdom." The sickle
can be explained as derived from Joel 4:13.

Vos's argument that Joel 4:13 does not describe the final judgment of the end-time, whereas Rev 14:14–20 does, is misleading. It
is to be granted that the perspective of Joel 4:13 and its context is
national, but it is also eschatological.[152] Furthermore, the author of
Revelation did not need to refer to the saying preserved in Matt
13:36–43 or to any specific saying of Jesus to interpret the passage

[147] J.C. Greenfield, "Prolegomenon," to H. Odeberg, *3 Enoch or the Hebrew Book of Enoch* (New York: 1973) XVII. See also J.C. Greenfield and M.E. Stone, "The Enochic Pentateuch and the Date of the Similitudes," *HTR* 70 (1977) 51–65; D.W. Suter, *Tradition and Composition in the Parables of Enoch* (SBLDS 47; Missoula, MT: Scholars Press, 1979) 32. A date in the early part of the first century CE is accepted also by George W.E. Nickelsburg, *Jewish Literature between the Bible and the Mishnah* (Philadelphia: Fortress, 1981) 223; and John J. Collins, *The Apocalyptic Imagination* (New York: Crossroad, 1984) 142–43.
[148] Cf. *1 Enoch* 45:3; 51:3; 55:4; 61:8; 62:1–2, 5–7. In 62:2 all the MSS read "the Lord of Spirits sat." Most commentators emend to "the Lord of Spirits set him" because the context requires some such emendation. These passages describe "the Chosen One" as seated on the throne of glory. In the present form of the work at least, the Chosen One and the Son of Man are identical.
[149] Cf. *1 Enoch* 55:4, 61:8, 62:3.
[150] The Similitudes most likely originated in the land of Israel/Palestine. See Yarbro Collins, *Crisis and Catharsis*, 46–49, for an argument that the author of Revelation was a native or resident of Palestine before traveling to the Roman province of Asia.
[151] Vos, *The Synoptic Traditions in the Apocalypse*, 146–47 and n. 173.
[152] Cf. H.W. Wolff, *Joel and Amos* (Hermeneia; Philadelphia: Fortress, 1977) 84–85.

in Joel in terms of apocalyptic eschatology. The community at Qumran and some early Christians interpreted even non-eschatological passages of the Jewish Bible in an eschatological way.[153] Although many commentators so assume, the harvest of Rev 14:14–16 does not necessarily refer to the ingathering of the elect. Rev 14:1–5 is indeed a vision of salvation and the 144,000 are called "first fruits for God and the Lamb" (vs 4). In 15:2–4 another vision of salvation appears, depicting the conquerors in a heavenly setting. Neither vision, however, implies that 14:14–16 represents a gathering of all the faithful to Christ or to heaven. The harvest in vss 14–16 is best understood as a visual representation of Joel 4:13a. The fact that the Hebrew קָצִיר is translated τρύγητος in the OG does not necessarily mean that the author of Revelation read the passage as a description of a single event, namely, vintage. קָצִיר often means a harvest of grain.[154] The author of Revelation may have recalled the Hebrew word or been familiar with a Greek recension which read θερισμός for קָצִיר.[155] Thus, the author of Revelation probably presented a vision of judgment in 14:14–20 with the double image of harvest and vintage, as he understood the text of Joel to do. Finally, it should be pointed out that it is misleading to describe this vision as referring to the *final* judgment. Vs 20 suggests, as noted above, that judgment here takes the form of a battle, for which harvest and vintage are metaphors. This battle is probably the same as the one described in 19:11–21.[156] This battle is analogous to that of Joel 4, namely, it is a battle of the champion of God's people against their enemies, epitomized in Revelation by Rome. The *final* judgment in Revelation takes place in 20:11–15.

In Matt 13:36–43 we have an allegorical interpretation of an older parable, which originally had a different application.[157] Jeremias attributed the interpretation to the work of the author of Matthew.[158] The elements of Matthew 13 pointed out by Vos as similar to Rev 14:14–19 are all in this later interpretation. Vos was incorrect in arguing that these elements are unique to the tradition associated

---

[153] See, e.g., 1 Cor 10:11.
[154] See BDB, 894.
[155] Compare Hatch-Redpath, 1. 649.
[156] Yarbro Collins, *Combat Myth*, 37.
[157] Joachim Jeremias, *The Parables of Jesus* (rev. ed.; New York: Scribner's Sons, 1963) 81–85, 223–27; E.P. Sanders, *Jesus and Judaism* (Philadelphia: Fortress, 1985) 114–115.
[158] Jeremias, *The Parables of Jesus*, 84–85.

with Jesus. In the Similitudes of Enoch, angels have a major role in the activities related to judgment. According to *1 Enoch* 54:1–2, "they" will throw the kings and the mighty into a deep valley with burning fire. This is most probably an allusion to the eschatological, final judgment.[159] "They" are probably angels. This eschatological judgment is an antitype of the judgment executed by the angels Michael, Gabriel, Raphael, and Phanuel upon the fallen angels just prior to the flood. This judgment consisted of throwing "them on that day into the furnace of burning fire" (vss 5–6). In *1 Enoch* 55:3–4, the final judgment is described in terms of the Lord of Spirits laying hold of the wicked "by the hand of the angels on the day of distress and pain." At the time of the final judgment, "the angels of punishment" will take the wicked ("the mighty kings, and the exalted, and those who rule the dry ground") and repay them for the wrong they did to the chosen ones of the Lord of Spirits (*1 Enoch* 62:9–11). This repayment is referred to in some manuscripts as "the flames of the torment of Sheol" (*1 Enoch* 63:1, 10).[160] As the author of Matthew interpreted an older parable in light of Jewish apocalyptic traditions known to him, so the author of Revelation, independently of Matthew, interpreted an older text, Joel 4:13, in light of the same apocalyptic traditions, including Daniel 7.

Vos is correct that the angel of Rev 14:15 should be understood as the agent of God, announcing the arrival of the time for the judgment against the nations. It is not necessary, however, to connect this incident in the vision with the saying of Jesus in Mark 13:32 par. Such a "subordination" of the one like a son of man to God through his agents is perfectly compatible with an early Christology in which the conception of the risen Christ is analogous to a high angel (Daniel 7) or the Son of Man in the Similitudes of Enoch.

The angel who has power over fire (vs 18) need not be explained as an allusion to Matt 13:40–42. The association of angels of punishment with fire in the Similitudes of Enoch was pointed out above. Further, the notion of angels appointed over certain elements occurs in this document as well. According to *1 Enoch* 60, there is a spirit appointed over the thunder and lightning (vs 14). Likewise, there is a spirit of the sea (vs 16), of the hoar-frost (vs 17), of the hail (vs 18),

---

[159] Note that the wicked and the adversaries of the faithful are sometimes described in similar terms in Revelation (6:15, 19:18).
[160] Cf. *1 Enoch* 67:9.

of the mist (vs 19), of the dew (vs 20), and of the rain (vs 21). In Rev 16:15, "the angel of the waters" is mentioned. It may be that the traditional schema of the four elements (earth, fire, water, and air) is reflected in Rev 16:15 and 14:18.[161] The angel of 14:18 may be associated both with the heavenly altar and with the created element fire; cf. 8:3–5. The appearance of the angel here recalls both the vision of 8:3–5 and that of 6:9–11 and thus suggests that the judgment-battle of 14:14–20 is divine vengeance upon those who have persecuted the faithful.

A comment remains to be made on the expression ὅμοιον υἱὸν ἀνθρώπου, which appears in Rev 14:14 and 1:13. The word ὅμοιον does not appear in any manuscript or citation of the OG of Dan 7:13 or in Theodotion. It is likely that the author of Revelation used it in these two passages as a translation of כְּ in the Aramaic text of Dan 7:13 known to him. It is likely that he knew of the translation ὡς for כְּ and used ὅμοιος here as its equivalent. This conclusion is supported by the fact that he uses ὅμοιος here similarly to ὡς both in meaning and construction.[162]

CONCLUSION

In Chapter Four I argued that the historical Jesus referred in his teaching to Dan 7:13 as an eschatological prophecy about to be fulfilled. In referring to the figure "one like a son of man" in that passage, Jesus used a definite form (the one like a son of man or that son of man) in order to point to the text already known to his audience. He understood that figure as a heavenly being, perhaps an angel, and associated his own teaching and activity with that being, although he probably did not identify himself with the "one like a son of man." The sayings which refer to a heavenly son of man and which are likely to go back in some form to the historical Jesus are Matt 24:44 par., Matt 24:37–39 par., and Matt 24:27 par. After

---

[161] H.D. Betz, "Zum Problem des religionsgeschichtlichen Verständnisses der Apokalyptik," *ZThK* 63 (1966) 391–409; ET, "On the Problem of the Religio-Historical Understanding of Apocalypticism," in R.W. Funk, ed., *Apocalypticism* (*JTC* 6; New York: Harper & Row, 1969) 140–42; cf. Adela Yarbro Collins, "The History-of-Religions Approach to Apocalypticism and the 'Angel of the Waters' (Rev 16:4–7)," *CBQ* 39 (1977) 374–79.

[162] So Charles, *The Revelation of St. John*, 1. 36–37.

Jesus' death, some of his followers, presuming his exaltation to heaven, identified him with the heavenly figure of Dan 7:13, as other Jews, possibly in the same century, had identified that son of man with their patron, Enoch.[163] I have also argued in another context that sayings regarding the heavenly Son of Man in an eschatological role are characteristic of the Synoptic Sayings Source (Q) at all the stages of its compositional history which can reasonably be differentiated, including the earliest stage.[164]

The discussion above of various passages in Revelation related to the son of man tradition suggests the following conclusions. The author of Revelation used the expression υἱὸς ἀνθρώπου only allusively; that is, when the phrase appears (1:13 and 14:14), other elements from Daniel 7 or even the wider context of Daniel 7–12 appear also. The phrase is not used in a titular or even quasi-titular manner. It is indefinite in both occurrences. It is clear, however, that the author of Revelation identified the one like a son of man in Dan 7:13 with the risen Christ. This is implied by the conflation of Dan 7:13 with Zechariah 12 in Rev 1:7 and by the saying in Rev 1:18 which clarifies 1:12–16. Thus, the author of Revelation uses the phrase from Dan 7:13 in a way similar to that posited for the historical Jesus above. It is assumed that the phrase refers to a particular heavenly being, but the phrase itself is allusive to a text and not titular.

The author of Revelation, nevertheless, does not simply reproduce the teaching of Jesus on the son of man. Revelation does not seem to contain a saying of Jesus on this topic in a form close to what Jesus plausibly may have said. Further, the author of Revelation identifies the son of man with the risen Jesus, an identification which Jesus probably did not make. At the same time, the author of Revelation did not take the step of using the form ὁ υἱὸς τοῦ ἀνθρώπου as the Q-tradition and the Gospels did. The use of the quasi-titular definite form of the phrase is apparently unknown to the author of Revelation. This difference suggests that the tradition known to the author of Revelation, with regard to this topic at least, has its roots in Palestinian Christianity in the early period after the experiences of the resurrection, but in a context in which Q had not yet been

---

[163] See Chapter Four above, "The Origin of the Designation of Jesus As 'Son of Man.'"

[164] Adela Yarbro Collins, "The Son of Man Sayings in the Sayings Source," in Maurya P. Horgan and Paul J. Kobelski, eds., *To Touch the Text: Biblical and Related Studies in Honor of Joseph A. Fitzmyer, S.J.* (New York: Crossroad, 1989) 369–89.

formulated or in which that tradition was unknown. Likewise, the Gospel of Mark and the other Gospels seem to have been unknown to the author of Revelation. In the book of Revelation then we seem to have an independent development of a very early Christological tradition.

CHAPTER SIX

THE POLITICAL PERSPECTIVE OF THE
REVELATION TO JOHN

Perhaps the hardest won and most dearly held result of historical-critical scholarship on the Revelation to John is the theory that the work must be interpreted in terms of the historical context in which it was composed.[1] Such an approach refers the images of Revelation to contemporary historical events and to eschatological images current at the time.[2] Probably the most widely accepted conclusions of this approach are that the beast from the sea of chapter 13 and the woman of chapter 17 represent the Roman empire in some way. Such allusions to the contemporary ruling power raise the issue of the political perspective expressed in these references. There are no doubt several ways in which that perspective might be elucidated. The one chosen here is the comparison of the political implications of the Revelation to John with those of Jewish writings and movements in the period immediately preceding the composition of Revelation, that is, the late Hellenistic and early Roman periods.

The second temple period of Judaism can be characterized as a time of tension between Jewish tradition, particularly eschatological expectation, and the realities of foreign rule. This tension occasionally erupted into conflict. One such situation of conflict was the Hellenizing crisis which led to the persecution of Jews by Antiochus IV Epiphanes and the Maccabean revolt. This crisis is particularly significant because it provided a variety of models for other groups in analogous situations in later times. In such a situation one might

---

[1] On the triumph in the last century of the historical-critical approach to Revelation over traditional modes of interpretation, see Wilhelm Bousset, *Die Offenbarung Johannis* (KEK 16; 5th ed.; Göttingen: Vandenhoeck und Ruprecht, 1896) 102–40.

[2] The studies of Hermann Gunkel (*Schöpfung und Chaos in Urzeit und Endzeit: Eine religionsgeschichtliche Untersuchung über Gen 1 und Ap Joh 12* [Göttingen: Vandenhoeck und Ruprecht, 1895]) and Ernst Lohmeyer (*Die Offenbarung des Johannes* [HNT 16; Tübingen: Mohr (Siebeck), 1926]) stand as correctives against any tendency toward a simplistic contemporary-historical interpretation because of their demonstrations of the universal character of many of Revelation's images with their roots in myth. But their polemic against the contemporary-historical approach was overstated and most commentators today regard that approach as an essential starting point.

of course choose to collaborate with the foreign authorities and as-similate their culture. Or, one might choose to resist. In the latter case, one has two basic options: 1) revolution or armed resistance and 2) active but non-violent resistance. In the crisis under Antiochus Epiphanes both types of resistance were exercised. Although the two types involved quite different modes of action, each made use of holy war tradition which has its roots in the ancient Near Eastern combat myth.[3]

I. MODELS OF RESISTANCE

Revolution

In the first model, the revolutionary option, holy war language is revived as an ideology for action or as a glorifying interpretation of events. The Lord will assist the Maccabees in battle against the Seleucids as he came to the aid of Israel in the wars of the conquest.[4] Typical holy war motifs are used in the accounts of the Maccabean battles.[5] In 1 Macc 4:30–33 the victories of David and Jonathan are cited as paradigms for Judas's second battle against the forces of Lysias. The idea current in the period of the judges and in the early monarchy, that a successful military leader had a special charisma from the Lord, is applied to the Maccabean family in 1 Macc 5:62.[6] In 2 Maccabees a further element of the holy war tradition becomes explicit; namely, the "two-story" conception of battle. That is the idea that above or alongside the human com-batants heavenly beings are also fighting.[7]

---

[3] Frank M. Cross, Jr., *Canaanite Myth and Hebrew Epic* (Cambridge, MA: Harvard University Press, 1973) 105–6; Patrick D. Miller, Jr., *The Divine Warrior in Early Israel* (HSM 5; Cambridge, MA: Harvard University Press, 1973) 64–65 and passim.

[4] Diego Arenhoevel, *Die Theokratie nach dem 1. und 2. Makkabäerbuch* (Walberger Studien 3; Mainz: Matthias-Grünewald-Verlag, 1967) 16–17, 35–39.

[5] Compare 1 Macc 3:16–22 with Judg 6:15, 7:2–4; 1 Sam 14:6 and 1 Macc 3:46–50 with 2 Sam 5:23, Num 10:9, Josh 6:4–5, Deut 20:5–8. On these motifs see Miller, *Divine Warrior*, 59, 157, and Gerhard von Rad, *Der heilige Krieg im alten Israel* (Zürich: Zwingli-Verlag, 1951) 6–7, 11.

[6] Cf. 1 Sam 10:1–3; 16:13; Cross, *Canaanite Myth*, 220–21; Arenhoevel, *Theokratie*, 47–49.

[7] 2 Macc 2:21, 5:1–4; 10:29–31, 15:8–16. The motif is already present in 1 Macc 7:41–42.

The successful revolt of the Maccabean movement later functioned as a model for the Zealot uprising. A number of Zealots had or took Maccabean names.[8] Both groups looked back to Phinehas as a model for action.[9] Related to the Phinehas motif is that of "zeal" which characterized both groups.[10] Explicit evidence for the ideology of holy war is lacking for the Zealots. But it is likely that the limited or "guerrilla" warfare waged from the time of Judas the Galilean to the outbreak of the revolt was seen as an early stage of holy war on the model of the raids of Jephthah and the initial campaigns of Mattathias the Maccabean patriarch.[11] The evidence also supports the contention that the Jewish war finally instigated by the Zealots was seen as the eschatological battle.[12] Finally, the Zealots allowed warfare on the sabbath, following the Maccabean precedent.[13]

In the model of resistance by revolution, holy war traditions function to stir up miliary action and to interpret its success. 1 and 2 Maccabees provide evidence, as we have seen, that this was the ideology of the successful Maccabean revolt. Later, this ideology seems to have been adopted by the Zealots. Since their revolt was unsuccessful, we have, as opposed to the positive accounts of the Maccabean revolt in 1 and 2 Maccabees, only the highly unsympathetic report of Josephus. But there are indications, as Farmer and Hengel have shown, that they claimed to be the heirs of the glorious holy war tradition. This model might be called "synergistic" in that both the Lord and the elect are thought to contribute to the victory.[14]

[8] W.R. Farmer, "Judas, Simon and Athronges," *NTS* 4 (1958) 147–55. On the distinction between militant anti-Roman movements in general, on the one hand, and the Zealots as a particular movement of this type, see Richard A. Horsley and John S. Hanson, *Bandits, Prophets, and Messiahs: Popular Movements in the Time of Jesus* (Minneapolis/Chicago/New York: Seabury/Winston, 1985) xiii–xvi, 190–243.

[9] W.R. Farmer, *Maccabees, Zealots, and Josephus* (New York: Columbia University Press, 1956) 177–78; Martin Hengel, *Die Zeloten* (AGJU 1; Leiden: Brill, 1961) 175–77; ET: *The Zealots: Investigations into the Jewish Freedom Movement in the Period from Herod I until 70 A.D.* (Edinburgh: T. & T. Clark, 1989) 171–77.

[10] Hengel, *Die Zeloten*, Chapter IV. "Der Eifer;" especially 154–56; *The Zealots*, Chapter IV. "Zeal," especially 149–54.

[11] Hengel, *Die Zeloten*, 288; *The Zealots*, 282.

[12] Hengel, *Die Zeloten*, 289–92; *The Zealots*, 283–87.

[13] Hengel, *Die Zeloten*, 294–95; *The Zealots*, 287–90.

[14] Miller, *Divine Warrior*, 156; Hengel, *Die Zeloten*, 127–32; *The Zealots*, 122–27.

Active but non-violent resistance

Within the model of active but non-violent resistance we can distinguish two types. One, represented by the book of Daniel, expresses
in literary and symbolic terms an interpretation of the situation of
conflict which involves a critical portrayal of the foreign overlord.
With regard to political action, the stance recommended is one of
endurance and waiting. A violent conflict leading to the destruction
of the oppressive power is expected. The imagery used is that of
holy war, but the elect will not participate in the final battle.[15] The
second type, illustrated by the *Assumption of Moses*, is like the first with
one important difference. The behavior of the elect vis-à-vis the
persecutors is the same, but a synergistic understanding of righteous
suffering is introduced. Both types involve a rejection of foreign rule
which is by definition either punishment for sin or an illegitimate
usurpation of the Lord's rule over his people. When such a regime
makes demands contrary to Jewish law and tradition it manifests its
illegitimacy. Resistance then focuses on refusal to cooperate with such
demands. This refusal is to be maintained even to the point of death.
The concept of martyrdom, later to play a significant role in both
Jewish and Christian contexts, arose from this type of response to
the Antiochan persecution.[16]

The classic example of this model is the book of Daniel. In the
tales, which probably antedate the crisis which led to the Maccabean
revolt, non-violent resistance is always followed by the rescue of the
individual(s) involved.[17] The part of the book which dates from the
persecution, however, presumes that some of the resisters will be killed
(11:33–35).

---

[15] The writings of the Qumran community are like the book of Daniel in that a
stance involving non-cooperation and critical interpretation, but not violence, is
advocated for the present (1QS 10:17–20), whereas a violent resolution is expected
which is described in holy war language (1QM). A notable difference between the
War Scroll and Daniel is that in the description of the eschatological battle in the
former the elect play an active role. Thus, the possibility is left open for violent
resistance at the appropriate time.

[16] Hengel, *Die Zeloten*, 262; *The Zealots*, 256. See also Norbert Brox, *Zeuge und Mär-
tyrer: Untersuchungen zur frühchristlichen Zeugnis-Terminologie* (SANT 5; München: Kösel-
Verlag, 1961) especially 132–73; J.W. van Henten, ed., *Die Entstehung der jüdischen
Martyrologie* (SPB 38; Leiden: Brill, 1989).

[17] On the date of the tales see W. Lee Humphreys, "A Life-style for Diaspora: A
Study of the Tales of Esther and Daniel," *JBL* 92 (1973) 218–19 and John J. Collins,
Daniel: A Commentary on the Book of Daniel (Hermeneia; Minneapolis: Fortress, 1993)
35–37. For non-violent resistance followed by rescue see, e.g., Dan 1:8–16, 3:13–27.

Readiness to die, however, is not peculiar to the non-violent option. It is obvious that the Maccabees and Zealots also willingly risked
their lives for the cause. It is likely that the deaths of many of the
Zealots were given atoning or eschatological significance by their
followers.[18] The distinctiveness of the non-violent model is the way
in which the holy war tradition is used. It is not the battles of Joshua
and David which are brought to mind as the paradigms for action
in the book of Daniel. Rather it is the ancient combat myth involving the struggle between the forces of creation and chaos which is
chosen to interpret the situation confronting the community.[19] There
is no new Joshua or David. The elect must wait for the creator-God
or his angelic agent to act. The only human actor in the cosmic
conflict is Antiochus who is assimilated to the forces of chaos. Since
the book of Daniel was written during the activity of Judas Macca-
beus, it is difficult to avoid the conclusion that the omission of the
active role of God's people in holy war is an expression of opposition to the Maccabean revolt. However one interprets the difficult
and vague statements in 11:34, the assertion made in 8:25 that
Antiochus will be broken *by no human hand* has a polemical ring to it,
given the historical context.[20] The role which ought to be adopted
includes "standing firm" (which involves keeping the covenant and
resisting pressure to do otherwise), "making many wise," suffering,
and "waiting" (11:32–35, 12:12).

In spite of the success of the Maccabean revolt in establishing Jewish
independence and the dominance of the Zealots in the first century
CE, non-violent resistance continued to be a live option. An incident
which should be assigned to this category is that in which students
of "national tradition," followers of two well-known rabbis, cut down
the golden eagle placed over the great gate of the temple by Herod
the Great. The resistance consisted in the refusal to tolerate an offense
against the current interpretation of the law. The resistance was open,
as is shown by the execution of the deed at midday; but non-violent,
as shown by the lack of any military action.[21] In addition to the

---

[18] Hengel, *Die Zeloten*, 265–77; *The Zealots*, 257–71.

[19] Aage Bentzen, *Daniel* (HAT 19; Tübingen: Mohr [Siebeck], 1952) 59; M. Delcor,
Le Livre de Daniel (SB; Paris, Gabalda, 1971) 144; Collins, *Daniel*, 280–94.

[20] See also 2:34, 45.

[21] Josephus *Bell.* 1.647–55; *Ant.* 17.149–63; Hengel, *Die Zeloten*, 264; *The Zealots*,
258–59; George Wesley Buchanan, *The Consequences of the Covenant* (NovTSup 20;
Leiden: Brill, 1970) 24.

incident regarding the eagle, Josephus relates two later incidents of bold non-violent resistance.[22]

The second type of non-violent resistance is represented by the *Assumption of Moses*, a rewriting of Deuteronomy 31–34 which dates to about 4 BCE–6 CE.[23] The review of history (in the form of prediction) given in chapters 2–6 culminates in a negative but rather vague description of the leaders at the dawning of the endtime (chapter 7). This is followed by a description of the eschatological woes (chapter 8) which take the form of a fierce persecution similar to that of Antiochus Epiphanes. The new element in this work is the description of the turning point from the final persecution to the manifestation of the kingdom of God. The voluntary deaths of Taxo and his seven sons, which they take upon themselves rather than transgress the commands of God (9:6), actually seem to bring about the appearance of the kingdom.[24] The commitment to non-violent resistance is here combined with the idea of synergism inherent in the Israelite concept and practice of holy war. The synergism of the *Assumption of Moses* 9 is based on the confidence that the voluntary death of a righteous person will be avenged: "our blood shall be avenged before the Lord" (9:7). The fulfillment of this expectation of vengeance is described in chapter 10 with language from the tradition of holy war. The angel (*nuntius*) appointed chief who will work vengeance (vs 2) is analogous to Michael in the *War Scroll*. In vss 3–7 the Lord is depicted as the Divine Warrior who does battle on behalf of his people.[25] In this type of non-violent resistance the suffering of the righteous is of central importance because it is the contribution which the elect can make toward the coming of the kingdom.

---

[22] *Bell.* 2.169–74; 2.195–98; *Ant.* 18.269–72.

[23] See George W.E. Nickelsburg, Jr., ed., *Studies on the Testament of Moses* (SBLSCS 4; Cambridge, MA: SBL, 1973); especially the introduction and the articles by Daniel J. Harrington, John J. Collins, George W.E. Nickelsburg, Jr., and David M. Rhoads.

[24] J. Licht, "Taxo, or the Apocalyptic Doctrine of Vengeance," *JJS* 12 (1961) 95–103.

[25] The expectation of divine vengeance against those who harm the people of God is also expressed in 2 Macc 7:36, 8:3. See also 4 Macc 6:28, 17:21–22. On the *nuntius* of *As. Mos.* 10:2 as warrior and analogue to Michael, see R.H. Charles, *The Assumption of Moses* (London: A. and C. Black, 1897) 38–39 and *APOT*, 2.421; George W.E. Nickelsburg, Jr., *Resurrection, Immortality and Eternal Life in Intertestamental Judaism* (HTS 26; Cambridge, MA: Harvard University Press, 1972) 28. The cosmic disturbances which accompany the appearance of the Heavenly One in 10:4–6 are motifs associated with the theophany of the Divine Warrior (see Cross, *Canaanite Myth*, 147–63).

Both types of non-violent resistance which we have examined expect an eschatological battle in which the Lord or his angelic representatives will defeat the adversaries of the elect. In one type of non-violent resistance (Daniel), the elect have no role in the battle and can do nothing to hasten its day. In the synergistic type (*Assumption of Moses*), the elect take no violent action, but they can take the initiative to bring on the Day of Wrath by sacrificing their lives and thus arousing the action of the deity to avenge them.

II.   RESISTANCE IN THE REVELATION TO JOHN

Prolegomena

A few words must be said about the literary character and date of the Revelation to John. The overall consistency of style alongside particular aporias of style and content is best explained by some form of the hypothesis proposed by Wilhelm Bousset.[26] The book in its present form is the composition of a single author who made use of some sources of limited scope as well as apocalyptic tradition in oral form.[27] It may not be possible to reconstruct all the sources, but there are indications of their use.

There is no unambiguous internal evidence for the date of the composition of the Revelation to John. Most scholars now accept the traditional dating first attested by Irenaeus, which assigns the work to the latter part of Domitian's reign (90–96 CE).[28] It is reasonable

---

[26] Bousset proposed his solution as a form of the "fragment hypothesis" (*Offenbarung*, 152–54). R.H. Charles also adopted a version of this hypothesis, but added the theory that since the author died when he had completed chapters 1–20:3, a redactor was responsible for the present ending and numerous minor alterations (*A Critical and Exegetical Commentary on the Revelation of St. John* [ICC; 2 vols.; New York: Scribner's Sons, 1920] 1. lxii). André Feuillet espoused a similar view in his review of the literature (*L'Apocalypse. Etat de la question* [Studia Neotestamentica Subsidia 3; Paris: Desclée, 1963] 27); he also allowed for subsequent redactions (26, 29). Heinrich Kraft returned to the *Überarbeitungshypothese*, i.e., the theory that there was originally a basic document (*Grundschrift*) which was expanded to its present form in a series of redactions (idem, *Die Offenbarung des Johannes* [HNT 16a; Tübingen: Mohr (Siebeck), 1974] 11–12); cf. Bousset, *Offenbarung*, 151–52.
[27] On the use of sources in Revelation 11 and 12, see Adela Yarbro Collins, *The Combat Myth in the Book of Revelation*, (HDR 9; Missoula, MT: Scholars Press, 1976) 166–70, 101–16. The understanding of the structure of the book of Revelation argued in the first chapter of that work is presupposed here.
[28] Irenaeus's comment on the date of Revelation is in *Adv. haer.* 5.30.3; see the

to accept this date since Irenaeus does not seem to have a vested interest in promulgating it and there is no compelling internal evidence for another date.[29] Lyder Brun's study of Revelation 17 demonstrated the likelihood that even this chapter was composed during Domitian's reign.[30]

Holy war and non-violent in the revelation to John

The mythic pattern of combat is used in Revelation to depict the religio-political conflict in which the author's community was involved as a dualistic cosmic struggle.[31] Such a depiction could be combined with a variety of programs for action. Given a situation of alienation from the contemporary ruling power, the book's particular use of holy war tradition would inevitably advocate or reinforce a position on the issue of resistance and violence to be adopted by its first readers.[32] That position may be defined first of all in terms of the two models illustrated above.

The first point to be made is that the holy war imagery is used in such a way as to encourage an acceptance of suffering in the eschatological conflict. In the paradigmatic narrative of chapter 12, the child and the woman are rescued from the attacks of the adversary. The story interprets the situation of the audience as part of a cosmic conflict and awakens trust in the power of heaven to protect and rescue. In chapter 13 images from Daniel 7 and 8 are adapted to depict the Roman empire as the beast of resurgent chaos rebelling

discussion in Adela Yarbro Collins, *Crisis and Catharsis: The Power of the Apocalypse* (Philadelphia: Westminster, 1984) 54–83.

[29] Barclay Newman disputed the theory that there was a significant persecution of Christians during the reign of Domitian; he did not, however, question the reliability of Irenaeus' dating of Revelation ("The Fallacy of the Domitian Hypothesis," *NTS* 10 [1963] 133–39).

[30] Lyder Brun, "Die römischen Kaiser in der Apokalypse," *ZNW* 26 (1927) 128–51. A Strobel revived the theory, but with less compelling arguments ("Abfassung und Geschichtstheologie der Apokalypse nach Kap. XVII.9–12," *NTS* 10 [1964] 433–45). B. Reicke also argued that Revelation 17 was composed under Domitian, but his theory regarding the identities of the other kings in vss 9–10 is rather arbitrary ("Die jüdische Apokalyptik und die johanneische Tiervision," *RSR* 60 [1972] 175–81).

[31] See Yarbro Collins, *Combat Myth*, 130–45; 157–90; 231–34.

[32] The "first readers" of the Revelation to John refers to the Christian communities for whom the book in its present form was intended; i.e., Christians of Asia Minor in the last decade of the first century CE.

against God.[33] That rebellion includes hostile actions toward the saints
(vs 7).[34] Vss 9–10 break out of the vision form with an allusion to Jer
15:2, which is framed by two direct addresses to the readers: "If
anyone has ears, let him hear" (vs 9) and "This is the endurance
and the faith of the saints" (vs 10c). The former is a formula used repeatedly in the messages to the seven churches and would thus be a
signal for a direct, hortatory address to the readers. The saying framed
by these hortatory comments has a complex textual history and its
translation is debated. There is consensus that vs 10a should be translated: "If any one is to be taken captive, to captivity he goes." The
major possibilities for the translation of vs 10b are: "if any one slays
with the sword, with the sword he must be slain" and "if any one is
to be slain by the sword, with the sword he is to be slain." The first
of these translations takes the assimilation of the Jeremiah-allusion to
Matt 26:52 to be original. If such is the case, then Rev 13:10 is an
explicit rejection of the militant option. In either case it is clear that
the elect are given a non-violent role in the eschatological conflict.[35]

No major role is taken by the elect in the final stage of the eschatological conflict; rather the adversaries are defeated by the risen
Christ and other heavenly beings. In 19:11–16 Christ appears with
the heavenly armies, angelic hosts presumably, to defeat the beast
and his allies. In 20:1–3 Satan is bound by an angel, and in 20:7–
10 the last resurgence of chaos—the attack of Gog and Magog—is
crushed by fire from heaven.

Rev 17:14 hints that the followers of the Lamb might have an
active role in the eschatological battle. In a context referring to the
battle between the beast and the Lamb, it is said "and those with
him [the Lamb] are called and chosen and faithful" (καὶ οἱ μετ᾽ αὐτοῦ
κλητοὶ καὶ ἐκλεκτοὶ καὶ πιστοί). This is the only time that κλητός and
ἐκλεκτός are used in the book. Πιστός is used elsewhere: three times
of Christ himself; twice of "the words [of this book, as a whole or in
part]," and twice of members of the community in a context of death
for the faith.[36] It is unlikely then that "those with him" in this pas-

---

[33] See n. 19 above and Yarbro Collins, *Combat Myth*, 161–74.

[34] Some MSS omit this statement, but the omission is probably due to haplography.
Cf. Bruce M. Metzger et al., *A Textual Commentary on the Greek New Testament* (London: United Bible Societies, 1971) 749.

[35] See the discussion by Charles, *Revelation*, 1. 355–57; and Metzger, *A Textual
Commentary*, 749–50.

[36] Rev 1:5, 3:14, 19:11 (of Christ); 21:5, 22:6 (of "these words"); 2:10 and 13 (of
Christians).

sage refers to angels. Rather, the reference is to the human followers of Jesus. The relevant question then is whether the Christians are mentioned as participants in the victory of the Lamb only, or in his battle as well.[37] "Those with [the Lamb]" in 17:14 calls to mind the 144,000 of 14:1–5 who are said to follow the Lamb wherever he goes (vs 5). The armies of heaven in 19:14 are also said to follow [the Word of God]. If the 144,000 are thought of as fighting along-side the angels in the final battle, the purity regulations relating to holy war would explain the otherwise rather isolated comment in 14:1—that they have not defiled themselves with women.[38] These two passages (17:14, 14:4) seem to show that the author was aware of the tradition that the elect would fight in the last battle. But they are just glimpses of such an idea and are not at all emphasized. The dominant conception of the final holy war is similar to that of Daniel, where the people will participate in the new order brought about by the eschatological battle but not in the battle itself.

Martyrdom in the Revelation to John

The terminological question regarding the process in which μάρτυς comes to mean "blood witness," that is, someone who has died for the faith, is not relevant to this study.[39] The point of interest here is the idea of a voluntary death in the context of persecution. The

---

[37] William Klassen asserts that the RSV has avoided the question by supplying the verb "are" rather than "they will conquer." It would be more accurate to say that the ambiguity lies with the author himself. The last verb used before this clause is "is" (ἐστίν); if the author had intended to be more specific about the role of the Christians he would presumably have used the appropriate verb (cf. Klassen, "Venge-ance in the Apocalypse of John," *CBQ* 27 [1966] 306).

[38] On the regulations at Qumran for ritual purity in connection with holy war, see Frank M. Cross, *The Ancient Library of Qumran and Modern Biblical Studies* (rev. ed.; Anchor Books; Garden City, NY: Doubleday, 1961) 98–99. Akira Satake, who in-terprets παρθένοι in 14:4 allegorically, mentions the context of holy war as one possible explanation for the use of this language (*Die Gemeindeordnung in der Johannesapokalypse* [WMANT 21; Neukirchen-Vluyn: Neukirchener Verlag, 1966] 45); Ernst Lohmeyer also refers to holy war tradition on this point (*Offenbarung*, 120). For a more detailed discussion of this comment, see Adela Yarbro Collins, *The Gospel and Women: The 1987 Fred O. Francis Memorial Lectures in Religion* (Orange, CA: Chapman College, 1988) 23–30; eadem, "Women's History and the Book of Revelation," in Kent H. Richards, ed., *Society of Biblical Literature 1987 Seminar Papers* (Atlanta: Scholars Press, 1987) 80–91.

[39] On the terminological issue see A.A. Trites, "Martyrs and Martyrdom in the Apocalypse: A Semantic Study," *NovT* 15 (1973) 72–80; the literature cited by Hengel,

terms "martyr" and "martyrdom," as shorthand expressions of this concept, will be used wherever the idea is present, regardless of the specific terminology in which the idea is expressed.

In the seven messages there is a repeated emphasis on the virtue of endurance or steadfastness (ὑπομονή).[40] In most cases the reference is not to a general characteristic of the life of faith, but to the stance to be taken in the context of persecution which is seen as the tribulation (θλῖψις) of the endtime. This theme is already enunciated in 1:9 where ὑπομονή is linked with θλῖψις.[41] The Ephesians are praised for their endurance which·is exemplified in their bearing up "on account of my name" (2:3). The latter phrase is an indication of persecution of some sort. In 2:10 and 13 various attitudes of steadfastness are praised or recommended in an explicit context of persecution: "Do not fear," "be faithful unto death," "you hold fast my name," "you did not deny my faith." Similar exhortation is given in 2:19, 25; 3:8, 10–11.

The only reference to a martyrdom which has actually taken place (2:13) is rather incidental to its context. The question then arises whether martyrdom in Revelation is a secondary matter, or, on the contrary, has a central function as in the *Assumption of Moses*. The following discussion is intended to show that the deaths of the elect mentioned in the body of the work (chapters 4–22) have a significance similar to that of Taxo and his sons in *Assumption of Moses* 9.

The first such reference is the vision of the souls under the altar which follows the opening of the fifth seal (Rev 6:9–11). They address the holy and true ruler (δεσπότης) saying, "How long until you will pass judgment (κρίνεις) and avenge (ἐκδικεῖς) our blood upon those who dwell upon the earth?" The association of the souls with the heavenly altar seems to imply that their deaths are conceived of as sacrifices offered to God. Such an idea seems to have been rather

---

Die Zeloten, 261–62, nn. 2–3; *The Zealots*, 256, nn. 130–131; Brox, *Zeuge und Märtyrer*. See also Satake, *Die Gemeindeordnung*, 97–119; Hans von Campenhausen, *Die Idee des Martyriums in der alten Kirche* (2nd ed.; Göttingen: Vandenhoeck und Ruprecht, 1964) 20–55; T.W. Manson, "Martyrs and Martyrdom," *BJRL* 39 (1957) 463–84; Eduard Lohse, *Märtyrer und Gottesknecht* (FRLANT 64; Göttingen: Vandenhoeck und Ruprecht, 1955) 203–13; Karl Holl, "Der ursprüngliche Sinn des Namens Märtyrer," and "Die Vorstellung vom Märtyrer und die Märtyrerakte in ihrer geschichtlichen Entwicklung," and *"Pseudomartys," Gesammelte Aufsätze zur Kirchengeschichte*, vol. 2, *Der Osten* (Tübingen: Mohr [Siebeck], 1928) 103–9; 68–102; 110–114.
[40] F. Hauck, "ὑπομένω, ὑπομονή," *TDNT* 4 (1967) 588.
[41] H. Schlier, "θλίβω, θλῖψις," *TDNT* 3 (1965) 143–48.

widespread.[42] The expectation that God would avenge innocent blood is attested elsewhere, as is the idea of a fixed number of souls which must go to their rest before the end could come.[43] What is distinctive about this passage is the combination of these elements, particularly the latter two. The result is the idea that there is a fixed number of martyrs who must meet their deaths before the end can arrive, and that the eschatological catastrophe is seen primarily as vengeance on the adversaries of the martyrs. From this point of view then, the role of the elect is not only to wait and endure; rather, there is the possibility of a kind of synergism. Each martyr's death brings the eschaton closer.

The cry of the martyrs (fifth seal) is immediately followed by a proleptic description of the final battle against the kings of the earth (sixth seal), which, as a theophany of the divine warriors, is accompanied by cosmic disturbances. This sequence suggests that, for the author of Revelation, the eschatological battle is to be an act of divine vengeance for the blood of the martyrs. This impression is confirmed in the second portion of the body of the work, chapters 12–22:5, where divine vengeance is described in more detail than in the first portion. Vengeance for the martyrs is not the only reason for the plagues on the earth and its dwellers, but it is a significant factor to which reference is repeatedly made.[44]

In the vision of the seven bowls in chapter 16, we find a heavenly commentary following the third bowl which is poured into the rivers and fountains of water and turns them into blood. This act of eschatological judgment calls to mind, on one level, the plague against Egypt when Moses turned the Nile to blood. Many of the plagues associated with the trumpets and bowls allude to the plagues on the

---

[42] Charles, *Revelation*, 1. 172–74; for another opinion see Lohse, *Märtyrer und Gottesknecht*, 196–97.

[43] On the prayer for or expectation of vengeance for the blood of the righteous, see 2 Macc 7:36; 8:3; *As. Mos.* 9:6–7; *1 Enoch* 47:2, 4; for further references, see Charles, *Revelation*, 1. 176. On the fixed number of souls, see *4 Ezra* 4:35–37, 41–43; *2 Bar.* 23:5 (cf. 30:2). Like Rev 6:9–11, *1 Enoch* 47:1–4 combines the two ideas. For similar conceptions of an eschatological measure, see Lohse, *Märtyrer und Gottesknecht*, 197, n. 9.

[44] I cannot agree with Klassen that "throughout the various developments [in the rest of Revelation after 6:9–11] the purpose is always to bring men to repentance through the tragedies of history (Ap 9, 20–21)" ("Vengeance," 304). 9:20–21 seems rather to illustrate the conviction that the lines have been drawn; the elect are to hold fast what they already have (2:25), and the wicked will continue to do wickedly (22:11). The only passage allowing for the repentance of some outsiders is 11:13, which probably refers to the Jews; cf. Charles, *Revelation*, 1. 292.

Egyptians which preceded the Exodus.[45] The typological function of
these allusions is clear: as divine judgment against the oppressors of
the people preceded the first deliverance and time of salvation, so
will it be at the end. But the particular point which the author wishes
to make with the image is expressed in the heavenly commentary
which follows:

> And I heard the angel of the waters saying, "You are just, you who
> are and who was, the holy one, because you decreed (ἔκρινας) these
> things; because they shed the blood of holy ones and prophets and you
> gave them blood to drink. It is their due." And I heard the altar say-
> ing, "Yes, Lord, God the Pantocrator, true and just are your judg-
> ments." (16:5–7)[46]

The acclamation of the angel of the waters indicates that at least this
aspect of the cosmic destruction is understood as divine vengeance
for the blood of the martyrs. The second acclamation is spoken by
the altar which calls to mind the vision of the souls under the altar
in 6:9–11. The third bowl is thus indirectly linked to the fifth seal as
the response to the cry for vengeance.

The next section of the book (17:1–19:10) focuses on the destruction of "Babylon." This section climaxes in the heavenly liturgy of
19:1–8, which begins with a judgment doxology (vss 1–2). There the
destruction is explicitly interpreted as an act of divine vengeance for
the persecution of the martyrs. Several other passages allude to this
theme earlier in the section (17:6; 18:20, 24).

The climax of the martyr theme comes in 20:4–6, the description
of the thousand-year messianic kingdom.

> And I saw thrones, and they sat upon them, and judgment was given
> to them, and [I saw] the souls of those who had been beheaded (τῶν
> πεπελεκισμένων) on account of the witness of Jesus and the word of
> God, and who [or whoever] (οἵτινες) did not worship the beast nor his
> image and did not receive the mark on the forehead and on the hand.
> They came to life (ἔζησαν) and reigned with Christ a thousand years.
> (20:4)

The text is ambiguous on the issue of participation in this messianic
reign. If οἵτινες retains its classical sense, it would refer to a wider

---

[45] Charles, *Revelation*, 1. 233–34; 242; 2. 43, 45, 53.

[46] On this passage see H.D. Betz, "On the Problem of the Religio-Historical
Understanding of Apocalypticism," *JTC* 6 (1969) 139 and Adela Yarbro Collins,
"The History-of-Religions Approach to Apocalypticism and the 'Angel of the Wa-
ters' (Apoc 16; 4–7)," *CBQ* 39 (1977) 367–81.

circle than the martyrs referred to in the τῶν πεπελεκισμένων clause. Thus participation would seem to be open to all faithful Christians.[47] But οἵτινες in NT Greek most often functions just like the ordinary relative, so the οἵτινες clause may be a further qualification of "the souls of those who had been beheaded."[48] Thus participation would be limited to the martyrs.[49] The argument that the οἵτινες clause refers at least in part to Christians still living is weak because it necessitates reading ἔζησαν in two different senses simultaneously.[50] Furthermore, the reference to the "rest of the dead" in vs 5 implies that those mentioned just previously were also dead in the usual sense.[51] Although it is not clear whether the thousand-year reign was limited to the martyrs, at least it is clear that they are singled out for special emphasis. The first resurrection and the exercise of kingly power with Christ are blessings by which those who share the fate of Jesus with regard to his death are also enabled to share in his glorious destiny.

R.H. Charles went beyond the evidence when he claimed that the body of Revelation (chapters 4–22) implied that all the followers of Jesus would be martyred.[52] But it is the case, as shown above, that martyrdom is singled out as a deed which helps to bring about the end and thus the kingdom, and is especially rewarded.

We began by raising the question about what stance Revelation advocates over against the contemporary ruling power. That question has been answered on one level, that is, what *action* is to be taken. The readers are not to take up arms in violent resistance, not even in the final battle. Rather they are to endure persecution including death and to hope for ultimate salvation (chapter 12; 2:10;

---

[47] So I.H. Marshall, "Martyrdom and Parousia in the Revelation of John," *Studia Evangelica* 4, ed. F.L. Cross (TU 102; Berlin: Akademie, 1968) 332; E.S. Fiorenza, *Priester für Gott* (Münster: Aschendorff, 1972) 305–6; D.C. Smith, "The Millenial Reign of Jesus Christ. Some Observations on Rev 20:1–10," *Restoration Quarterly* 16 (1973) 219–30.

[48] Charles, *Revelation*, 1. cxxii; 2. 183; F. Blass and A. Debrunner, *A Greek Grammar of the New Testament and Other Early Christian Literature* (ed. Robert W. Funk; Chicago: The University of Chicago Press, 1961) § 293.

[49] See Charles, *Revelation*, 2. 183; Satake, *Die Gemeindeordnung*, 100–1.

[50] So Satake (ibid.) against Bousset (*Offenbarung*, 502) and Mathias Rissi (*Zeit und Geschichte in der Offenbarung des Johannes* [AThANT 22; Zürich: Zwingli, 1952] 155); Rissi is not fully clear on whether he considers the second group (καὶ οἵτινες) to be Christians still living at the time of the parousia or Christians who have died but not as martyrs. The same unclarity persists in the second edition of the work cited (*Was ist und was geschehen soll danach* [AThANT 46; Zürich: Zwingli, 1965] 120).

[51] Charles, *Revelation*, 2. 183.

[52] See the critique of Charles by Marshall, "Martyrdom and Parousia."

13:10). A certain synergism is possible according to Rev 6:9–11. The death of each martyr brings the eschaton nearer.

But we have not yet fully understood a "stance" when we take note of which actions are rejected and which are advocated. Non-violent resistance and a high regard for martyrdom might be combined with a variety of total worldviews. Given a situation of persecution, a variety of responses is possible. One might decide to write an apology for the Christian faith rather than an apocalypse. The fact that the author chose to write an apocalypse and one which involves such a thorough-going attack on the authority of Rome is an indication that he shared the fundamental theological principle of the Zealots: that the kingdom of God is incompatible with the kingdom of Caesar.

III. THE REVELATION TO JOHN AND THE ZEALOTS

That the radical critique of the Roman state in Revelation shares a fundamental theological principle with the Zealots is supported by Rev 13:16–17 which reflects another principle advocated by the Zealots.

> And he causes all (καὶ ποιεῖ πάντας), the small and the great, and the rich and the poor, and the free and the slave, to be marked (ἵνα δῶσιν αὐτοῖς χάραγμα) on the right hand or on the forehead, and [he brings it about] that (καὶ ἵνα) no one is able to buy or sell unless he has the mark, the name of the beast or the number of his name. (13:16–17)

Marking those loyal to the beast is, as often noted, a parody of the sealing of the elect in 7:1–8. The seal (σφραγίς) of the living God (7:2) is a guarantee of protection from the natural and demonic plagues of the endtime (7:3, 3:10, 9:4), while the mark (χάραγμα) of the beast marks its bearers for such plagues (16:2) and for eternal punishment (14:9–11). This is clearly eschatological imagery influenced by Ezekiel 9 and possibly by *Ps. Sol.* 15:9–10. But it is also apparent that in painting this eschatological image, the author of Revelation made use of certain elements which had contemporary cultural associations and thus enhanced the effect of the image. The choice of the term χάραγμα, for example, is significant since it was the technical term for the imperial stamp.[53] The eschatological idea of sealing was

---

[53] Adolf Deissmann, *Light from the Ancient East* (New York: Harper, [1927]) 341 and fig. 62.

traditionally thought of as a mark on the forehead.[54] The addition in our text of a reference to the right hand may be a parodying allusion to the Jewish practice of wearing phylacteries on the head and left hand.[55] This nuance would fit the general theme of the book whereby the beast and his followers parody the Lamb and his followers, since the author and first readers of Revelation apparently claimed the title "Jews" ('Ιουδαῖοι), and followed Jewish practice on at least some points.[56]

Vs 16 thus contains two probable allusions to the current historical situation. It is a matter of debate whether vs 17 also contains a contemporary reference. Bousset argued that Rev 13:17 reflects a widespread mythic motif about the signs of the antichrist, according to which only those sealed by the antichrist are allowed to buy (and sell).[57] The use of a traditional mythic or eschatological motif is not incompatible with allusion to the contemporary historical situation, as was noted above in the discussion of vs 16. Thus, even if vs 17 does reflect a mythic motif, we should still ask how the image may have been shaped by the situation of the author.

It is unlikely that the inability to buy or sell refers to "a ruthless economic warfare" waged by the state against the elect.[58] As Caird points out, our author was probably aware that Roman hostility to non-Roman religious practice did not normally take the form of economic sanctions.[59] It seems rather that the juxtaposition of buying and selling with the mark of the beast refers to the fact that Roman coins normally bore the image and name of the current emperor. The inability to buy and sell would then be the result of the refusal to use Roman coins. Such a refusal is analogous to the Zealot refusal to carry, look at, or manufacture coins bearing any sort of image.[60] The explicit reason given is a strict interpretation of the law against images.

---

[54] Cf. Ezek 9:4; *Ps. Sol.* 15:10.
[55] Charles, *Revelation*, 1. 362. The inversion from the left to the right hand is presumably part of the parody.
[56] On the title "Jews," see Rev 2:9, 3:9; on Jewish practice, cf. Rev 2:14, 20 with Acts 15:29.
[57] Wilhelm Bousset, *Der Antichrist* (Göttingen: Vandenhoeck und Ruprecht, 1895) 132–33.
[58] So Charles, *Revelation*, 1. 363.
[59] G.B. Caird, *A Commentary on the Revelation of St. John the Divine* (New York: Harper, 1966) 173.
[60] Hengel, *Die Zeloten*, 195–201; *The Zealots*, 190–96. Various exegetes have sug-

214214 CHAPTER SIX

Another aspect of the Zealot program was the refusal to pay taxes to Rome.[61] The question put to Jesus in Mark 12:13–17 and parallels—"Is it lawful (ἔξεστιν) to pay taxes to Caesar, or not?"—reflects the debate instigated by the Zealots who argued that such payment was equivalent to apostasy.[62] Jesus' response implies that whoever participates in the Roman economic system by using Roman coins is bound to pay the tax; it is Caesar's due. Those who accepted Rome as the political authority ordained by God would thus read the story as a legitimation of limited cooperation with Rome and of the practice of paying taxes. The story and the saying of Jesus with which it culminates could be read quite differently, however, by those who saw Rome as a rebellious and blasphemous power analogous to the reign of Antiochus Epiphanes. In such a context the images and inscriptions of Roman coins would be idolatrous and thus contact with them was to be avoided. The relevant saying of Jesus would then have been read dualistically and as a mandate for separatism and possibly even economic boycott.[63]

IV. MARTYRDOM AND POLITICAL CRITIQUE

The high regard for martyrdom in Revelation might appear rather incompatible with the book's thoroughgoing denunciation of the contemporary political order. The political critique would seem to

---

gested that the χάραγμα in vs 17 should be understood as a reference to Roman coins; Bousset (*Offenbarung*, 427–28) cites earlier exegetes who made this suggestion. Bousset himself rejects this interpretation, though he has no other to suggest. More recent commentators who interpret the "mark" in vs 17 as a reference to coins include Ethelbert Stauffer (*Christ and the Caesars* [Philadelphia: Westminster, 1955] 126, 179); Caird, (*Revelation*, 173); Kraft (*Offenbarung*, 182–83). To my knowledge, however, no commentator has linked this apparent allusion to Roman coins with Zealot theology and practice.

[61] Hengel, *Die Zeloten*, 132–45; *The Zealots*, 134–40; S.G.F. Brandon, *Jesus and the Zealots* (New York: Scribner's Sons, 1967) 32–33; idem, *The Trial of Jesus of Nazareth* (New York: Stein and Day, 1968) 28–30, 33.

[62] Brandon, *Jesus and the Zealots*, 345–47.

[63] According to Oscar Cullmann, Jesus' response was intentionally ambiguous (*Jesus and the Revolutionaries* [New York: Harper, 1970] 45). Hengel links the tribute pericope with the Zealots' refusal to use coins with images; for the Zealot who did not use Roman coins, Jesus' saying would not imply an obligation to pay the tax (*Die Zeloten*, 198–200; *The Zealots*, 194–95; cf. also idem, *Was Jesus a Revolutionist?* [FBBS 28; Philadephia: Fortress, 1971] 33). Brandon argued that a Zealot would have approved Jesus' saying, since from the former's point of view, the Jewish people and land belonged to God, not to Caesar (*Jesus and the Zealots*, 347).

manifest a communal religiosity, while martyrdom emphasizes the individual. There are a number of points at which the theology of martyrdom relates primarily to the individual. It has been noted that the desire for vengeance on enemies and for a special reward are important elements of the idea of martyrdom in Revelation. Such natural human desires are not particularly admirable in themselves. But in the overall context they do serve the worthy purpose of making allegiance to transcendent values psychologically possible in difficult circumstances.

A further factor in the importance of martyrdom in Revelation is certainly the example of Christ. In the opening vision in which the seer is commissioned, Christ says, ". . . I am . . . the living one; I died, and behold I am alive for evermore, and I have the keys of Death and Hades" (1:17–18). This statement is repeated in briefer form in 2:8 in the introduction to the message to the church in Smyrna, who are being exhorted to "be faithful unto death" (2:10). The model of Christ who suffered, died and rose from the dead makes suffering and death tolerable, gives them value, and allows hope which transcends death.[64] The assimilation of the martyrs to Jesus is most clear in 12:11 and 20:4–6.

Martyrdom in Revelation, however, is not simply a matter of individual salvation. H. von Campenhausen's remark that the fate of the individual martyr must be seen as part of a supra-individual, eschatological process[65] is valid for this work. As noted above, the deaths of the martyrs bring the end nearer. The eschatological process for Revelation involves destruction of the earth, torture and destruction of the dwellers on earth, and suffering and death for the martyrs. These various manifestations of the wrath of God which amount to the destruction of creation are seen as necessary by the author because of his perception of the cosmos as pervasively corrupted.

---

[64] Compare the suggestion of John J. Collins that the primary function of the apocalyptic type of eschatological language is to transcend death ("Apocalyptic Eschatology as the Transcendence of Death," *CBQ* 36 [1974] 21–43).

[65] H. von Campenhausen, *Die Idee des Martyriums*, 106. Donald W. Riddle argued that there is a new element in Revelation compared to Jewish apocalypticism, i.e., a more direct appeal to individual readers. He saw this as part of a shift in early Christianity from the genre apocalypse to martyrology, due to the change in audience or environment (Jewish communal interest to Greek individualism). See his "From Apocalypse to Martyrology" *ATR* 9 (1927) 260–80, especially 274–75 and idem, *The Martyrs. A Study in Social Control* (Chicago: University of Chicago Press, 1931) 164–70; a discussion of this hypothesis is unfortunately beyond the scope of this chapter.

H.D. Betz has pointed to texts which illustrate the widespread perception in the ancient world that the unrighteous behavior of humanity has corrupted the elements.[66] The seven trumpets and the
seven bowls may be seen from this perspective as a process of purg-
ing by destruction in preparation for a new creation. A similar attitude is expressed in 2 Peter where the destruction by fire of the
present heavens and earth is linked to the judgment of ungodly men
(3:7) and the new heavens and earth are associated with righteousness (3:13). The understanding that the present order is corrupted is
expressed most clearly in Rev 19:2—"[God] judged the great harlot
who corrupted the earth with her fornication. . . ." Here we have the
solidarity of the natural and social realms expressed; the earth is
corrupt because of the reprehensible character of the social order as
determined by Rome.[67]

If we look once again at 14:1–5 from this perspective the role of
the martyrs can be further clarified. The fact that this group is called
the 144,000 and the first fruits indicates that they are to be understood as those who have died as a result of their faith. The "144,000"
refers back to 7:1–17 and the "first fruits" forward to 20:4–6 (the
first resurrection). The way that this group is described in vss 4–5
especially indicates that they are conceived of as a special group, set
apart. They represent purity over against the defiled earth: "they are
spotless" (ἄμωμοί εἰσιν). This purity is expressed in speech ("and in
their mouth no lie was found"), by celibacy ("for they are virgins"—
παρθένοι) and finally by death. Death has a purifying significance for
themselves (7:14) and, as part of the eschatological process, contrib-
utes to the coming of the new creation.

SUMMARY

Given a situation of persecution or alienation from the ruling power,
Jewish tradition of the late Hellenistic and early Roman periods
developed two basic models for resistance. One was violent revolution; the other, non-violent resistance. In the revolutionary model,
holy war traditions are revived and function to stir up revolt or to

---

[66] Betz, "On the Problem of the Religio-Historical Understanding of Apocalypticism," 143–53.
[67] See also Rev 17:2, 5; 18:3, 9, 23.

interpret its success. Two types of non-violent resistance can be distinguished. In one type, holy war traditions function as the mythic context in which the current conflict is understood and as the expression of certainty regarding the victory of the elect. The elect, however, take no initiative either in the present or in the expected violent resolution of the conflict. They wait in hope of sharing in the blessings which will follow the victory. In the second type, some of the elect act synergistically with the divine power, because the deaths suffered by members of the community are thought to play a role in bringing about the turning point, the eschatological battle.

The Revelation to John makes use of holy war traditions to interpret the situation of its first readers. In doing so it advocates non-violent resistance of the second type. The faithful are to suffer persecution and death in the present. They expect a violent resolution of the conflict in which heavenly forces will defeat their adversaries. Their contribution to this outcome may be made in the form of a martyr's death, which hastens the end, because a fixed number of martyrs must die before the eschatological battle can be initiated. The value of the martyr's death is greatly enhanced by the example of Christ.

Thus martyrdom in Revelation is part of the eschatological process. The view of this process expressed in Revelation has several elements in common with the theological views of the Zealots. The major difference between the two is, of course, the attitude toward violent resistance. But they share the idea that some synergism is possible for the faithful and a willingness to die for the cause. They also share a fundamental critique of the rule of Rome as incompatible with the rule of God and the rejection of images as a form of protest against Roman rule.

CHAPTER SEVEN

THE ORIGIN OF CHRISTIAN BAPTISM

The aim of this chapter is to reflect on the origin of the Christian practice of baptism in the context of Jewish tradition and ritual. By "ritual" I mean a culturally patterned activity intended to create interaction between human and divine beings and performed in accordance with a perception of the divine will.[1] Rather than limiting the discussion to the NT, I shall draw upon Jewish, extracanonical Christian and other texts that illuminate the early Christian ritual of baptism, its origin and significance.

I. THE BAPTISM OF JOHN

Since the late nineteenth century, students of the NT have recognized that the history of early Christianity begins in an important sense with John the Baptist.[2] However much Jesus may have differed from John in lifestyle and teaching, the fact that he was baptized by John suggests that the Jesus-movement had its roots in the activity of John. All four Gospels begin the account of Jesus' public life with his baptism; the point is most vividly dramatized in Mark and is made explicit in Acts 1:21–22: the one to replace Judas among the Twelve had to be one who had been with them "beginning from the baptism of John until the day when [Jesus] was taken up from us."[3] I would suggest that Christian baptism also had its origin in the baptism performed by John.

In order to understand the origins of Christian baptism, therefore, it is important to understand the nature of the baptism performed by John. The primary sources for the reconstruction of the historical John the Baptist are the Synoptic Sayings Source (Q) that is recov-

---

[1] See the brief theoretical discussion of religion and ritual in Wayne Meeks, *The First Urban Christians: The Social World of the Apostle Paul* (New Haven, CT: Yale University Press, 1983) 140–42.

[2] See, for example, Hendrikus Boers, *Who Was Jesus? The Historical Jesus and the Synoptic Gospels* (San Francisco: Harper & Row, 1989).

[3] Translations of passages from the NT are taken from the RSV.

erable through a comparison of the Gospels of Matthew and Luke, the four canonical Gospels (Mark, Matthew, Luke, and John), the book of the Acts of the Apostles, and Josephus.[4] Josephus discusses John the Baptist in book 18 of the *Antiquities of the Jews*. The most important part of the account is as follows:

> ... he was a good man and had exhorted the Jews to lead righteous lives, to practise justice towards their fellows and piety towards God, and so doing to join in baptism. In his view this was a necessary preliminary if baptism was to be acceptable to God. They must not employ it to gain pardon for whatever sins they committed, but as a consecration of the body implying that the soul was already thoroughly cleansed by right behaviour. When others too joined the crowds about him, because they were aroused to the highest degree by his sermons, Herod became alarmed. Eloquence that had so great an effect on mankind might lead to some form of sedition, for it looked as if they would be guided by John in everything that they did. Herod decided therefore that it would be much better to strike first and be rid of him before his work led to an uprising, than to wait for an upheaval, get involved in a difficult situation and see his mistake.[5]

This passage is authentic, since it displays no Christian tendencies and coheres with Josephus's usual content and style. Its reliability is qualified by Josephus's well known biases, namely, that he consistently avoided any mention of Jewish eschatology and that he attempted to present Jewish ideas and practices in as clear and rational a manner as possible and in Greco-Roman terms, often philosophical terms. The first bias is clearly at work here. In stark contrast to the Christian texts, Josephus makes no mention of John's orientation to the future.[6] The reasons given for Herod's execution of John may

---

[4] Other, less reliable, sources are Justin Martyr, the *Protevangelium of James* (2nd century CE) and other infancy gospels dependent on it, Tertullian, Hippolytus, Origen, the *Gospel of the Ebionites* (whose tradition may go back to the 2nd century) as cited by Epiphanius (4th century), the *Gospel of Nicodemus* or *Acts of Pilate* (4th or early 5th century), the *Clementine Homilies* and *Recognitions* (3rd century), the Mandaean literature (8th century), and the Slavonic manuscripts of Josephus' *Jewish War* (15–16th century). On the Christian apocryphal works, see Wilhelm Schneemelcher, ed., *New Testament Apocrypha* (2 vols.; rev. ed.; Cambridge, UK: James Clarke; Louisville, KY: Westminster/John Knox, 1991 and 1992); on the Mandaean literature see Charles Scobie, *John the Baptist* (Philadelphia: Fortress, 1964) 23–31.

[5] Josephus *Ant.* 18.116–119; translation cited is by Louis H. Feldman in idem, ed., *Josephus* (9 vols.; LCL; Cambridge, MA: Harvard University Press; London: Heinemann, 1965) 9. 81, 83.

[6] Although Bo Reicke mentions the fact that the baptism of John was eschatological, he also minimizes this characteristic, in order to fit John and Jesus into a theological framework of Law and Gospel; see idem, "The Historical Setting of John's Baptism,"

reveal indirectly the political effect of John's eschatological teaching. The second bias may be behind Josephus's emphasis that the ablution was not meant to be effective in itself. This emphasis could be a distortion meant to impress Josephus's enlightened and skeptical Gentile readers, his own importing into his understanding of John ideas foreign to John himself, or a rationalizing understanding of John's teaching that the ritual required appropriate preparation and disposition.

The passage from Acts that presents the baptism of John as the beginning of Jesus' public life has already been cited (1:21–22). The bias of the book of Acts on this issue comes through most clearly in its repeated contrast between the baptism of John with *water* and the baptism through Christ with *spirit*.[7] In a speech of Paul, Acts describes John as one who "preached a baptism of repentance to all the people of Israel" (13:24). This brief description is compatible with Josephus's account and is probably reliable. It is embedded, however, in a context which portrays John as the forerunner of Christ (Acts 13:23–25).

The idea that John consciously prepared the way for Jesus the Messiah is a typical Christian bias and is probably not historical. This Christian interpretation of the significance of John is present already in the oldest narrative gospel, Mark, in the announcement placed in John's mouth, "After me comes he who is mightier than I, the thong of whose sandals I am not worthy to stoop down and untie. I have baptized you with water; but he will baptize you with the Holy Spirit" (Mark 1:7–8). The Gospel of Matthew minimizes the authority of John by having him demur at baptizing Jesus (Matt 3:14). Luke refrains from describing the actual baptism of Jesus by John, presumably for a similar reason. In the gospel of John, the Baptist's role as the forerunner of Christ is elaborated and his inferiority to him is emphasized (John 1:6–8, 19–37; cf. 3:22–30, 4:1–3).[8]

The Synoptic Sayings Source (Q), which is probably as old as and independent of Mark, also included a saying in which John identifies himself as a forerunner.[9] According to this form of the saying, the one who comes after John, the mightier one, will baptize not only

---

in E.P. Sanders, ed., *Jesus, the Gospels, and the Church: Essays in Honor of William R. Farmer* (Macon, GA: Mercer University Press, 1987) 209–24.

[7] Acts 1:5, 11:16, 18:24–25, 19:1–7.

[8] See further Walter Wink, *John the Baptist in the Gospel Tradition* (Cambridge, UK: Cambridge University Press, 1968).

[9] This saying has been preserved in Matt 3:11 and Luke 3:16.

with holy spirit, but also with fire. To this saying is added another: "His winnowing fork is in his hand, to clear his threshing floor, and to gather the wheat into his granary, but the chaff he will burn with unquenchable fire" (Luke 3:17; cf. Matt 3:12).

Behind the Christian picture of John pointing ahead to Jesus the Messiah there may well be a historically accurate tradition that John presented himself as a forerunner. Rather than a human messiah, however, it is likely that John spoke of a direct divine intervention.[10] Support for this hypothesis lies in several considerations. The Gospel of Mark (1:2–3) quotes Malachi 3:1 and Isa 40:3 and implies that John the Baptist is the messenger spoken of and Jesus is the Lord who is coming. If John the Baptist alluded to Scriptures like these, he probably interpreted the Coming One as God, an interpretation which is closer to the original sense than the Christian reading. Jewish texts written relatively close to the time and place of John's activity make plausible the hypothesis that he used imagery of spirit and fire for the future activity of God. According to the *Rule of the Community* from Qumran:

> at the time of the visitation . . . God will then purify every deed of Man with his truth; He will refine for Himself the human frame by rooting out all spirit of falsehood from the bounds of his flesh. He will cleanse him of all wicked deeds with the *spirit* of holiness; like purifying waters he will shed upon him the *spirit* of truth. . . .[11]

Book 4 of the *Sibylline Oracles* was composed by a Jewish writer around 80 CE.[12] Its call for righteousness and its eschatological perspective are similar to the message of John the Baptist as it can be reconstructed from the accounts of Josephus, Acts, Mark, and Q. Divine punishment by fire plays an important role in this work. A climactic passage reads:

> But when faith in piety perishes from among men,
> and justice is hidden in the world,
> untrustworthy men, living for unholy deeds,
> will commit outrage, wicked and evil deeds.

---

[10] Albert Schweitzer argued that John the Baptist considered himself to be the forerunner of the forerunner, Elijah; see idem, *The Mysticism of Paul the Apostle* (New York: Seabury, 1931) 162–63, 231.

[11] 1QS 4; translation cited is by Geza Vermes in idem, *The Dead Sea Scrolls in English* (3rd ed.; New York: Penguin Books, 1987) 66; emphasis added.

[12] See John J. Collins, "The Sibylline Oracles," in J.H. Charlesworth, ed., *The Old Testament Pseudepigrapha* (Garden City, NY: Doubleday, 1983) 1. 381–82.

No one will take account of the pious, but they will even
destroy them all, by foolishness, very infantile people,
rejoicing in outrages and applying their hands to blood.
Even then know that God is no longer benign
but gnashing his teeth in wrath and destroying the entire
race of men at once by a great conflagration.
Ah, wretched mortals, change these things, and do not
lead the great God to all sorts of anger, but abandon
daggers and groanings, murders and outrages,
and wash your whole bodies in perennial rivers.
Stretch out your hands to heaven and ask forgiveness
for your previous deeds and make propitiation
for bitter impiety with words of praise; God will grant repentance
and will not destroy. He will stop his wrath again if you all
practice honorable piety in your hearts.
But if you do not obey me, evil-minded ones, but love
impiety, and receive all these things with evil ears,
there will be fire throughout the whole world, and a very great sign
with sword and trumpet at the rising of the sun.[13]

The Q-saying preserved in Matt 3:11–12 and Luke 3:16–17, that
describes metaphorically judgment to be executed by the Coming
One with spirit and fire, may therefore be a Christian application to
Jesus of a saying spoken by John with reference to divine judgment.

The question of the origin of the baptism of John has been disputed. One theory is that it was based on the ritual ablutions at
Qumran. Some scholars have argued that the Qumran community
required a ritual immersion connected with initiation into the community, that is, a baptism.[14] One form of this hypothesis is based on
a passage in the *Rule of the Community* declaring that any hypocritical
member of the congregation could not be cleansed by any ablution
(1QS 3:4–9).[15] The argument is that this text is in proximity with the
description of the ceremony of entry into the covenant community
(1:16–2:18) and that it precedes the instruction on the two spirits
that may have been part of the instruction given to members about
to be initiated. The problems with this view are that no immersion
is mentioned as part of the ceremony and the ablutions referred to

---

[13] *Sib. Or.* 4. 152–174; translation cited by John J. Collins, ibid., 388.
[14] W.H. Brownlee, "John the Baptist in the New Light of Ancient Scrolls," in
Krister Stendahl, ed., *The Scrolls and the New Testament* (New York: Harper & Row,
1957); see J. Gnilka, "Die essenischen Tauchbäder und die Johannestaufe," *RevQ* 3
(1961–62) 185–207 for a discussion of this issue and further bibliography.
[15] Otto Betz, "Die Proselytentaufe der Qumransekte und die Taufe im Neuen
Testament," *RevQ* 1 (1958) 213–34, especially 216–17.

are the repeated ritual washings practiced by the group. Another passage used to support this view is the remark that the men of falsehood shall not enter the water to partake of the pure meal of the saints, that is, the members of the community.[16] This passage, however, more likely refers to the daily immersion of full members of the community before the main meal that was eaten in a state of ritual purity. The ablutions at Qumran then did not include an initiatory baptism. Rather, they were Levitical washings related to ritual purity.[17] Admission to the regular ablutions and the meal symbolized the conviction that those admitted were pure and free of sin and were living in a holy manner and thus widely separated from sinful and impure people.

The baptism of John did have certain similarities to the ritual washings at Qumran: both involved withdrawal to the desert to await the Lord; both were linked to an ascetic lifestyle; both included total immersion in water; and both had an eschatological context. These features, however, were not unique to John and the community at Qumran.[18] The differences are at least equally striking: a priestly, exclusive community versus the activity of a prophetic, charismatic leader in a public situation;[19] a ritual practiced at least once daily

---

[16] 1QS 5:7–15; the paraphrase given above is based on Vermes's translation, *The Dead Sea Scrolls in English*, 68; this is Brownlee's argument (see n. 14).

[17] At some point, immersion also became a symbol of higher purification and consecration. See the remark that "None may enter the Temple Court for [an act of the Temple-]Service, even though he is clean, until he has immersed himself. On this day the High Priest five times immerses himself and ten times he sanctifies [his hands and his feet], each time, excepting this alone, in the Temple by the Parwah Chamber" in the Mishnaic tractate *Yoma* 3.3. "This day" is, of course, Yom Kippur; the translation cited is by Herbert Danby, *The Mishnah* (London: Oxford University Press, 1933) 164. On this point, see L. Finkelstein, "The Institution of Baptism for Proselytes," *JBL* 52 (1933) 205–206. See also idem, "Some examples of the Maccabean Halaka," *JBL* 49 (1930) 37–38. This new understanding may have been operative already in the higher ablutions at Qumran.

[18] According to Acts 21:38, a charismatic leader called simply "the Egyptian" assembled a large following in the desert; Josephus calls him a false prophet and says that he led his followers from the desert to the Mount of Olives, proposing to take Jerusalem by force (*Bell.* 2.261–63; cf. *Ant.* 20.169–70 where Josephus says that he promised to make the walls of the city collapse). Bannos, Josephus's teacher for three years, lived in the desert and practiced frequent ablutions in cold water, by day and night; he was also ascetic, wearing only what the trees provided and eating only things which grew of themselves (Josephus *Vita* 11). Eschatology was apparently widespread at this time (see, e.g., the *Psalms of Solomon* and the *Assumption of Moses*). Total immersion had long been practiced by priests and other Jews for purification and at this time the ritual was becoming more common.

[19] On John the Baptist as a prophet, see Richard A. Horsley and John S. Hanson,

versus an apparently once and for all ritual; and a self-enacted ritual versus a ritual administered by John.

Proselyte baptism

Other scholars have argued that proselyte baptism provides the key for interpreting the baptism of John. There are certain important similarities. Proselyte baptism is at least witnessed and may be understood as administered. It is a once and for all ritual understood as a sign of an inner transformation. On the assumption that the practice of proselyte baptism is older than the time of John, some scholars have argued that his baptism was a reinterpretation of that ritual: his intention was to signify that the whole Jewish people had become like the Gentiles; since they were apostates from the covenant, they too were unclean.[20] John's baptism thus meant a re-entry into the covenant relationship or an initiation into an eschatological community, prepared for the visitation of the Lord.

If, however, proselyte baptism originated later than John, it cannot provide a context for the interpretation of John's ritual. The date of the origin of proselyte baptism has been much discussed. The issue is complex, because the notion and practice of proselyte baptism seem to have evolved gradually, rather than to have been instituted *de novo* at a particular point in time. The discussion has been confused because of a lack of clarity over what is being talked about. A major root of this confusion is the fact that, in the rabbinical writings, the noun טבילה is used in two ways: to mean the ordinary ritual bath and the immersion that was part of the initiation of proselytes. The problem is how to determine when the second meaning is present. If the notion and ritual of proselyte baptism evolved gradually, one must distinguish between the first ordinary ritual ablution of a convert to Judaism and an immersion that is part of an initiation ceremony. One important criterion is that proselyte baptism is present only when the ritual is administered or at least witnessed.

There have been three major theories in the literature about the origin of proselyte baptism. Gedalyahu Alon represents the position

---

Bandits, Prophets, and Messiahs: Popular Movements at the Time of Jesus (Minneapolis, MN: Seabury/Winston, 1985) 175–81.

[20] J. Leipoldt and Robert Eisler argued along these lines; see the discussion in Scobie, *John the Baptist*, 101 and n. 1.

with the earliest date for the ritual. He has argued that the immersion of proselytes goes back to the early Second Temple period. The purpose was to remove the uncleanness of the Gentiles that derives from idols.[21]

The second major view, held by Israel Abrahams, H.H. Rowley, Joachim Jeremias, and Lawrence Schiffman, is that proselyte baptism was a widespread practice at least prior to John the Baptist.[22] Jeremias stated that the older Jewish view was that the priestly purity laws were not binding on Gentiles. Therefore, only circumcision was necessary for the proselyte. This view was still dominant in the second century BCE, as Judith 14:10 shows. When Achior joined the house of Israel, he was circumcised, but no mention is made of baptism. Jeremias suggested that the newer view arose in the first century BCE, namely, that all Gentile women were impure because they did not purify themselves after menstruation. Therefore, all Gentile men were also impure because of their contact with Gentile women. To support this hypothesis, Jeremias pointed to a text in the *Testament of Levi*, part of the patriarch's speech to his children, the beginning of the priestly line of the nation:

> with harlots and adulteresses will you be joined, and the daughters of the Gentiles shall you take to wife, *purifying them with unlawful purifications*; and your union shall be like unto Sodom and Gomorrah (*T. Levi* 14:6).[23]

Jeremias also pointed to rabbinic texts in support of his view.[24]

---

[21] Gedalyahu Alon, *Jews, Judaism and the Classical World* (Jerusalem: Magnes Press, 1977) 146–89.

[22] Israel Abrahams, *Studies in Pharisaism and the Gospels* (1st series; Cambridge, UK: Cambridge University Press, 1917; reprinted New York: Ktav, 1967) 30–46; H.H. Rowley, "Jewish Proselyte Baptism and the Baptism of John," *HUCA* 15 (1940) 313–34; Joachim Jeremias, *Infant Baptism in the First Four Centuries* (Philadelphia: Westminster, 1960); Lawrence Schiffman, *Who Was a Jew?* (Hoboken, NJ: Ktav, 1985). T.F. Torrance also takes this position; idem, "Proselyte Baptism," *NTS* 1 (1954) 150–54.

[23] Jeremias, *Infant Baptism in the First Four Centuries*, 25–28; quotation is from p. 26; emphasis added. The emphasized phrase (καθαρίζοντες αὐτὰς καθαρισμῷ παρανόμῳ in the Greek manuscripts) was excluded from the critical edition by Robert Henry Charles (*The Greek Versions of the Testaments of the Twelve Patriarchs* [Oxford: Clarendon, 1908; reprinted Hildesheim: Georg Olms Verlagsbuchhandlung, 1960] 57) and thus from the translation by Howard C. Kee (*OTP*, 1. 793). The reading is present, however, in most of the older manuscripts and is included in the critical edition of M. de Jonge (*The Testaments of the Twelve Patriarchs: A Critical Edition of the Greek Text* [Leiden: Brill, 1978] 42).

[24] *Mishnah Pesaḥim* 8.8 and *Eduyoth* 5.2; *b. Pesaḥim* 92a; *t. Pesaḥim* 7.13.

In his treatment of the issue, Lawrence Schiffman admitted that
there is no definite attestation of immersion for conversion before
the early Yavnean period.[25] Nevertheless, he concluded that it is
necessary to date the Jewish ritual prior to John the Baptist in order
to explain his baptism and that of the early Christians.[26]

The third major theory is that proselyte baptism developed in
Judaism in the second half of the first century or in the second century CE. Among those holding this position are Charles Scobie and
S. Zeitlin.[27] The studies of A. Büchler have suggested to some that
the immersion of proselytes was instituted in about 65 CE with the
enactment of the eighteen decrees, one of which declared (for the
first time) that Gentiles were intrinsically unclean. Büchler viewed
this decree as a precautionary measure against Roman sodomy.[28]
Scobie argued that the rabbinic texts regarding proselytes which are
early have no explicit allusion to immersion as part of the initiation
ceremony. The rabbinic texts which speak explicitly of such an immersion date to the late first or early second century CE. He suggested that, after the destruction of the temple, the ritual of immersion
could have risen in importance as the only available ritual for female
proselytes.

All modern scholars who have addressed the subject agree that
there is no proselyte baptism in the Jewish Tanakh, which is also the
Christian Old Testament. With regard to Alon's theory, it is possible
that some proselytes observed ritual washings in the early Second
Temple period. In some cases, the first ablution may have been
thought to counteract impurity contracted by Gentile life. But there
is no evidence that such ablutions, if they occurred, were "baptisms,"
since there is no reliable evidence that they were tied to an initiation
rite, administered, or performed in the presence of witnesses.

Jeremias's appeal to the *Testament of Levi* does not demonstrate that
proselyte baptism was instituted in the first century BCE. The *Testaments of the Twelve Patriarchs* is virtually impossible to date. It is not
even certain that the document was originally Jewish, since its present

---

[25] Schiffman, *Who Was a Jew?*, 29.

[26] Ibid., 26, 29.

[27] Scobie, *John the Baptist*, 95–102; S. Zeitlin, "The Halaka in the Gospels and its
Relation to the Jewish Law in the Time of Jesus," *HUCA* 1 (1924) 357–63; idem,
"A Note on Baptism for Proselytes," *JBL* 52 (1933) 78–79.

[28] A. Büchler, "The Levitical Impurity of the Gentile in Palestine Before the Year
70," *JQR* n.s. 17 (1926/27) 1–81; Schiffman, *Who Was A Jew?*, 26, 85, n. 44.

form is Christian. Further, the comment about "purifying them with an unlawful purification" is not a certain allusion to proselyte baptism.

In the proselytizing of the Maccabean period, admission to Israel was always simply by circumcision, according to the evidence.[29] Furthermore, Philo often speaks of proselytes, but never mentions proselyte baptism. Josephus discusses the admission of proselytes, but mentions circumcision only. The rabbinic texts cited by Jeremias which relate to the Passover contain no indication that the immersion mentioned was part of a ceremony of initiation.[30]

The oldest clear reference to proselyte baptism is in the *Babylonian Talmud, Yebamoth* 46a. The relevant passage begins with the question of the status of children conceived by Jewish women from proselytes who had been circumcised but had not performed the required ritual ablution. If the fathers were proper proselytes, the children were Jews; if the fathers were not proper proselytes, the fathers were idolators and the children bastards. In the course of the discussion, the opinions of Rabbi Eliezer ben Hyrcanus and Rabbi Joshua ben Hananiah are cited. These two rabbis apparently belonged to the second generation of the Tannaim, active from about 90 to 130 CE.[31] Rabbi Eliezer is quoted as teaching that a proselyte who was circumcised but had not performed the prescribed ritual ablution was a proper proselyte. Rabbi Joshua is said to have taught that a proselyte who had performed the prescribed ablution but had not been circumcised was a proper proselyte. This tradition is evidence, at most, that around the end of the first and the beginning of the second century, proselyte baptism was beginning to be recognized as an essential part of the initiation into Judaism, but was not yet recognized as such by all authorities.[32]

A saying of Epictetus, preserved by Arrian, implies that baptism was an essential part of the process of conversion to Judaism.[33] Some scholars have argued that Epictetus is referring here to Christians and not to Jews.[34] Menahem Stern argues that the philosopher was

---

[29] Josephus *Ant.* 13.257–58 and 318–19.

[30] See the discussion by Scobie, *John the Baptist*, 98.

[31] Hermann L. Strack, *Introduction to the Talmud and Midrash* (New York: Atheneum, 1969) 110–111.

[32] See the discussion in Scobie, *John the Baptist*, 99.

[33] Text, translation and notes are given by Menahem Stern, *Greek and Latin Authors on Jews and Judaism* (Jerusalem: The Israel Academy of Sciences and Humanities, 1976) 1. 542–544.

[34] Scobie, *John the Baptist*, 99, n. 2.

indeed referring to Jews. Following Fergus Millar, he places this
discourse at Nicopolis and dates it to about 108 CE. Even if Stern
is correct, this bit of evidence does not support the emergence of
proselyte baptism before the end of the first or the beginning of
the second century.

The origin of John's baptism

Schiffman's argument that proselyte baptism must be dated before
John the Baptist in order to explain his baptism and that of the
early Christians is unwarranted. Only two elements have a firm claim
for consideration on the question of the origin of the baptism of
John. Without these two elements, this baptism would be unintelli-
gible. One of these is the tradition and practice of Levitical ablutions. This ritual is the ultimate source of the form of John's ritual
which apparently involved total immersion in water. The other element is the prophetic-apocalyptic tradition.[35] One aspect of this tradition important for John's baptism was the expectation of a future,
definitive intervention of God. Another significant aspect was the
ethical use of ablution imagery. For example, Isaiah 1:16–17 exhorts
the people:

> Wash yourselves; make yourselves clean;
> remove the evil of your doings from before my eyes;
> cease to do evil, learn to do good;
> seek justice, correct oppression;
> defend the fatherless, plead for the widow.[36]

In some texts, such as Ezekiel 36:25–28, ablution imagery was used
both ethically and eschatologically. God's transformation of the people
in the eschatological restoration was to involve a new spirit and a
new heart. This new creation was to begin with a divine sprinkling
of clean water upon the people to cleanse them from their sins and
acts of idolatry. The tradition of prophetic symbolic actions may have
played a role. The baptism of John may have been intended to signify God's approach as purifier before the promised judgment and
transformation. As has already been noted, ritual ablutions were

---

[35] Schweitzer believed that the prophetic tradition alone, along with John's
eschatological orientation, was sufficient to explain the origin of John's baptism (*The
Mysticism of Paul the Apostle*, 231–32).

[36] Translations from the Tanakh/OT are according to the RSV.

growing in importance in John's time. This development is attested by the literature from Qumran, the traditions about the Pharisees and about meal-associates, and traditions about ascetic individuals, like Bannos, the teacher of Josephus. The tradition of the prophetic symbolic action and the growing importance of ritual ablutions were contributing factors in making John a baptizer rather than simply a preacher or oracular prophet.[37] The significance of John's baptism is best understood in terms of a prophetic reinterpretation of the sense of defilement in ethical terms and of an apocalyptic expectation of judgment.

II. JESUS AND BAPTISM

One of the few strong points of consensus on the historical Jesus is that he was baptized by John. The fact that Jesus sought baptism by John is evidence that Jesus recognized the authority of John as an agent of God. The Synoptic tradition reflects that recognition on the part of Jesus, in spite of its subordination of John to Jesus.[38] Presumably, Jesus, by accepting the baptism of John, accepted its prophetic-eschatological significance. Many students of the NT conclude that Jesus's eschatology was more oriented to the present time of fulfillment than to the future consummation.[39]

The relationship between the activity of John and that of Jesus is portrayed differently in the Synoptics than in the Gospel of John. According to Mark, Matthew, and Luke, Jesus's activity of teaching and healing began only after John was arrested.[40] There is no indication in these Gospels that either Jesus or his disciples baptized during the life of the historical Jesus.[41] The Gospel of John describes Jesus's public activity as overlapping with John's.[42] It differs from the

---

[37] John's activity of baptizing calls into question his identification as an "oracular prophet," rather than an "action prophet," by Horsley and Hanson; see n. 19 above.

[38] Matt 11:9–19/Luke 7:26–35; Mark 11:27–33/Matt 21:23–27/Luke 20:1–8; Matt 21:32.

[39] See, for example, Boers, *Who Was Jesus?*

[40] The point is explicit in Mark 1:14 and Matt 4:12–17; it is implicit in Luke 3:18–23.

[41] Baptizing is not one of the activities enjoined by Jesus on the disciples during his earthly life; see Mark 3:13–19, 6:7–13; Matt 10:1–15; Luke 9:1–6, 10:1–12. It is only after the resurrection, according to Matthew, that the command to baptize was given: 28:16–20.

[42] John 3:22–30, 4:1–3.

Synoptics also in stating (three times) that Jesus was baptizing many people.[43] These statements, however, are corrected, perhaps by a later hand, with a parenthetical remark that Jesus himself did not baptize, but only his disciples.[44] Whether the Synoptics or John present the historically more reliable picture has been disputed. One theory is that the picture of the Gospel of John is unreliable, because it is a literary composition reflecting rivalry between the followers of John the Baptist and those of Jesus at the time the Gospel was written.[45] Another point of view is that the Gospel of John is more accurate than the Synoptics on this point, because there is no plausible theological reason why the tradition that Jesus and his disciples once baptized would be invented. The practice of Christian baptism did not need such support. If there were followers of the Baptist around who rivalled the Christians for whom the Gospel was written, the information that Jesus had imitated John would provide them with ammunition against the independence and authority of Jesus.[46] A further argument in favor of the reliability of the Gospel of John is that the report of Jesus's baptizing creates a problem for the evangelist. In 1:33 Jesus was presented as the one who baptizes with holy spirit. But the description in chapters 3–4 does not imply that Jesus's baptism was different in kind from John's. According to 7:39, the spirit is given only after Jesus's "exaltation." The appropriate conclusion seems to be that the Gospel of John is historically accurate on this point and that the authors of the other Gospels were unaware of, or suppressed, the tradition that Jesus baptized.

If Jesus administered baptism of a kind similar to John's, one would expect continuity between the baptism of John and early Christian baptism. The discontinuity is as great as the continuity in the cases of the Gospel of Matthew and the letters of Paul, but there is striking continuity between John's baptism and the baptism to which Peter invited the Jews assembled in Jerusalem on Pentecost according to the second chapter of Acts.

---

[43] John 3:22, 26; 4:1.
[44] John 4:2.
[45] Rudolf Bultmann, *The Gospel of John: A Commentary* (Philadelphia: Westminster, 1971) 167.
[46] Raymond E. Brown, *The Gospel According to John (i–xii)* (AB; Garden City, NY: Doubleday, 1966) 155.

III. CHRISTIAN BAPTISM

The origin of Christian baptism has been disputed. The traditional view of course is that the practice of baptism in the early Church was the result of the command of the risen Lord as reported in the Gospel of Matthew (28:16–20). There are problems with the assumption that this passage is authentic.[47] Even if the passage is assumed to be authentic, it is still necessary to place the command in a context, to ask what the early Christians understood themselves to be doing.

Students of the NT who assume that Jesus did not baptize have usually taken one of three basic positions. Some have hypothesized that the early Christians reverted to the baptism of John and reinterpreted it.[48] Others have argued that the metaphor of baptism in the spirit in the teaching of John gave rise to a baptismal ritual associated with the gift of the spirit. Many have taken the position that the early church simply borrowed the ritual of proselyte baptism from the Jews. Another possibility is that there was an unbroken continuity from the baptism of John, through the baptism associated with the activity of Jesus, to the baptism practiced by the early Christians. The first fundamental change occurred in the context of the Gentile mission under the increasing influence of Hellenistic culture.

Baptism in Acts 2

The assumption of unbroken continuity has two main advantages. It explains why the 120 or so persons referred to in Acts 1:15 are not said to have undergone any particularly Christian baptismal ritual. It also explains why the basic function of baptism as reflected in Peter's Pentecost sermon is so similar to the baptism of John. New elements are added, but the starting point is the same.[49]

Peter calls for repentance, just as John is said to have done.[50] Peter indicates that the baptism is for the forgiveness of sins. The same

---

[47] G.R. Beasley-Murray, *Baptism in the New Testament* (London: Macmillan, 1962; reprinted 1972).

[48] This is the position taken by Schweitzer (*The Mysticism of Paul the Apostle*, 233–34).

[49] This essential continuity was recognized by Schweitzer (*The Mysticism of Paul the Apostle*, 236).

[50] Cf. Acts 2:38 with Mark 1:4; Matt 3:2, 11.

association is made in Mark and Matthew regarding the baptism of John.[51] Peter exhorts his Jewish audience, "Save yourselves from this crooked generation." Their response is to submit to baptism.[52] According to Matthew, going to John for baptism was a means of fleeing from "the wrath to come" (Matt 3:7). The images of trees being cut down and thrown into the fire and of chaff being burned in unquenchable fire also point to a coming judgment.[53] Thus, on the most basic level, the meaning of the ritual of baptism in Acts 2 is similar to that of John the Baptist and to the ablutions called for in book four of the *Sibylline Oracles*: wrath is coming on this evil generation; members of this generation may be saved by repenting and receiving baptism; this baptism is a metaphorical cleansing so that the fire of judgment will, at worst, further refine and not destroy.[54]

There are two new elements in the function and meaning of baptism in Acts 2. One is that baptism occurs "in the name (ἐπὶ τῷ ὀνόματι) of Jesus Christ" (vs 38). There has been a debate over the origin of this phrase. Albrecht Oepke, following A. Deissmann, argued that it has a Greek cultural origin and that the phrase εἰς τὸ ὄνομα[55] was a technical term in commerce. The literal meaning was "to the account of."[56] Here the metaphorical meaning is that the person baptized belongs to Christ. Others argued that the phrase derived from Greek culture, but that its original provenance was magic. Abrahams and Jeremias argued for a Semitic cultural origin.[57] They suggested that it expressed the intention of a cultic action. For example, in *Gerim* 1.7 it is said, "Whoever is not a proselyte in the name of heaven is no proselyte." In *b. Yebamoth* 45b and 47b it is said that slaves after becoming free are rebaptized in the name of freedom.

The variation in the wording of the phrase counts against Deissmann's thesis.[58] The variation could be explained by differing translations of a Semitic phrase. Whatever its origin, the meaning of the phrase in Acts 2:38 is to associate baptism with acceptance of the

---

[51] Cf. Acts 2:38 with Mark 1:4 and Matt 3:6.
[52] Acts 3:40–41.
[53] Matt 3:10, 12.
[54] Cf. 1 Cor 3:15.
[55] Cf. 1 Cor 1:13, 15; Matt 28:19.
[56] Albrecht Oepke, "βάπτω, βαπτίζω," *TDNT* 1 (1964) 539 and n. 51.
[57] Abrahams, *Studies in Pharisaism and the Gospels*; Jeremias, *Infant Baptism in the First Four Centuries*; cf. Billerbeck 1. 1054–55; 4. 744.
[58] In Acts 10:48 it is ἐν τῷ ὀνόματι; in Acts 2:38, as noted above, it is ἐπὶ τῷ ὀνόματι.

proclamation about Jesus. The reception of baptism becomes an outward sign of faith in God through Jesus. When John baptized, reception of that baptism implied acceptance of his message of the wrath to come and of repentance. It further implied the recognition that the will of God was manifest in the preaching of John. When Jesus and his disciples baptized, reception of that baptism implied acceptance of the proclamation about the nearness of the kingdom of God. It also implied recognition that the will of God was manifest in the teaching of Jesus. After the crucifixion and the appearances of the risen Lord, the followers of Jesus did not have the same direct authority that John and Jesus had. Reception of baptism at their hands implied acceptance first of all that there was a need for repentance in the face of the wrath to come or in preparation for the full manifestation of the kingdom of God. It also implied the recognition that the will of God was manifest in the death of Jesus and that God had raised him from the dead. The ritual of baptism for John, and probably for Jesus, was primarily an individual matter, although it took place in the context of the covenant people of God. But among the early Christians, because of the link of baptism with acceptance of what God had done with Jesus, the ritual became an initiation rite into a community. Acceptance of the proclamation about Jesus meant joining a group whose *raison d'être* was faith in Jesus as the mediator of salvation. The group was proselytizing, and the outsiders, those who refused to join, were those who did not accept Jesus' role as the primary mediator. Although the picture in Acts of the Christian community in Jerusalem is an idealized one, there is no reason to doubt that a new group identity formed early.

The other new element is the association of baptism with the gift of the Holy Spirit (Acts 2:38). In Acts 1:5 the prophecy of John the Baptist is alluded to, that the Coming One would baptize "with the Holy Spirit and with fire" (Luke 3:16). The metaphorical fulfillment of that prophecy, with regard to the 120 or so followers of Jesus, is narrated in the beginning of Acts 2. Thereafter, the ritual of baptism in the name of Jesus Christ is associated with the gift of the Holy Spirit. Peter's sermon, however, does not quote John the Baptist. Instead, there is a pesher-like interpretation and application of Joel 3:1–5 (2:28–32 in the RSV). The prophecy of Joel, that God would pour out the divine spirit on all humankind, is explicitly declared to be fulfilled in the reception of the spirit by the band of Jesus' followers. In the biblical tradition, the Spirit of God rested only on certain charismatic individuals and on those appointed to a particular office, such as kings, prophets, and judges. The prophecy of Joel looked forward to the day when the gift of the spirit would be democratized. The early Christians claimed that the day had come. Not only free men, but slaves and women as well, now receive the spirit of God. The letters of Paul give evidence for the early association of the gift of the spirit with baptism and for its universal character.[59]

Variety in interpretation

The early Christian community had a somewhat different eschatological schema than John the Baptist. They understood themselves to be farther along the eschatological trajectory because one human being had already been raised from the dead. For those associated with the risen Christ, that event meant for them a proleptic resurrection from the dead. The implication for baptism is that, as an expression of faith, it transforms human nature and makes possible in the present the living of a supra-human life. But in Acts' account of Christian beginnings and baptism in that context, the operative symbol is still cleansing.

The basic, fundamental meaning of the ritual of baptism as a washing, a cleansing from sin, originated with John the Baptist and continued to be expressed in early Christian writings on into the second century. It is present, as we have seen, in Acts 2. It was presupposed by Paul.[60] It is expressed in Ephesians[61] and in the *Shepherd of Hermas*.[62]

Other interpretations arose and developed alongside the original one. The notion of baptism as God's seal on Christians, authorizing, ratifying them and guaranteeing their protection, occurs in Paul's letters[63] and in the deutero-Pauline letter to the Ephesians.[64] This interpretive image is also found in the *Shepherd of Hermas*.[65]

---

[59] 1 Cor 6:11, 12:13; Gal 3:27–29.

[60] See 1 Cor 6:9–11; 1 Cor 15:29 presupposes that baptism is a kind of expiation for sin; cf. 2 Macc 12:39–45. See also the speech attributed to Paul in Acts 22, especially vs 16.

[61] Ephesians 5:25–27.

[62] *Hermas Mandates* 4.3.1.

[63] 2 Cor 1:21–22; cf. Rom 4:11.

[64] Ephesians 1:13–14; 4:30.

[65] *Hermas Similitudes* 9.16.1–4.

As was suggested earlier, Christian baptism early on developed connotations of an initiation ritual, initiation into the community of those who accepted Jesus as the Messiah, who believed that God had raised him from the dead. This sense is implied, as we have seen, by the phrase "in the name of Jesus Christ" in the account of Acts 2 (vs 38). It is also implied by the narrator's remark that "there were added that day about three thousand souls" (vs 41). The following comment, that "they devoted themselves to the apostles' teaching and fellowship, to the breaking of bread and the prayers" (vs 42), is an indication that "adding souls" does not refer only to a heavenly tally of the "saved" but to the growth of the Christian community. The notion of baptism as a ritual of initiation is implied also by Matt 28:18–20. The command of the risen Lord associates baptism with "making disciples" and "teaching them to observe all that I have commanded you." Clearly one aspect of baptism here is initiation into the community of the disciples of Christ. The function of initiation is implicit in some of Paul's remarks on baptism also. In 1 Cor 12:12–13, baptism is the means whereby Jews and Greeks, slaves and free people are joined into one body. Similarly, according to Gal 3:26–29, baptism overcomes distinctions between Jews and Greeks, slaves and free, men and women, and makes them all one in Christ. By the time of the deutero-Pauline Colossians, baptism's character as a ritual of initiation can be taken for granted to the extent that it can be presented as a new circumcision, a circumcision made without hands (2:11).

Baptism as death and resurrection

Two sayings attributed to Jesus in the Synoptic tradition seem to use the word baptism metaphorically to mean death, especially the death of Jesus.[66] In these sayings, the operative symbol has shifted from cleansing that leads to a pure and holy life to death that leads to new life. These sayings are close to Paul's interpretation of baptism in Romans 6, one of the most important passages on baptism in the NT.

Since the publication of Richard Reitzenstein's *Die Hellenistischen Mysterienreligionen* in 1910, a debate has raged continually on the relation

---

[66] Mark 10:38–39; Luke 12:50.

between Romans 6 and the Greco-Roman mystery-religions.[67] Reitzenstein argued that baptism had already been shaped by Hellenism in
the pre-Pauline tradition. Paul did not therefore reinterpret baptism
in the language of the mysteries. The similarity was already present.
Paul himself, according to Reizenstein, was familiar with the language of the mysteries. Thus his formulations of basic powerful images are informed by the mysteries and he borrowed particular terms
from their traditional terminology.[68] Another leader of the history of
religions school, Wilhelm Bousset, argued in more detail that Christian faith and ritual were already Hellenized in the tradition that
Paul received. He suggested that the process began in the Christian
community of Antioch in Syria.[69] In the Forward to his book, Bousset
responded to the criticism that the Hellenistic texts cited by the historians of religion as analogues to Romans 6, for example, were later
than the date of Romans by stressing that it was not a question of
literary dependence. The history of religions school did not take the
position that Paul had read the Corpus Hermeticum, or even Philo.
Rather, they were concerned to show broad intellectual connections
between certain forms of early Christianity and the Hellenistic mystery religions. They wanted to reconstruct and illustrate a form of
piety that grew quite early in its own soil (the Hellenized ancient
Near East) and later fused with the gospel of Christ. They did not
assert that particular forms of Christian faith and ritual were dependent, for example, on the Mithraic cult, but that both made use of
common, earlier ideas. Most of those who have denied that Paul
was dependent on the mystery religions missed the point that the
history of religions school was making.[70]

---

[67] The third edition was published in 1927; see also the ET, Richard Reitzenstein,
(Pittsburgh: Pickwick, 1978).

[68] J.H. Randall (*Hellenistic Ways of Deliverance and the Making of the Christian Synthesis*
[New York: Columbia University Press, 1970]) and Joscelyn Godwin (*Mystery Religions in the Ancient World* [New York: Harper & Row, 1981]) have also concluded
that Paul was influenced by the mystery religions.

[69] Wilhelm Bousset, *Kyrios Christos: A History of the Belief in Christ from the Beginnings
of Christianity to Irenaeus* (Germ. ed. 1913; Nashville: Abingdon, 1970). Ernst Käsemann
(*Commentary on Romans* [Grand Rapids: Eerdmans, 1980]) and Robert C. Tannehill
(*Dying and Rising with Christ* [BZNW 32; Berlin: Topelmann, 1967]) also conclude
that Hellenization took place prior to Paul.

[70] Those who have argued against the influence of the mystery religions on Paul
include Arthur Darby Nock, "Early Gentile Christianity and Its Hellenistic Background," in A.E.J. Rawlinson, ed., *Essays on the Trinity and Incarnation* (London:
Longmans, Green, & Co., 1928) 51–156; idem, *Early Gentile Christianity and Its Hellenistic Background* (New York: Harper & Row, 1964) 109–145; Günter Wagner, *Pauline*

In Romas 6:1–14 the ritual of baptism is explicitly interpreted as a reenactment of the death and resurrection of Jesus in which the baptized person appropriates the significance of that death for him- or herself. In this understanding of the ritual, the experience of the Christian is firmly and vividly grounded in the story of the death and resurrection of Christ. These qualities of reenactment of a foundational story and the identification of the participant with the protagonist of the story are strikingly reminiscent of what is known about the initiation rituals of certain mystery religions, notably the Eleusinian mysteries and the Isis mysteries.[71]

One of the distinctive features of Romans 6 is that Paul avoids saying "we have risen" with Christ; rather he speaks of "newness of life." The implication of Paul's restraint is that the transformation is not complete. There is still an apocalyptic expectation of a future, fuller transformation into a heavenly form of life. This expectation fits with Paul's use throughout the passage of the imperative alongside the indicative. "Newness of life" is a real, present possibility, both spiritually and ethically, but the actualizing of that possibility requires decision and commitment as well as grace.[72]

At some point, at least forty years after Paul's death, the notion of death and rebirth was also attached to proselyte baptism in Judaism. Two passages in the *Babylonian Talmud* mention the opinion that one who became a proselyte is like a child newly born.[73] The rebirth of the rabbinic proselyte baptism, unlike the Christian form, was not

Baptism and the Pagan Mysteries: The Problem of the Pauline Doctrine of Baptism in Romans VI.1–11, In the Light of Religio-Historical "Parallels" (Edinburgh: Oliver & Boyd, 1967) and Ronald H. Nash, *Christianity and the Hellenistic World* (Grand Rapids: Zondervan, 1984) 115–59.

[71] For the story or ἱερὸς λόγος of the Eleusinian mysteries, see the Homeric Hymn to Demeter. An English translation of this hymn, along with an introduction and bibliography, has been published by Marvin W. Meyer, *The Ancient Mysteries: A Sourcebook* (New York: Harper & Row, 1987) 17–30. For an account of an initiation into the mysteries of Isis, see Apuleius, The Golden Ass, Book 11. See also Plutarch's On Isis and Osiris. Meyer has included book 11 of the Golden Ass and selections from Plutarch's work (ibid., 176–93 and 160–72).

[72] Note that the author of Colossians does not hesitate to say that Christians have risen with Christ (2:12, 3:1). Baptism is also linked to the resurrection of Christ in 1 Pet 3:21. See also the related interpretation of baptism as rebirth in John 3:3–8 and Titus 3:5.

[73] *Yebamoth* 62a; *Bekoroth* 47a; see George F. Moore, *Judaism in the First Centuries of the Christian Era: The Age of the Tannaim* (Cambridge, MA: Harvard University Press, 1927; New York: Schocken, 1971) 1. 334–35. See also *Yebamoth* 48b, m. *Keritoth* 8b, t. *Shekalim* 3.20, *Gerim* 2.5; Jeremias, *Infant Baptism*, 33, n. 8; Rowley, "Jewish Proselyte Baptism and the Baptism of John," 329.

eschatological. No direct link to immortality was made. As Israel
Abrahams put it, proselyte baptism did not ensure sinlessness nor
the transformation of human character. Such, according to the rabbis,
was not possible in the pre-messianic age.[74] The image of rebirth
thus shows the gulf between life within and life outside the covenant
people.

Christian and rabbinic baptism both have their ultimate roots in
the ritual washings of Leviticus. Both came to function as rituals of
initiation. The major difference is the relation of this ritual to eschatology. Both expect a fulfillment, but the two communities place themselves on different sides of the turning point between the two ages.

---

[74] Abrahams, *Studies in Pharisaism and the Gospels*, 42; in support of his point, he
cites *Gen. Rab.* 70.8, *b. Qiddushin* 30b, and *Midr. Tanḥuma*, Meṣora 17–18.

INDEX OF ANCIENT PERSONS AND TEXTS

I. ANCIENT PERSONS

II. ANCIENT TEXTS

INDEX OF MODERN AUTHORS

SUBJECT INDEX

Subjects easily located by means of the table of Contents are not
listed here.

SCHOLARS' LIST

*Through its Scholars' List Brill aims to make available
to a wider public a selection of its most successful
hardcover titles in a paperback edition.*

Titles now available are:

AMITAI-PREISS, R. & D.O. MORGAN, *The Mongol Empire and its Legacy*.
2000. ISBN 90 04 11946 9, price USD 29.90

COHEN. B., *Not the Classical Ideal*. Athens and the Construction of the Other
in Greek Art. 2000. ISBN 90 04 11712 1, price USD 39.90

GRIGGS, C.W., *Early Egyptian Christianity* from its Origins to 451 CE.
2000. ISBN 90 04 11926 4, price USD 29.90

HORSFALL, N., *A Companion to the Study of Virgil*. 2000.
ISBN 90 04 11870 5, price USD 27.90

JAYYUSI, S.K., *The Legacy of Muslim Spain*. 2000.
ISBN 90 04 11945 0, price USD 54.90

RUTGERS, L.V., *The Jews in Late Ancient Rome*. Evidence of Cultural
Interaction in the Roman Diaspora. 2000.
ISBN 90 04 11928 0, price USD 29.90

TER HAAR, B.J., *The Ritual and Mythology of the Chinese Triads*.
Creating an Identity. 2000. ISBN 90 04 11944 2, price USD 39.90

THOMPSON, T.L., *Early History of the Israelite People* from the Written &
Archaeological Sources. 2000. ISBN 90 04 11943 4, price USD 39.90

WOOD, S.E., *Imperial Women*. A Study in Public Images, 40 BC – AD 68
2000. ISBN 90 04 11950 7, price USD 34.90

YARBRO COLLINS, A., *Cosmology & Eschatology in Jewish & Christian
Apocalypticism*. 2000. ISBN 90 04 11927 2, price USD 29.90

―――――